CULTURE AND THE BILINGUAL CLASSROOM
Studies in Classroom Ethnography

Henry T. Trueba
San Diego State University

Grace Pung Guthrie
Center for the Study of Reading, University of Illinois

Kathryn Hu-Pei Au
Kamehameha Early Education Program, Honolulu, Hawaii

Editors

Newbury House Publishers, Inc. / Rowley / Massachusetts / 01969
ROWLEY • LONDON • TOKYO

1981

Library of Congress Cataloging in Publication Data
Main entry under title:

Culture and the bilingual classroom.

(Bilingual multicultural education; book 2)
Bibliography: p.
1. Education, Bilingual--United States--Addresses,
essays, lectures. 2. Minorities--Education--United
States--Addresses, essays, lectures. 3. Acculturation
--Addresses, essays, lectures. 4. Interaction analysis
in education--Addresses, essays, lectures. I. Trueba,
Henry T. II. Guthrie, Grace Pung. III. Au, Kathryn
Hu-Pei. IV. Series.
LC3731.B553 book 2 371.97 80-27912
ISBN 0-88377-182-9

NEWBURY HOUSE PUBLISHERS, INC.

Language Science
Language Teaching
Language Learning

ROWLEY, MASSACHUSETTS 01969
ROWLEY • LONDON • TOKYO

Cover design by Diana Esterly

This work was developed under a grant [to the Midwest Organization for Materials Development, College of Education, University of Illinois, Urbana, Illinois 61801] from the U.S. Office of Education, Department of Health, Education and Welfare. However, the content does not necessarily reflect the position or policy of that Agency, and no official endorsement of these materials should be inferred.

First printing: May 1981
Printed in the U.S.A.   5   4   3   2

A Series on

BILINGUAL MULTICULTURAL EDUCATION

Because bilingual education is a relatively young field, there is, still, a paucity of materials available for the training of professionals. Most of the materials developed to date have concentrated at the basic classroom level to the exclusion of materials for institutions of higher education. The Midwest Organization for Materials Development at the University of Illinois, Urbana-Champaign, concerned with this void in the field, has developed a series of curricular texts for practicing and future professionals in the field. This series, written for teachers, teacher trainers, administrators, supervisors, faculties in institutions of higher education, government officers, legislators and others who are concerned with the quality of education for linguistic minorities, presents a compendium of knowledge about bilingual education, both theoretical and applied, from what has been — to what is — to futuristic projections of what may be.

Each book in the series, although highly readable for a number of different audiences, has been carefully directed toward specific professionals. The series, in total, makes a basic library for those in bilingual education and related fields.

Acknowledgments

We would like to thank all the ethnographers, scholars, colleagues and friends who helped in the gestation and birth of this volume. We would like to express our gratitude to Mary Glockner for copy editing, and Lucille Gallegos-Jaramillo for the compilation of the bibliography. Last, but not least, we thank Pamela G. Wright for the endless hours she spent in proofing, correcting and completing the entire volume, particularly the bibliography.

Preface

The increasing investment of federal monies in ethnographic research and the substantial investment of energy and resources on the part of research organizations necessitates an overview and a critical evaluation of the status quo, relevance, and implications of the most recent microethnographic studies.

This volume, *Culture and the Bilingual Classroom*, carries the promise that ethnographic research can help lay a more concrete and realistic foundation for a pluralistic philosophy of education. The most recent microethnographic, classroom studies support previous contentions regarding the structural complexity of child/child and child/teacher interpersonal interactions and the miscommunication that often develops in interethnic settings. Ethnographic findings are also being used to monitor and improve classroom teaching practices.

The readers will recognize valuable insights and substantial progress towards an understanding of the learning processes in culturally different children vis-a-vis bilingual and/or regular classrooms. These pages contain important implications for teacher training and evaluation, for bilingual program implementation, and for subsequent classroom research methodology.

We hope this volume will enhance the heuristic value, descriptive validity, functional relevance, and overall worth of microethnographic research. As Erickson has stated: "It is an issue of 'reality control' which is also one of 'quality control'" (Erickson, 1978:1). The ultimate test of microethnography as a useful research tool in educational research will be in its capacity to impact the reality and the quality of the educational process.

Henry Trueba

Contents

1

INTRODUCTION

The contemporary bilingual education movement is largely a result of the struggles of linguistic minorities for equal educational opportunity. One of the basic assumptions underlying this movement is that linguistic differences and the consequent response to them are major factors behind minority children's school failure, and that such differences should not be considered as deficits to be compensated for, but strengths to be capitalized upon, in educating these children. Because linguistic differences in the classroom are readily apparent, they have been the natural focus of bilingual education.

However, in recent years, increasing amounts of attention have been paid to cultural factors other than language to explain educational difficulties of minority children. As a result, various attempts have been made to rename this educational reform movement from *bilingual* to *bilingual/bicultural, bilingual/multicultural*, or even to *multicultural education*. Our intention here is not to participate in a debate on terminology, but rather to emphasize the importance of cultural factors in influencing the outcomes of schooling for minority children. For the sake of clarity and convenience, we use the term *bilingual classroom* to refer to any classroom where minority children are present.

An outgrowth of the increased emphasis on nonlinguistic factors of culture has been the gradual introduction of cultural components into the curricula of bilingual programs. However, these so-called cultural curricula are too often no more than celebrations of ethnic festivals and holidays, featuring song and dance, cooking and tasting ethnic foods, or national costume shows. These activities may well have some educational value, and they may promote intercultural under-standing, but such emphasis on the overt aspects of culture tends to obscure more subtle, implicit, and invisible differences which may have just as much, or more, impact on the educational success or failure of children. It is these differences we are concerned with in our discussion of cultural diversity in the classroom.

To provide a proper context for the papers in this volume, we devote the first part of this chapter to a clarification and definition of the concept of culture. Various scientific and operational definitions of culture are reviewed in order to reach a composite definition. In the second section, we point out the realities of cultural and structural pluralism in this society to make our discussion of minority cultures more meaningful. The third section presents various approaches to the treatment of cultural differences in our society. These approaches are often a result of the structurally stratified nature or prevailing ideology of the society. We suggest that only a pluralistic view of the different cultures within this society will ensure true equality of educational opportunity for minority culture members. In the fourth section, we focus on the importance of basic ethnographic research in educational settings which, we believe, can help not only educators and policy makers, but the public in general to acquire a more enlightened attitude toward the minority cultures in this country, and shed new light on the educational problems and difficulties of minority children in American schools. Finally, we introduce the rationale and organization of this volume, and briefly discuss each chapter.

What is Culture?

The term *culture*, as used in this volume, comes from the field of anthropology. However, even though culture has long been used by anthropologists as the central concept in their study of human behavior and custom, its meaning is still rather unclear. Recognizing this, a number of scholars within the discipline have attempted to formulate a "scientific" or "operational" definition of culture (Cf. esp. Kluckhohn and Kelly, 1945; Kroeber and Kluckhohn, 1952). Kroeber and Kluckhohn have compiled evidence of some 400 such attempts; nevertheless, a standard scientific definition is still lacking.

We will not be presumptuous enough here to attempt such a definition. We will, however, discuss briefly some of the more significant and better-known definitions by leading anthropologists—definitions which have enjoyed wide acceptance at one time or another. Furthermore, we will develop a working definition of culture for the purposes of this book—a definition which we feel emphasizes the important aspects of culture as it applies to the classroom.

It is generally acknowledged by anthropologists that the earliest definition of culture was E.B. Tylor's: "Culture or civilization, taken in its widest ethnographic sense, is that complex whole which includes knowledge, belief, art, morals, laws, customs, and any other capabilities and habits acquired by man as a member of society" (Tylor, 1871). To Tylor, culture was broad enough to cover all of human activity and was, in essence, indistinguishable from civilization.

The usefulness of such a general characterization is limited, however, and consequently, this definition has been modified and revised again and again in order to achieve more scientific rigor and clarity. With each modification, different aspects of human experience are emphasized. For example, a distinction is often made between *learned* behavior and genetic behavior, with learned behavior thought of as culture: "The sum total of the knowledge, attitudes and habitual behavior patterns shared and transmitted by the members of a particular society" (Linton, 1940). An interest in this distinction naturally led to the decidedly behaviorist terminology of definitions such as Kroeber's: "The mass of learned and transmitted motor reactions, habits, techniques, ideas, and values—and the behavior they induce" (1948). Taking a different tack, Kluckhohn and Kelly (1945) emphasized the patterns for behavior, but excluded the behavior itself (Leach, 1967):

> By culture, we mean all those historically created designs for living, explicit and implicit, rational, irrational, and nonrational, which exist at any given time as potential guides for the behavior of men.

Still another approach was to focus on the artifacts of culture, the physical evidence that man leaves behind, "the man-made part of the environment" (Herskovits, 1955).

All these definitions have in common the fact that they reflect popular trends in social sciences at the time. More recently, the influence of developments in cognitive psychology and Chomskian linguistics is evident; anthropologists now define culture in more cognitive terms. Among these attempts to characterize culture, Goodenough's definition (1971) is perhaps the most widely quoted. He sees culture as a "system of standards for perceiving, believing, evaluating, and acting."

According to Goodenough, different cultures use different systems of perceiving, believing, evaluating, and acting. The individual who comes into contact with different groups of people will eventually develop a sense of the system under which these people operate; this system will be perceived as the culture of the other group. Different cultures are recognized as those groups of people which an individual sees as having different systems (Goodenough, 1971).

The traditional view of culture is that it applies only to faraway exotic societies and that there is only one culture to each society. According to Goodenough, however, culture applies equally to our own industrialized societies. Furthermore, not only may a variety of cultures be present in one society, but an individual may be competent in more than one culture. Just as individuals can have varying degrees of competence in more than one language, so can they have varying degrees of competence in more than one culture. In other words, just as individuals may have a "communicative repertoire" (Hymes, 1972), so can they have a *cultural repertoire* when they have developed or acquired competence in more than one culture. An example would be a Chinese-American who is competent not only in mainstream American culture, but also in the unique culture of a Chinatown community, including traditional Chinese cultural values and interaction rules.

We believe the notions of cultural competence and cultural repertoire are important in investigating the match or mismatch of home/school culture of minority children and in answering the question of whether the school and home environments are sufficiently congruent to allow children to use their own cultural competence successfully in the school environment. An interesting case in point is the success of the reading instruction in the Kamehameha Early Education Program (KEEP). The KEEP program's effectiveness in teaching Hawaiian children how to read seems to lie in the structuring of the reading lesson in such a way as to permit the application of the children's native cultural competence (See Au and Jordan, this volume).

Many definitions of culture contain a reference to culture as communication. Communication and interaction are at the hub of human existence, and accordingly, should appear in any comprehensive definition of culture. For example, the notion of culture as communication is implicit in Goodenough's definition: Our perceptions, beliefs, evaluations, and actions all relate to aspects of human communication and the sending and receiving of thoughts, feelings, and information. Other scholars have expressed this idea more explicitly. To facilitate discussion of his theory of culture, Edward T. Hall treats "culture in its entirety as a form of communication" (1959). Edmund Leach refers to culture as a "communication system." Recognizing the importance of language in culture, he stresses mutual intelligibility as a "fundamental necessity for any cohesive social group" (Leach, 1967). Members of a group, in order to remain a group, must be mutually intelligible; they must communicate.

Having examined a number of definitions of culture, we will now attempt to define culture in a specific way so as to clarify the meaning and purpose of this volume. At least within the confines of this book, culture as communication seems to possess several advantages over other definitions. Culture as communication avoids the traditional emphasis on the products of human activities as culture and calls into mind the dynamic processes through which a person acquires, maintains, and transmits his culture. Because communication is a construct common to sociology, psychology, anthropology, and linguistics, this treatment of culture highlights the interdisciplinary efforts entailed in a successful study of culture. And as this volume represents a new interdisciplinary approach toward understanding the cultural diversity and complexity within classrooms, it is fitting that communication be included in our definition of culture. In fact, this book is basically about communication and miscommunication in intercultural situations in the classroom.

Anthropological theories of culture have repeatedly hypothesized that culture exists on two levels. Linton (1940), for example, makes a distinction between *overt* and *covert* cultures: the former is easily visible and described; the latter, not visible and difficult to describe. Kluckhohn (1949) introduces a similar distinction and refers to *explicit* and *implicit* cultures. What people can talk about and be specific about, such as traditional customs and laws, constitutes their overt or explicit culture. What they take for granted, or what exists beyond conscious awareness, is their covert or implicit culture. It is the covert or implicit culture which is of interest to us here, because it is most often a factor in miscommunication. Since one important goal of this book is to call attention to the "out-of-awareness" aspects of communication in bilingual multicultural classrooms, we must attend to these aspects in our definition of culture.

Taking into consideration Goodenough's definition, the treatment of culture as communication, and the notions of explicit and implicit culture, we can now attempt to formulate a working definition of culture for the purpose of this book: Culture is essentially a form of communication with learned and shared, explicit and implicit rules for perceiving, believing, evaluating, and acting.

It seems obvious, from this definition of culture, that many different cultures must exist within a society as big and complex as our own. Indeed, as Goodenough (1976) points out, "multiculturalism is present to some degree in every human society." However, the extent of the cultural diversity and complexity of this society is not commonly recognized; we discuss this point in the next section.

Culture within the Greater American Context

According to the melting pot theory, American culture is created by people from diverse cultures and is unique and distinctive from the contributing cultures (Baratz and Baratz, 1970). In reality, however, there are many different cultures dominated by the mainstream Anglo culture. The failures of researchers in social science and education to recognize the existence of these dominated and often oppressed cultures has led to many erroneous conclusions regarding minority children. We will return to this point later in our discussion.

In order to understand minority cultural experiences and to interpret correctly the results of social science research, Hall and Freedle (1975) suggest that distinctions be made among holistic, embedded, and encapsulated cultures. This formulation is at variance with that traditionally maintained in, for example, cross-cultural psychology, where the focus has been upon the comparison and contrast of holistic cultures. Little attention has been given to subcultures. In order to make studies of these subcultures meaningful, proper contextualization within the holistic culture is necessary. Hall and Freedle make a further distinction between embedded and encapsulated subcultures:

> The embedded subculture is one that must function as if it were an integral part of the larger culture with few of the rights and privileges of that larger culture; the encapsulated subculture is allowed to maintain its cultural practices in such a way that their impact on those of the prevailing culture is minimal or nonexistent. (p.4)

Black-American and Spanish-American cultures are examples of embedded subcultures; American-Indian and Chinese-American, encapsulated subcultures. Traditionally, Black-Americans have been constantly influenced by the mainstream culture, yet have few of the privileges of that culture. In contrast, American Indians on reservations are much more isolated from the dominant culture of White America.

This scheme of classification is based not only on cultural differences among the groups but also on the structural pluralism of this society. Structural pluralism refers to the "differential distribution of rights, privileges, and scarce resources in the public domain" (Sanday, 1976; p. 54)—a sad but real fact of present day American "democracy." Subcultural groups in America are typically short on political power and oppressed economically by the dominant cultural group.

Being a member of such a dominated subculture often causes a person to behave and perceive in certain characteristic ways, inviting more prejudice, oppression, and discrimination (Hall and Freedle, 1975).

Since the schools of a society tend to reflect its social structure, American school and classroom culture has typically been that of the Anglo group. It is, then, imperative that those concerned with minority education take into consideration the compatability or incompatability of the home and school cultures of minority cultural children. It also follows that teacher/child and peer communication or miscommunication is an important area of investigation which can uncover the underlying sociocultural rules of classroom interaction.

Useful and important as it is to classify the subcultural groups within the American context and to recognize cultural differences in the classrooms, we have to be conscious of the danger of pigeonholing and stereotyping minority students by assuming a one-to-one relationship between culture and ethnicity. Even though members of an ethnic group may share a culture, the individuals of a particular ethnic group can also acquire competence in the cultures of other ethnic groups. Furthermore, members of a social class, through constant interactions in social settings, tend to develop and share a system of standards of perceiving, believing, evaluating, and acting across ethnic boundaries. Upper or upper-middle-class Blacks and Spanish-Americans may have more in common with the dominant Anglo culture than with their own ethnic groups. Garcia (1974), in the same vein, points out the cultural diversity in Chicano communities across the country. Anthropologists have also amply investigated and documented the cultural diversity among American Indian tribes.

This warning of general cultural stereotyping must not be taken too lightly. Treatment of cultural grouping as isomorphic with racial grouping has resulted in mistaking cultural differences for racial (genetic) ones. Indeed, the deficit/difference and nature/nurture debates in education and the social sciences can be traced back to such a misconception. In the following section, we will discuss the major assumptions underlying these debates.

Cultural Deficit, Cultural Difference, and Cultural Pluralism

The lower test scores, and school failure of minority children have frequently been attributed to cultural or genetic deficit (Jensen, 1969, 1971; Bereiter et al., 1966; Deutsch et al., 1967); the cultural bias of achievement and IQ tests has too often been ignored. This deficit approach assumes cultural homogeneity in this country and, thus, treats any difference from the "all-American" culture and standard English usage as deficiency and pathology. In this deficit model, children of linguistic and cultural minorities have been said to have either an inferior, pathological variety of language and culture or none at all. Compensatory educational remedies and early childhood intervention programs such as Head Start are usually based on this erroneous assumption (Baratz and Baratz, 1970; Valentine, 1971). Unfortunately, such rejection of the minority child's language and culture is often perceived by the child as a rejection of herself or himself. Even more un-fortunately, the child is often punished for his native linguistic and cultural com-petence. Such repression and discrimination, compounded with the resulting low self-concept suffered by the minority child, has given the ethnocentric deficit view the power of self-fulfilling prophecy.

Recently, social scientists have repeatedly "discovered" and documented the logic and richness of the so-called "deprived" minority children's language and culture (Labov, 1970; Baratz, 1970; Cazden et al., 1972). In light of these new findings, a new approach, or rather, a new attitude has been advocated for the study of the educational difficulties of minority children. This new approach, labeled the Cultural Difference Model (Lee and Gropper, 1974), recognizes group differences without imposing any value judgment. All differences must be treated with equal respect and understanding. Cultural diversity within the society is to be considered a unique source of strength instead of weakness.

However, this more enlightened attitude among social researchers and educators is obviously not enough. Under the present circumstances of structural pluralism in the society, the cultural difference model can easily be turned into an ethnocentric deficit model (Lee and Gropper, 1974). A case in point is the con-temporary bilingual education movement. The proponents of the movement had hoped to solve the educational problems of linguistic minority children and to guarantee the equality of educational opportunity of these children by utilizing and including the richness of their linguistic and cultural heritages in the school curriculum. But unfortunately, bilingual programs in the schools have character-istically followed the deficit model and have more or less become yet another compensatory educational reform.

To avoid the danger that bilingual education may become merely a new sort of compensatory education and to achieve their stated goals, a number of proponents have argued for "maintenance" as opposed to "transitional compen-satory" programs (Fishman, 1977) to elicit the support of the mainstream culture.

It is not our purpose here to get into the controversies of this educational reform movement. (For a comprehensive review, see *Bilingual Education: Current Perspectives, Vols. I-V*, Center for Applied Linguistics.) We would like to suggest, however, that equality of educational opportunity in our racially stratified society (Ogbu, 1979) will be achieved only through the promotion of cultural pluralism.

By cultural pluralism we refer to that situation in a society where different cultures coexist on an equal basis, and ethnic and cultural minorities are neither dominated nor polarized into ethnic interest groups. Cultural pluralism would allow each and every child of majority or minority cultures to develop not only a positive concept of self and group identity, but a larger cultural repertoire as well. In American society today, it is primarily minority culture members who develop competence in another—the dominant—culture through necessity, not choice, and at the expense of their own identity. Many minority educators, therefore, con-sider cultural pluralism a necessary strategy not only toward true equality of education for minority children, but also toward intergroup cooperation and inte-gration (Leacock, 1977; Lewis, 1976).

Fortunately, it now appears that attitudes toward minority cultures in the United States are changing. Cultural deficit has given way to cultural difference, and cultural pluralism is gaining momentum, at least among some educators and social scientists. Cultural pluralism in the society at large still remains a distant reality, however. One way educators and social science researchers can contribute to this change is by studying cultural diversity in the classrooms and the wider community. In this regard, we see great promise in the use of ethnography as a research methodology.

Ethnography and Microethnography

Ethnography, as defined by Bauman (1972), is "the process of constructing through direct personal observation of social behavior, a theory of the working of a particular culture in terms as close as possible to the way members of that culture view the universe and organize their behavior within it." Hymes (1977, p. 172) defines ethnography in terms of its application to educational research:

> What happens to children in schools appears to depend on how the children interpret their world, given such categories as they have available. To find out what they see and do, to convey that knowledge in a way that permitted some of the texture of their lives and world to come through, would be what I mean by ethnography.

Inherent and essential to these and other definitions of ethnography is an open-minded attitude toward the studying of cultures. Ethnographers try not to impose their own cultural categories but describe the culture under study in terms that correspond to its members' categories.

Because of the nature and philosophy of its qualitative and holistic approach (Rist, 1977), ethnography can be important in combatting the ethnocentric aspects of traditional research and in contributing to the understanding of minority cultures within this country. Ethnographers can provide vital information regarding what minority children bring to schools, and educators can then build on what the children have already acquired and experienced. In fact, recent ethnographic work in sociolinguistics and anthropology has documented significant cultural differences and their influences on the teaching and learning of minority children (Cazden et al., 1972). We believe that more ethnographic studies of minority children in the classrooms and the wider community are needed before any substantial improvement can be made in their education.

Thanks to the recent advancement in technology in the audiovisual field, ethnographers have refined their methodology, conducting "constitutive ethnography" (Mehan, 1978, 1979, and this volume), "microethnography" (Erickson, 1977) or "ethnographic monitoring" (Hymes, this volume). In contrast to ethnography in general, microethnography is much more focused, narrower in scope, and extremely fine-grained in analysis. (For a more detailed discussion on this methodology, see Mehan, this volume, and Erickson and Shultz, 1977). Studies using microethnographic analysis of videotape data have managed to capture very subtle and usually out-of-awareness aspects of classroom interaction and communication (Byers and Byers, 1972; McDermott and Gospodinoff, Van Ness, this volume). Evident in these studies is the joy and excitement of discovery — especially in uncovering the implicit or unconscious cultural rules which, according to Hall (1959, 1966, 1976), bind us and control us in many unknown ways. Such studies can not only bring the child's culture into the consciousness of the teacher but also bring the teacher's culture into his own consciousness: As Bernstein puts it (1972), "If the culture of the teacher is to become part of the consciousness of the child, then the culture of the child must first be in the consciousness of the teacher."

The implications of microethnographic studies to the education of minority culture children are far-reaching indeed. Carrasco's, Au and Jordan's, and Mohatt and Erickson's papers in this volume demonstrate what direct benefits can be reaped through such basic microethnographic research.

As Erickson (this volume) points out, entailed in the methodology of microethnography in the classrooms is the close collaboration necessary between the teacher and researcher. Both are sensitized and are transformed in the process (See Florio and Walsh, and Carrasco, this volume). This new research methodology has unintentionally opened up a new avenue toward more effective teacher education and teacher self-evaluation of his or her own classroom behavior (Mohatt and Erickson, this volume).

Because of the above-mentioned implications of microethnography to the education of minority culture children, we have decided that this book on culture and the bilingual classroom should provide a forum for microethnographic research in the classroom. We believe the studies in this volume will help move the discussion of culture in the classroom from its vague and uncertain terms toward a more precise documentation of cultural diversity in our classrooms.

Rationale and Organization

The papers in this volume are grouped into two sections: (1) General Theoretical and Methodological Issues, and (2) Microethnographic Studies of Minority Culture Children in the Classroom. This division may be a bit arbitrary, since some of the papers in the first section are based on specific case studies, and some in the second address theoretical and methodological issues. The division is not clear-cut, but for the sake of clarity and easy reference, we consider this partition necessary. The case studies in Section II are further grouped according to the population under investigation (Native Americans, Hawaiian Americans, etc.). These groupings are also arbitrary, to a certain extent, but since this volume is largely concerned with culture, we feel it is important to emphasize the variety of cultures represented here. Certainly, the arguments of the papers go far beyond any ethnic or cultural labeling, a case in point being the McDermott and Gospodinoff paper. The subject of the study *is* Puerto Rican, but that fact really has little do to with the main point of the paper, which will be discussed later.

I. General Methodological and Theoretical Issues

Erickson's paper provides theoretical background for most of the papers in this volume, and, therefore, is a logical starting point. Erickson reviews three strategies for research which are qualitative in nature, yet can be made quantitative so as to be useful to other social science researchers. Two of these three strategies — "ethnographic monitoring" and "studies deriving from a cognitive theory of culture and social competence" — are the methodologies used extensively in the case studies in this volume. These two strategies involve "focused primary data collection," and Erickson argues for the validity and generalizability of studies based on these (qualitative, yet quantitative) methods. Erickson's paper is especially important as an introduction to the Mohatt and Erickson, and Van Ness papers. His call for a dialogue across disciplines also highlights one purpose of this volume.

While Erickson addresses the validity of ethnographic approaches to educational research in general, Mehan argues for the validity and importance of ethnography for bilingual education *per se*. Mehan first criticizes the traditional correlational approach to classroom research which tends to preclude a scrutiny of classroom dynamics. After reviewing existing ethnographic studies in educational settings, with particular emphasis on studies done on classroom organization, Mehan concludes that "basic ethnographic research on the linguistic situation of the community in relation to that of the school" is necessary before any successful and meaningful implementation of a bilingual program.

Hymes' paper further elaborates the importance of ethnographic research in bilingual education. He does not hesitate to claim that ". . . of all forms of scientific knowledge, ethnography is the most open, the most compatible with a democratic way of life"; this is precisely our sentiment in dedicating this book to studies of classroom ethnography which, we believe, will help to combat the traditional ethnocentric approach in educational research and encourage an open-minded pluralistic view. Like Mehan, Hymes considers ethnography essential in providing "initial knowledge" in the implementation of bilingual programs; beyond an initial state, however, "ethnographic monitoring" is needed to study the conduct, evaluation, and justification of bilingual programs. Eventually, ethnography will be essential to the evaluation and justification of the bilingual education movement itself.

Mehan provides an extensive review of ethnographic work in educational research to argue for the efficacy of such a methodology; Hymes presents the same argument in a more theoretical and philosophical manner. Taking a different tack, Cazden and Leggett, from an applied point of view, recommend ethnography as one way to achieve Lau Remedies II. This paper is addressed specifically to the creation of culturally responsive education; the authors find that "there is probably no more powerful way" to do so than through "ethnographic monitoring." They suggest that monitoring be carried out immediately as part of evaluation procedures in all bilingual programs, and that community-specific ethnographic research be conducted and supported whenever possible. This paper also contains a thorough, yet concise, literature review in cultural differences in cognitive and interactional styles and, thus, serves very well as background reading for the papers in this volume.

Florio and Walsh's paper is based on a longitudinal ethnographic case study. It traces the development of the collaborative relationship of the teacher and researcher in classroom research. It is an interesting, insightful, and personal account of the development of a new methodology. A microanalysis of a case study is presented to demonstrate the application of this methodology. Similar procedures are followed in the Van Ness, Mohatt and Erickson, and Carrasco studies in the second part of the book.

II. Microethnographic Studies of Minority Culture Children in the Classrooms

Mohatt and Erickson describe cultural differences in the way an Odawa Indian teacher and a non-Indian teacher organize participation structures in the classroom. Van Ness analyzes the social organization of behavior in getting ready for reading in an Alaskan classroom with one native teacher and seven students (all but one are native Koyukon Athabaskan). Both papers uncover the implicit cultural patterns of interaction and present them in precise descriptive statistical terms; they find culture to be a critical variable in cross-cultural classrooms. A particularly important point regarding bilingual education is made by Mohatt and Erickson: ". . . invisible cultural rules survive and remain quite strong long after the children lose their referential language." Of interest to practitioners is Mohatt and Erickson's report on the successful application of microethnographic or ethnographic monitoring methodology in the training of school personnel. The training procedures reported in the paper should prove very useful in other settings as well.

Au and Jordan's paper analyzes a successful reading program for Hawaiian children. This culturally responsive solution toward Hawaiian children's reading problems is a result of ongoing interdisciplinary research efforts combined with the intuition and experience of the classroom teacher. The authors demonstrate how ethnographic study of the native culture and of instructional contexts can contribute to culturally appropriate strategies for the education of minority culture children. Once again, the importance of teacher/researcher cooperation in classroom ethnography is emphasized.

The paper by Carrasco documents the discovery of the "out-of-teacher-awareness" communicative competence of a Chicano bilingual child. This paper testifies to the importance of videotape and its analysis in educational settings. Carrasco suggests that teachers pay attention to "appropriately behaved" children in their classrooms, especially in the assessment of these children's social and intellectual competence, for they tend to become invisible to the teachers. Carrasco, in documenting his personal research experience as a classroom ethnographer, shows once again the validity of ethnographic monitoring and the value of teacher and researcher collaboration. Most of all, he demonstrates that an ethnographic monitoring study does not have to be time-consuming to be worthwhile.

LeCompte's paper is unique in this collection in the sense that it is the only study conducted without the use of videotape analysis. Its approach is a more traditional type of classroom ethnography. LeCompte attempts to identify the hidden curriculum — norms, values, and behavior patterns important for the socialization into the adult society — which tends to be different from the culture of minority children and cause difficulties for these children in the classrooms. However, outside the hidden curriculum (i.e., "management core"), LeCompte discovers the discretionary area of behavior which often depends on the personality and philosophy of the individual teacher and generally allows a certain degree of flexibility for the teacher to help lessen the possibly negative impact of the "management core" on the minority culture children. LeCompte concludes that, besides the teachers' adapting the learning style of the school to that of the minority children (in the discretionary area), the hidden curriculum should be made explicit to these children so that they can successfully cope with the management core. However, as the other studies in this collection have pointed out, the management core is often implicit and invisible; we believe that the use of microethnography and ethnographic monitoring can make the hidden curriculum better understood.

Ludwig's paper follows the "tradition" of participation structure analysis set by Philips (1972, 1974), Mehan (1974, 1978), and Erickson and Shultz (1977). Ludwig identifies four verbal participation structures: Posing the Problem, Feeling Around, Redirection, and Finding the Problem. Then she focuses on the analysis of metaphrasing — a strategy used by students to set up a Feeling Around time in order to change the nature of the interaction patterns in the classroom. Ludwig's data indicate that, even though both black and white students use metaphrasing, there seem to be differences between black and white students in the functions this strategy serves. Due to the limited scope of the data, the conclusion is only tentative; more research into the verbal participation structures in the classroom is needed. Nevertheless, Ludwig has identified a potentially fertile area (like the discretionary area for the teachers in LeCompte's paper) in which students can become active participants in the organization of classroom structures. Teacher and student can then jointly create an environment more conducive to learning.

So far, all the papers in the volume have identified various differences between the school and classroom culture and that of minority children. They have attributed the difficulties and problems encountered by these children to such differences. Most of the papers have called for culturally responsive or culturally appropriate solutions in the school systems. McDermott and Gospodinoff, on the other hand, present a completely different interpretation of the surface differences in interaction rules or styles. These differences are far more than cultural; they are socially and politically designed and encouraged to maintain ethnic borders. This interpretation brings to mind the discussion of structural pluralism in the second section of this introduction and echoes the sentiment in Hymes' paper: "In sum, small differences can become symbols of hostility, and large differences can be accepted and ignored. The causes are outside of language (and culture)." Only when the structure and attitudes of the society at large are changed can educational innovation for the sake of minority children succeed. McDermott and Gospodinoff's microethnography of the reading group is focused on a specific Puerto Rican child's interaction with his teacher. However, due to their interpretation which transcends cultural categorizations, we should, perhaps, put a big question mark right next to "Puerto Rican Americans" in our Table of Contents.

Finally, because we do not intend to leave our readers on a pessimistic note, Kimball's reflection on the potential contributions of anthropology to educational research is included. We hope that the findings from anthropology, cross-cultural psychology, sociology, and other relevant disciplines will contribute to our knowledge of minority culture children in the classroom and in the larger community, and help make this society more truly democratic. Certainly more ethnographic and microethnographic studies such as those described in this volume are needed. We hope this book will inspire teachers, researchers, administrators, and policy makers to move in this direction.

Grace Pung Guthrie
William S. Hall

PART I
General Theoretical and Methodological Issues

2

SOME APPROACHES TO INQUIRY
IN SCHOOL-COMMUNITY ETHNOGRAPHY*

Frederick Erickson

I have a conviction that the art and the science of qualitative field research can articulate with forms of research generally employed in the study of education. It is important to recognize, however, that when researchers of differing orientations come together to discuss collaboration, there are real differences in premises and methods — in cultures of inquiry — that are likely to make not only for genuine conflict among positions but also for mutual misinterpretation of what the positions of "others" are. In short, one can expect problems of cross-cultural miscommunication and methodological ethnocentrism in symposia of this kind.

Consequently, I begin this paper by considering some of the differences between "qualitative" and "quantitative" types of research. Then I suggest three kinds of strategies for identifying qualitatively derived models and data that could be useful in collaboration across orientations and conclude with some remarks on implications.

An Attempt to Define Some Terms

In emphasizing differences among research orientations it might seem that I am suggesting that the distinction between the *qualitative* and the *quantitative* is the most appropriate way to characterize differences in approach to educational research. I am not sure this is so. There seems to be a distinction among approaches that would be worth making, but it's not clear what that distinction is. The dis-

*Reproduced by permission of the Council on Anthropology and Education from the *Anthropology and Education Quarterly* 8(2):58-69, 1977.

tinction between experimental and naturalistic methods may be a more useful one, but that's not entirely satisfactory either. Feinberg's term "psychostatistician" may become a useful label for those who have a "mainstream" orientation to educational research. However one defines the terms, it seems that the differences among approaches lie not in the presence or absence of quantification *per se* (if one thinks of quantification simply as a means of summarizing information) but in the underlying assumptions of method and proof.

In developing strategies for collaboration across orientations, a fundamental issue is how to get from qualitative study of naturally occurring events in everyday life, that which is essential to such work, without making use of it in logically inappropriate ways, or so changing the processes of data collection and analysis that the approach we call "qualitative" or "ethnographic" becomes something other than what made it potentially useful and interesting in the first place. This is a concern shared by Hammel who suggests that anthropologists need to learn the languages of other social scientists, notably statistics, not only because quantitative techniques are useful in their own right but also because they enable one to argue in the other people's language, "to point out in no uncertain terms when the assumptions of . . . mathematical models are violated by the ethnographic facts" (Hammel, 1976:32).

As one who knows next to nothing about quantitative methods — just enough to have had numbers demystified for me — I am impatient with qualitative researchers whose fear of "number crunching" stems from their knowing absolutely nothing about quantitative methods. But some researchers who, like Hammel, are mathematically sophisticated are still concerned that quantitative approaches (and their usual traveling companions, the verification procedures borrowed by social scientists from the physical sciences) may do violence to "ethnographic facts." What are such facts, and what is such violence? What are some good reasons for researchers whose orientation can be labeled "qualitative" to be suspicious of other orientations?

I think that what is essential to qualitative or naturalistic research is not that it avoids the use of frequency data, but that its primary concern is with deciding what makes sense to count — with definitions of the quality of the things of social life. The reluctance of many qualitatively oriented researchers to count things may be related to a theoretically based reluctance to follow Durkheim's injunction (1895:1) to consider social facts as things. Researchers of the Malinowskian tradition in anthropology (and "fieldwork sociologists," "symbolic interactionists," and most recently "ethnomethodologists" in sociology) have been concerned with social *fact* as social *action*; with social *meaning* as residing in and constituted by people's *doing* in everyday life. These meanings are most often discovered through fieldwork by hanging around and watching people carefully and asking them why they do what they do, sometimes asking them as they are in the midst of their doing. Because of this orientation toward social meaning as embedded in the concrete, particular doings of people — doings that include people's intentions and points of view — qualitative researchers are reluctant to see attributes of the doing abstracted from the scene of social action and counted out of context.

I agree with Feinberg (1977): if qualitative researchers really want to do science and address the problem of the generalizability of insights derived from fieldwork (and if they also have the less disinterested aim of surviving in the arena of policy research), they must become able and willing to count social facts, too. The trick lies in defining carefully what the "facts" are in ways that are precise, reliable, and capable of quantitative summary, yet articulate with the meanings the facts have, to the people engaged in everyday life.

The "classical" way qualitative researchers state the social meaning of social facts is through descriptions whose terms have functional relevance within a model of system process. These are descriptions grounded in some theory of the event being described; no such descriptions are *mere* descriptions.

There are many ways to describe what happens in a social event other than in functionally relevant terms. We could, for example, describe the playing of chess in terms of movement in millimeters forward, backward, and sideways on a plane. The behavior of chess pieces on the board could be coded by observers this way with high inter-coder reliability, and the resulting data could be manipulated statistically. Yet by itself, this would tell us nothing about what was going on in the game of chess. We need descriptive categories with functional relevance for the game — checkmate, defense — terms for the *qualities of things* (in an etymologically literal sense) for the *kinds of kinds of things* that are meaningful for an understanding (a working theory) of the game as a whole (cf. Wittgenstein, 1953). To use Eisner's metaphor of *connoisseurship*, no connoisseur would describe chess in functionally irrelevant terms. It should be noted here that by "function" I do not mean it as the term is used by sociologists and anthropologists of various "functionalist" theoretical orientations. Rather, I mean "function" in the sense meant by linguists. This point will become clearer in the subsequent discussion.

Because the statement of functional relevance considers relations between parts and the whole, such work involves systems thinking. It is in this sense that ethnographic work is "holistic," not because of the size of the social unit but because units of analysis are considered analytically as wholes, whether that whole be a community, a school system and its political relations with its various "publics," the relations among those in a school building, or the beginning of one lesson in a single classroom.

Each of these wholes can be considered as a game. Qualitative research seeks to tell us what the game is: what attributes of "things" in the game are functionally relevant to playing the game, what appropriate relations among things there are in the game, and what the game related purposes of the players are. This may seem to researchers trained in other ways to be a claim to omniscience, but there do exist conventional rules of evidence and verification in qualitative analysis. On the basis of our definitions of the quality of things in functionally relevant terms, we can make predictions of how the game will unfold. The test of validity of the qualitatively "grounded" theory of the game is its predictive power; given a finite set of circumstances the theory can tell us what the players could appropriately do next.

I think part of the anxiety of qualitatively oriented researchers about quantification stems from the fear that what will be counted will be functionally irrelevant attributes of the things people are attending to in everyday life. Past history of interethnic conflict among the social sciences may make such anxiety understandable, especially when qualitatively derived models are met by researchers from different orientations shooting from the hip with such questions as, "Where's the evidence?" or "Why are there no verification procedures?" or "What's the sample?" without any reference to the qualitative researcher's main question, which is something like, "What's the game, and how can it be described?"

Qualitative researchers might respond by saying, "But my description works — it has predictive validity." This answer overlooks the fact that other researchers were not there in the field to see how events actually did unfold as the researcher finally learned through field experience — a socialization experience — to expect they would. It also ignores the deep distrust or ordinary, unmediated sense impressions that is an epistemological underpinning of standard scientific procedures of verification.

There are genuine differences across research orientations, but they may not be antithetical. One approach to articulation involves considering a distinction analogous to that between functionally relevant and irrelevant terms for description — the distinction between the "emic" and the "etic."

As a way of defining the difference between the "etic" and the "emic", we can consider a difference between kinds of variation among phenomena that can be summarized quantitatively: continuous variation (height, rate of heartbeat) and discontinuous or categorical variation (being tall, medium or short, left and right, presence and absence). In social life, people often treat continuous variation as if it were categorical, chopping up continua into meaningful chunks as if there were discontinuous thresholds — cutting points — along the continua. These perceived thresholds are meaningful in that people in everyday life take action with regard to them so habitually that the actions (and meanings) are conventional.

In everyday interaction, for example, people may treat the phenomenally continuous variable of *height* as if it were discontinuous, categorizing people as short, average, and tall in stature. Units of *stature*, then, would be social facts, defined in terms of people's discriminations of thresholds and the actions they take toward each other on the basis of those discriminations. The continuous variable, *height*, could be measured formally by an arbitrarily defined unit such as the inch or millimeter, capable of reliable use by observers in making low inference judgments. These units of description could be used in valid and reliable ways within a system of technical categorization independent from functional categories or discontinuous "chunks" used by people in thinking of stature.

The distinction between height and stature is analogous to the distinction linguists make between the "etic" and the "emic" — between phenomena considered from the point of view of standardized measurement of form (or if not in terms of measurement, at least in terms of systematic ways in which scientists as external observers define units) and phenomena considered from the functional point of view of the ordinary actor in everyday life (Sapir, 1925; Pike, 1967:35-

72; Pelto, 1970:67-87; and the discussion of Sapir's principle of *contrastive relevance* in the comments by Hymes in this volume).

Modern anthropology, sociology, and linguistics have shown great variation among human groups in the emic discrimination and emic salience of physical and social phenomena. Researchers in these disciplines can state systematically what is emic in everyday events and how people take action with regard to the emic. From my point of view, this is what is qualitative about research — statements of the quality of things and relations, descriptions of events in functional terms. Unfortunately, the "literary" narrative form of reporting traditional qualitative research sometimes obscures systematic statements about emic relations. And there is a difference between the particular procedures of discovery and verification employed in deriving and validating such statements of *quality* and those used by other social scientists. The two approaches to verification can articulate, it seems to me, at the point of correspondence between things considered in terms of their form and in terms of their function — the point of correspondence between the etic and the emic. Some aspects of the emic — of thresholds and "chunking" of experience for social use — can be operationally defined and measured etically, technically, in ways that permit low levels of inference in observer judgments.

One can do this for a piano. The intervals of pitch between keys can be specified etically in terms of cycles of vibration per second, like the etic measurements of distance in the example from chess. Such etic measurement of sound is not useful for playing the piano or for analyzing *as a game* the playing of pianos. But if we want to know if two pianos on which piano games are being played are comparable in tuning (so we can state some formal correspondence between the two games), then it is useful and appropriate. While etic measurement cannot tell us what the game *is* (which is a problem of emic, qualitative analysis), it can establish that features of two games are similar in form or different. If one piano were tuned in half steps and the other in quarter tones, we would show evidence in clearly defined operational terms that the game played on the quarter tone piano was not part of the Western European cultural system of music.

I think this working back and forth between etic and emic units of analysis can also be done in studying social events and social knowledge. Some key elements or features can be described etically and become grist for the mills of social scientists from different orientations. (Granted, some key features can't be described etically without doing violence to the uniqueness and spontaneity of everyday life.) This does not relegate qualitative research to initial states in scientific inquiry — to the primitive phase of "exploratory," "intuitive" work. Qualitative researchers have their own procedures for proof, for testing the predictive power of their "working theoretical" models, which can be used to judge the adequacy of qualitative work within the community of discourse and culture of inquiry of qualitative researchers. Work defined as adequate within this community can be used by the community to frame theory at more general levels. At the same time, researchers from different traditions of inquiry can make use of qualitatively derived insights. By learning more about how such insights are derived and stated, those researchers would be in a better position to judge the usefulness of qualitative data and methods for their own work.

For it is not as if researchers whose orientation is not primarily "qualitative" have a malevolent and perverted desire to quantify and derive theory from social "facts" defined in ways that are functionally irrelevant to actors in social life. At that level of generality, I think, the aims of social scientists are similar (with the possible exception of radical behaviorists). What "qualitative" researchers have to offer others is potentially valid insight into functionally relevant definitions of social facts. What "quantitative" researchers have to offer the "qualitatives" is ways of determining the generalizability of qualitative insights, ways of escaping from that tyranny of the single case.

In the next section, I will consider the first of three strategies discussed in this paper by which information derived from qualitative research can be made useful to other social scientists.

Textual Analysis of Ethnographic Reports

In his introduction to *Argonauts of the Western Pacific*, Malinowski called on ethnographers to report three kinds of descriptive information: (1) an outline of the social anatomy, (2) "imponderabilia of actual life and everyday behavior," and (3) members' points of view, especially as determined from a collection of typical narratives, utterances, folklore, and magical formulae, "as a *corpus inscriptionum*, as documents of native mentality" (1922:22,24).

I think what qualitative research does best and most essentially is to describe key incidents in functionally relevant descriptive terms and place them in some relations to the wider social context, using the key incident as a concrete instance of the workings of abstract principles of social organization.

It is from Malinowski's middle level of "imponderabilia" that the key incidents are derived, usually from field notes. In the research report the generic features of these incidents are highlighted with as much concrete detail as is necessary to make a statement of the relation of the instance to the pattern of the whole. The qualitative researcher's ability to pull out from field notes a key incident, link it to other incidents, phenomena, and theoretical constructs, and write it up so that others can see the generic in the particular, the universal in the concrete, the relation between part and whole (or at least between part and some level of context) may be the most important thing he does. Such selection, description, and interpretation is very emic — indeed, ontological. It involves massive leaps of inference over many different kinds of data from different sources — field notes, documents, elicited texts, demographic information, unstructured interviews, and very possibly survey data. This is a decision process analogous to that of the historian or biographer deciding which incidents among many in a person's life to describe.

Classic examples are Whyte's description of the bowling matches between the corner gang and another young men's club in *Street Corner Society* (1955:

318-320) and Malinowski's (1922) description of various incidents involved in the Kula trade network across a number of Melanesian islands. A recent example is Ogbu's story of how rumors spread in a multiracial, multiethnic school community (Ogbu, 1974:133-170). Such incidents of great "working-theoretical" salience may tie together the whole qualitative account. This is so for Whyte's bowling match. As Whyte described it, social relations were played out within and between groups in forms that he claims to have seen repeated in the neighborhood in widely differing group contexts. By describing the bowling match in rich detail, Whyte helps us to see how this instance is generic and how it related to many others.

I have described this process of selective reporting in producing a whole ethnography as *caricature* (Erickson, 1973): an abstraction from the diversity of phenomena as experienced so as to emphasize some features and deemphasize others. To say an image is a caricature is not to deny its validity. Indeed, caricatures in the graphic arts and in literary description can be "truer" than the "actual" life the caricaturist attempts to represent, as all art is in one way or another "truer" — more coherently organized — than life. However, the caricature's validity is of a different epistemological order from that of standard science. It would be fruitless to look for empirical evidence in the phenomenal world for the shape of Richard Nixon's nose as portrayed by some political cartoonists. There may be a "truth" in such portrayal, but it is not amenable to empirical investigation. Still, despite the tendency of ethnographic caricatures to go beyond the bounds of the empirical, the insights they report can have uses for researchers of other orientations.

By what means could these insights be codified and summarized without doing violence to their uniqueness? This is an issue of cross-case comparison in which the unit of analysis is the qualitative research report. The strategy that comes immediately to mind — the approach toward coding "ethnographic facts" across case studies taken by the Human Relations Area Files — may not be the most appropriate.[1]

The qualitative case study is a literary form potentially amenable to some kinds of "text criticism." Perhaps panels of readers with differing points of view — practitioners, policy planners, "quantitatives," and "qualitatives" — could go through a set of case studies and abstract from them key incidents and the interpretations of those incidents that together constitute the author's "working theoretical" models of social organization in the setting. While working models would vary both in the scale and complexity of the phenomena they attempt to account for, and in orientations of substantive, qualitatively grounded theory (and perhaps general theory) out of which they were constructed, such a review process could suggest common dynamics in operation across individual classrooms, schools, and school communities. It could point to fruitful directions for further research using strategies other than qualitative and might lead to research on aspects of educational processes that had not been considered before. But in addition, such foraging operations over the qualitatively defined "field" phenomenon *education in community life* might simply provide qualitative insight of a kind directly useful for varying audiences concerned with the study and practice of education — new ways of thinking about educational practice, everyday life in schools and communities, everyday aspects of attempts at change.

This is a process of cross-case comparison by panel review somewhat similar to that used by Tikunoff, Berliner, and Rist (1975) to identify potentially useful classroom interaction variables from the field notes of participant observers. The results of their subsequent research using reviewer defined variables suggest that review strategies may be useful in articulating the work of qualitatively oriented researchers with that of researchers with differing orientations.

The approach I am suggesting differs from that of Tikunoff, et al., in two ways. First, it differs by entering the process of qualitative, emic definition and modeling at a later stage, after the qualitative researcher has produced a final report by a process of inference and emphasis that gives the report a characteristic shape — the coherence of a caricature. (The decision processes that produce such shape are, I think, intrinsic and essential to the "classic" way of doing qualitative research.) Second, this approach differs by identifying as units of analysis not simply variables but models — ways of thinking about things and their relations that we might for some purposes choose to call *variable sets* and hypotheses, amenable to etic operationalization and testing, but which we might for other purposes choose to consider more loosely and less formally.

Since there seems to be a paucity of new ideas about how to think about what happens in educational, sociocultural, and political processes among actual children, teachers, administrators, and parents in school communities, this approach to finding out what qualitative researchers have to tell us may have considerable merit.

Focused Strategies of Primary Data Collection — An Apologia

The two remaining strategies to be discussed here for collaboration across research orientations involve more focused approaches to qualitative data collection. They may be more compatible with the methods of "psychostatistical" researchers than the textual analysis of qualitative research reports prepared by the "classic" hypertypical lone researcher, working for the most part through informally systematized methods of data collection. Before detailing these two strategies, an explanation is in order.

The decision to use more focused approaches changes the field experience of the researcher. It requires that fieldwork be conceived as a process of actively and consciously directed inquiry in which decisions about researchable problems and the statement of researchable questions are made while the researcher is in the field, rather than at some time after having left it.[2] Specification of data collection strategies while in the field presupposes a conscious theoretical orientation by the researcher — a conscious awareness of one's commitment to points of view derived from substantive theory in social science and from personal theory. Focused data collection also requires knowing something about the setting one is studying through information gathered before entering the setting as well as from first hand experience. This point is made very strongly by Hammel (1976) who, in speaking to anthropologists in particular, says that in the study of complex modern societies it is not useful as a research strategy to pretend to know nothing in advance about the setting one is studying.

Focused data collection strategies are incompatible with the "hypertypical" view of the field research process — in which one begins atheoretically with no prior conceptions about the setting, then "hangs around" letting the setting "tell you what's going on," and finally decides what the problems were after returning from the field. Systematic strategies would seem to leave too little room for intuition and happenstance, for the unmediated richness of field experience. Certainly, there is a danger that focused data collection can freeze the research process prematurely. But greater danger lies in adopting the hypertypical view of field research as highly spontaneous, for I think this view is based on a wrong-headed interpretation of what actually happens in the field. No setting, I would argue, "tells" anybody anything; no questions are generated directly from experience — there are no pure inductions. Research questions come from interaction between experience and some kind of theory, substantive or personal. It is extremely important that qualitative researchers make that interaction as explicit as possible both to their audience in reporting and to themselves while in the field. In no other way can qualitative researchers cumulate knowledge, and in no other way can they avoid a "credibility gap" with other social scientists (cf. Pelto, 1970:1-46).

In short, I am arguing that research on schools can be both qualitative and systematic. We have theory in sociology and anthropology relevant to what happens in American schools. We know a lot already about what happens, and there is no need to pretend methodologically that we don't know anything. On the basis of both kinds of knowledge — the theoretically derived and the experientially derived — we can identify phenomena of emic salience to persons in the setting and operationally define those phenomena in etic terms for systematic procedures of data collection and analysis.

Strategies for doing this can be thought of in two main streams of approach to focused data collection. The first involves working with definitions of what is relevant taken from the existing conscious awareness of school practitioners and from existing literature in social science and educational research. Following Hymes, I will call this approach "ethnographic monitoring." The other approach involves discovering new phenomena of functional relevance — new variables and relationships among variables that may not be accounted for in the conscious awareness of school practitioners but may be suggested by recent research and theory development in the social sciences.

Ethnographic Monitoring

To monitor anything one needs: (1) a working model of the whole system or subsystem that is to be monitored and (2) some means of measuring functionally critical features of system process. For example, in constructing a cybernetic system to monitor a home heating plant, one needs a model that specifies some relations between the fuel consumed in the furnace firebox on the one hand and room air temperature on the other and a way to measure amounts of fuel and room air temperature. In a jury-rigged man-machine cybernetic system like the old-fashioned home heating plant, tolerances are fairly wide and the measurement operations can be very informal, approximate, and "emic." One waits until the air temperature is "too cold," then goes to the basement and shovels "enough" coal into the furnace. Not only is precise measurement capability unnecessary but a general theory of system dynamics is not necessary either; one doesn't need a fully developed theory of heat and heat transfer or of combustion to make the system work.

Learning environments, as social systems, are such jury-rigged operations, capable of useful monitoring in fairly crude ways so long as what is measured is functionally critical to the system. The relatively loose ebb and flow of everyday operations in classrooms and other learning environments, together with adaptive learning strategies of children and adults in such settings, results in adaptive knowledge of system processes by members of the setting. They can tell the researcher some of the phenomena that are relevant to monitoring system processes.

In sum, relevant phenomena can be identified on the basis of (1) prior qualitative research in the same or similar settings, (2) the concerns of participants in the setting, or (3) a combination of (1) and (2). These methods of identification resemble those advocated for "formative" evaluation of educational settings (cf. House, 1973; Provus, 1971). Such a focus on issues of value to those affected by and involved in the research makes possible humane and genuinely collaborative relationships between the researcher and the practitioner (cf. Hymes). After relevant phenomena are identified, they can be "monitored" through systematic, focused observation that generates data capable of quantitative summary.

An example of ethnographic monitoring is the work of Shultz and Harkness (Shultz, n.d.). They were interested in the social contexts in which children spoke Spanish or English in bilingual education programs. This was a salient issue for the program's administrators who were concerned that despite their aim of maintaining children's use of the Spanish language spoken at home, tests showed that the longer the children were in the program the less well they used Spanish. The administrators and researchers wanted to see what "formative" aspects of the children's experience in the bilingual program might be producing these "summative" test results. Such an issue is appropriate for investigation by ethnographic monitoring both because of its salience for program personnel and because an existing body of knowledge — the discipline of linguistics — provides a system of description by which relevant phenomena (in this case "which language is being spoken") can be reliably categorized and monitored.

Shultz and Harkness put a cassette tape recorder in a child's backpack, had each Spanish-speaking child in a bilingual classroom wear it for a half hour, and recorded the child's naturally occurring speech. Analysis of the tapes revealed that the children who had been in the program longest spoke English most frequently to other children (frequency measured in percent of time the child was speaking each language in freely initiated conversation with other students). Monitoring the bilingual teachers, the researchers found that while the teachers conducted the formal "content" instruction half in each language, they gave "procedural" instructions almost exclusively in English. English speaking ability thus became a valuable commodity in the social and political economy of the classroom. The children who had been in the program longer became "brokers" between the newcomers and the teacher, translating the teacher's instructions into Spanish for the newcomers and "speaking up for them" to the teacher in English.

Similar dynamics in the politics of speaking were found in a Center for Applied Linguistics study of a classroom in another state. Thus, by turning up in two classrooms, a finding from ethnographic monitoring has escaped the tyranny of the single case. At this point, it would be possible to check generalizability across a number of classrooms. Moreover, the potentially key factor in the system, the teacher's giving procedural instructions entirely in English, can probably be controlled, making possible experimental manipulation of the variable. Or more simply, some teachers might decide to give procedural instructions in Spanish, try to change their behavior, and monitor themselves by wearing the backpack occasionally. They then would control the techniques of the research process and the information generated by it.

There are a number of other aspects of social relations in learning environments that can be operationalized and monitored in quite straightforward ways.

1. *The amounts of time children spend listening to the teacher.* Aspects of listening behavior that culture members interpret as showing attention — features such as eye contact and postural orientation and stability — can be monitored reliably in detailed coding from videotapes or crude but reliable coding *in situ* by classroom observers. Issues of who pays attention, how much, and the relation of children's attention behavior to teachers' perceptions of their intelligence and motivation can be addressed, as can culturally patterned differences in ways of showing attention, interest, and comprehension.

2. *The topical relevance of children's discourse with the teacher and with other children.* This variable, mentioned in Cooley's discussion of research on effective teaching, involves both the topical relevance of children's classroom talk and teachers' strategies of fostering topical relevance. Audiotape probably would be necessary and, given the complex ways the meanings of ordinary talk are embedded in the social situation of the moment, videotape recording might be desirable.

3. *Teacher assessment of the intellectual competence of children on the basis of social performance.* This recalls Cazden's "mini-tests" by which teachers informally size up the children, Rist's approach to the same point, and Leacock's "we-they" dichotomy in teachers' folk taxonomies of children. At issue are: (1) the cues teachers employ to make judgments of competence — e.g., how children talk, listen, sit, respond to procedural instructions (and, following Rist, how they smell); (2) the relative differentiation of the teacher's typology of children in the class — the range of "taxons" or dimensions of contrasts in the teacher's cognitive

map of the kind of students in the class; and (3) the relative stability of the teacher's typology over time. While monitoring procedures for this topic are not as well developed as for the previous two, and while the judgments required of researchers are more complex, recent literature suggests that the topic is important. Detailed observational records, derived from participant observation alone or in combination with videotaping, as well as interview data would be necessary.

4. *The regularity of classroom activity rhythms.* This can be monitored by timing the speech and body motion of students and teachers and the sustainment of postural configurations by classroom groups. Irregular rhythms of speech and body motion and aperiodic sequences of group postural configurations seem to have social significance. Such occurrences were judged "uncomfortable moments" with high interrater reliability in studies of dyadic encounters (Erickson, 1976; Shultz, 1974), and we have found analogous patterns in recent research in classrooms. Ruiz, in a study of videotapes of 100 Head Start classrooms, found that the variable that discriminated best between inexperienced and experienced teachers was the periodicity of the teacher's movement around the room — the duration of each "passage" from one child or group to the next and the duration of time spent with the child or group at a "destination." For experienced teachers there was little variation in the durations of "passages" and "destinations," while for inexperienced teachers there was great variation. We have found similar patterns of temporal regularity among experienced teachers in classrooms in Boston suburbs and in an Indian reservation school in northern Ontario.

Studies Deriving from a Cognitive Theory of Culture and Social Competence

Most of the studies to be reviewed here are recent. They approach issues of the sociocultural organization of learning environments — some of which are new to educational practitioners and researchers and others of which have been addressed before in thinking about education, but in different ways.

The studies share an overall theoretical frame of reference that is emerging from theoretical and empirical work in anthropology, sociology, linguistics, and social psychology. One way this general approach has been articulated in anthropology is in a cognitive theory of culture. Goodenough has defined culture ideationally as "a system of standards for perceiving, believing, evaluating, and acting" (1971:41). What one has to know in order to act appropriately as a member of a given group includes knowing not only what to do oneself but also how to anticipate the actions of others.[3]

Related definitions can be found in linguistics and sociology. Hymes (1974b) notes that knowing how to speak appropriately involves much more than *linguistic competence,* which is Chomsky's (1965) term for a speaker's capacity to employ the sound system and grammar of a language in generating sentences. For Hymes, *linguistic competence* must necessarily entail *social competence,* since acceptable speaking requires the ability to produce not only grammatically appropriate speech but also situationally appropriate speech. Less closely related, but still comparable, is the emphasis on "member's work" — the exercise of practical reasoning in everyday social life — found in the emerging field of sociology called ethnomethodology (Garfinkel, 1967). All these theoretical positions have in common an emphasis on what people need to know in order to do what they do in ordinary social interaction. They emphasize not simply behavior but the knowledge necessary to produce the behavior.

Educational settings, in schools and families and communities, are especially appropriate for study from this theoretical perspective because they aim to transmit knowledge about how to perceive, believe, evaluate, and act. This transmission takes place largely through the medium of face-to-face interaction (Gearing and Sangree, in press). School classrooms are settings in which special attention is paid to appropriate ways of behaving. Appropriate behavior may be explicity encouraged, an inappropriate behavior — or the absence of appropriate behavior — may be explicitly pointed out and negatively sanctioned. A general question for classroom interaction research is, "What do teachers and children have to know in order to do what they are doing?"

There are two main ways by which we can study people's cultural knowledge — by asking them and by watching them. First I will describe approaches based primarily on asking, then approaches based primarily on watching.

Questionnaires are one way to elicit people's cultural knowledge. In a recent attempt by Jacob and Sanday (1976), questionnaire items were constructed on the basis of Goodenough's general theory of culture and designed to elicit expectations for appropriate school behavior. The instrument was administered to 266 Puerto Rican students and dropouts and 15 teachers in New York, Philadelphia, and Vineland, New Jersey. Interestingly, Jacob and Sanday found through simple statistical analysis that the categories *low hooky—high hooky* discriminated student responses better than the categories *dropout—stayin*, i.e., the responses of some dropouts and stayins were very similar. By moving to this more differentiated classification, they found that the responses of high hooky dropouts and stayins were more similar to those of teachers than were the responses of low hooky students. Low hooky students saw fewer behaviors as acceptable, relative both to teachers and high hooky students. Their low risk strategy of showing up for school is consonant with this view of what is expected of them. One would expect them to adopt low risk strategies in everyday life in the classroom as well.

While the authors acknowledge a number of technical problems involving possible sample and instrument bias, the study is interesting because it reveals a potentially salient dimension of analysis that was not intuitively obvious when the research was begun. Such results can inform further fieldwork, e.g., to see if low hooky students do indeed adopt low risk strategies in the classroom, if high hooky students use their knowledge of the classroom game to make themselves highly visible, and if low versus high hooky dropouts report different kinds of reasons for leaving school. These insights could then be combined with a redesigned questionnaire for further investigation. In such ways, focused primary data collection can inform the researcher during the course of fieldwork, and participant observation can inform the design of focused data collection.

Another approach to eliciting similar information is that of Spradley and his students (Spradley and McCurdey, 1972). They combined field observation with format interviews to elicit the "ethnosemantic" judgments of students about what kinds of activities and social roles there were in classrooms and at school recess. From the interviews, the authors constructed models of emic cultural knowledge about social relationships. They state their models of students' and teachers' "cognitive maps" of rules and plans for everyday school interaction in formal ways whose clear specification of variables could form the basis for further research. While there are serious problems with the use of ethnosemantic elicitation techniques apart from fieldwork, the work of Spradley's undergraduate students is compellingly attractive and its theoretical orientation is clearly articulated. I think this represents a useful approach for fieldworkers and has great potential for researchers from other orientations as well.

I turn now to approaches based primarily on watching — to inferring people's social competence from their social performance. Another implication of the general theoretical position of Goodenough and the others referred to above is that socialization is not simply a matter of reinforcement. The theory assumes that children and adults are actively engaged in constructing emic models of the social worlds in which they find themselves. Especially among ethnomethodologists, an assumption is that socialization is a never ending process, that as people of any age interact they are continuously engaged in telling each other, nonverbally as well as verbally, what is going on. Thus from the study of social behavior (performance) one can infer the social knowledge (competence) necessary to produce the behavior, just as a connoisseur of the symphony orchestra can rigorously and objectively infer the musical knowledge necessary to write a symphony and produce a performance of it. This premise suggests observational methods as a means of primary data collection.

One example of such work is that of Philips (1972, 1974) in which the key analytic notion is *participation structure*, the characteristic "games" or modes of organization by which children and adults conduct everyday interaction. Philips investigated culturally different forms of participation structure through the classic method of participant observation, carefully observing and comparing the interaction of children and adults at home and school on the Warm Springs Indian reservation. The theoretical orientation was that of Goodenough, Hymes, and Goffman. Two salient aspects of this work are: (1) the comparison of customary participation structures outside school with those inside school and (2) the fully "interactional" character of the analytic model, i.e., the model accounts for what all parties to an interactional event are doing — what one person does while others do what they do.

Philips identified a range of characteristic ways that rights and obligations governing speaking and turn-taking were organized and showed cultural differences between participation structures most commonly occurring inside and outside school. A major difference involved the role of the adult or other leader. At school, the leader (the teachers, who were always white) attempted to control all activity, communicative and otherwise, functioning as a switchboard operator, to whom much talk was addressed and by whom all allocation of legitimate turns at speaking was granted. In such a participation structure, the Indian students performed much more situationally inappropriate behavior than did white students in the classroom. For Indian students and adults outside the classroom, Philips reports that participation structures in which one person controls all activity did not occur: "The notion of a single individual being structurally set apart from all others, in anything other than an observer role, and yet still a part of the group organization, is one that [Indian] children probably encounter for the first time in school" (Philips, 1972:391).

Such propositions and working theoretical models are stated in a form entirely appropriate for further focused investigation. They are etic statements of the emic organization of everyday activity. Those who do field research in educational settings can benefit from attempting to state their models as clearly as does Philips.

Currently, Gerald Mohatt and I are using Philips's notion of participation structure to organize our study of the interaction of children and adults on an Odawa reservation in northern Ontario. Using a portable radio microphone and a minimum of visual "camera editing" we have been making continuous videotapes of interaction at home and in two school classrooms. All the school children are Indian; one of the teachers is Indian, the other White. We are interested in the extent to which (1) the white teacher organizes participation structures involving all or some children in ways similar to Philips's models of teacher-student interaction and (2) the Indian teacher organizes participation structures differently from Philips's models. Philips's work would lead one to expect that the Indian teacher might organize participation structures without putting herself constantly in a position of absolute control over all activity, and on the basis of preliminary analysis of our tapes, that seems indeed to be the case. Moreover, our tapes of family interaction at home show participation structures Philips found characteristic of interaction outside school at Warm Springs.

By direct analysis of minimally edited behavior records (audiotapes, videotapes, cinema film), models of the social organization of interaction can be tested carefully for validity and generalizability. Systematic sampling of recurrent events in the daily rounds of teachers and students is possible, and the data generated can be operationally defined in etic terms for which high interrater reliability can be demonstrated (cf. Erickson, 1976a). Such data is amenable both to carefully controlled logical analysis as done by linguists and to quantitative summary and analysis.

Interaction analysis directly from behavior records enables the researcher to observe repeatedly each "strip" of interaction being investigated. This can prevent premature "typification" in constructing models. One can stay in touch with discrepant cases that do not quite fit an initially undifferentiated analytic model, adjusting the model to take account of variation that is not trivial by stating "variable rules" and "exceptions to the rules," as well as more general patterns. The work of Mehan, et al., (1976) is exemplary in this regard. In their analysis of instructional sequencing in classroom lessons, they are able to account for systematic variation in their data, accounting for every case in their sample by methods of discrepant case analysis.

While Mehan, et al. have focused primarily on verbal interaction, Mc-Dermott (in press) has investigated nonverbal interaction in a comparative study of the social organization of taking turns at reading in "high" and "low" reading groups in a first grade classroom. In a related approach Gumperz has studied "con-textualization-cueing" — the verbal and nonverbal cues by which people signal each other how to interpret what they are saying as they say it (Gumperz and Herasimchuk, 1970; Gumperz, 1976).[4]

A final example of current research in these directions can be characterized as eclectic in the extreme. Shultz, Florio, Walsh, Bremme, and I have been investi-gating the participation structures and social competence of one kindergarten–first grade teacher and her students (Shultz, 1976). Over a two-year period, we have videotaped in the classroom for a total of 72 hours of tape and, to a much lesser extent, in children's homes.

A relationship of close collaboration with Walsh, the teacher, has evolved (Florio and Walsh, 1976), enabling us to integrate the humane relationship of dialogue with a key informant that has been essential to much ethnographic re-search with the more systematic and "distanced" observational methods em-ployed in the direct analysis of behavior records.

We also have interviewed the teacher in spontaneous conversation, in formal interviews, and in "viewing sessions" in which we watch and discuss videotaped excerpts of classroom happenings identified as potential "key incidents." Shultz, Bremme, and Florio have analyzed the videotapes, preparing intensive case studies of verbal and nonverbal behavior in key incidents that highlight fine details of par-ticipation structure: how children get turns at speaking, how the mutual rights and obligations of those engaged in interaction shift from moment to moment (cf. Cicourel 1972), and how brief and transient "subcontexts" are played out within larger strips of activity — moments in which what was socially appropriate the moment before is no longer appropriate.

To get on in school, teachers and children need a social "radar" for monitor-ing the culturally patterned contextualization cues that signal subtle shifts in con-text of situation from moment to moment. Researchers studying the role of com-municative competence in classroom interaction need methods for the empirical investigation of such contextual shifting. Because of the relative indeterminacy of segment boundaries or "junctures" between emically salient "chunks" of every-day interaction, the empirical study of contextual shifting is a problem deserving continuing basic research. School classrooms are highly appropriate settings for such research.

Case studies of classroom participation structure derived from direct analy-sis of behavior records are a means of producing etic data which can be quantita-tively summarized yet which also can be articulated with categories of emic structures relevant to the point of view and purposes of teacher and students. Units of data and combinations of units that are identified through videotape analysis and operationally defined in etic terms can be tested in "viewing sessions" for congruence with the teacher's ways of talking about the events. Thus for a given classroom event, points of formal correspondence can be shown between (1) the teacher's emic model of the event, as elicited in interviews, (2) the researcher's "emic/etic" model of the event identified from direct analysis of the behavior record, and (3) etically defined measurement operations that produce frequency data. Note the correspondence of this approach with Bartlett's ladder diagram for the process of scientific inquiry found in Feinberg's paper (1977).

All of the studies reviewed in this section have addressed the relationship of social or communicative competence to the enactment of everyday life in classrooms.[5] The theoretical and methodological orientations of most of these studies allow the researcher to stay in touch not only with the concrete details of the enactment of social life, and with the "rules" for enactment that are usually studied and reported by social scientists — the customary patterns or normative order according to which social scenes are played out day after day — but also with the creativity and spontaneity involved in recurrent performance by which the old and familiar is continually made new and chosen. Using a variety of methods, most of which permit quantitative summary of data, these researchers are attempting to discover new qualitative knowledge — new aspects of what children need to know in going to school and of what teachers need to know in doing teaching.

In concluding, it is appropriate to ask how all this relates to issues in the mainstream of educational research and to issues of quantitative method. Despite surface differences, there seems to be considerable convergence between the work reviewed in the previous section and the work of Smith and Geoffrey (1968), Smith and Carpenter (1972), and Kounin (1972), on the one hand, and of Barker and Gump and their associates on the other (Barker, 1965, 1968; Gump, 1969; Gump and Ross, 1975; Gump and Good, 1976).

In attempting to conceptualize the process of teaching, Smith has emphasized ringmastership and its components — awareness, pacing, sequential smoothness, and teaching in motion. Kounin has identified similar dimensions of the process of classroom management — momentum, "withitness," smoothness, overlapping, and variety. Both these conceptual schemes emphasize the timing of activity and point up what may be one of the most salient ethnographic "facts" about life in classrooms — that there always seems to be more than one thing at a time happening. Effective teachers seem to be able to handle this multiplicity of events. Some students, whether because of differences in culture, temperament, or ability, seem to be able to handle the multiplicity better than others and to perform more effectively, socially and academically. As Rist reports (1970), the social behavior of children in classrooms establishes social identities for them from the point of view of the teacher, and these social identities seem to correlate with academic achievement and form a basis for tracking students in the early grades (see also Mehan, 1975, and Leiter, 1975).

Philips (1972) provides another way of formally describing the social organization of the multiplicity of events in the classroom — a way that permits specification of variation across different structures of participation, different social environments for learning. Those environments may be the key unit of analysis for the study of classroom interaction. This point is made in different terms by Kelly (1969) and by Gump (1969:201), who notes: "The root problem in ecological psychology is conceptualization of the environment. The study of the subject's behavior in his natural habitat is *not* the same as the study of natural habitats." In recent work, Gump has reported ways of characterizing whole environments using quantitative data (Gump and Ross, 1975; Gump and Good, 1976).

We are approaching the time when we can construct comparative typologies or models of whole classroom learning environments and identify styles of classroom management by teachers and classroom behavior by children within the context of the overall classroom environment. When this becomes possible, we can investigate what styles of being a student "go with" what styles of teaching and how these different forms of social relationship in classrooms correlate with the outcomes measures of achievement traditionally measured in educational research. Then we can begin to learn ways of matching kinds of teachers, kinds of children, and kinds of learning environments that result in optimal outcomes.

The other issue I want to address briefly as a postscript concerns methods of quantification. On this subject I have only minimal technical knowledge. But provided one collects primary data so there is some correspondence between the emic ways people have of ordering interaction in everyday life and etic ways of operationalizing variables, it would seem that there is no inherent contradiction in using quantitative methods in qualitative research. I have argued elsewhere that the statistical techniques appropriate for the analysis of qualitatively derived models and data may well be extremely simple techniques — the chi-square, the Mann-Whitney two-tailed test in the analysis of "categorical" data, and two and three way analysis of variance.[6]

The purpose of such quantitative analysis is simply to demonstrate the validity of one's analytic models — models in which, because of their grounding in qualitative observation, one knows a good deal about the expected variation before conducting statistical analysis. I have arrived at this contention in collaboration with Shultz and find support for it from Pelto, who has suggested that if, in addition, one wants to use more elaborate statistical techniques in the analysis of qualitatively derived data, the approaches of Bayesian statistics — in which one can specify expected ranges of variation and adjust these expectations during the process of analysis — may be more appropriate than the approaches of classical statistics (personal communication, July 11, 1976).

Of this last point I am not technically competent to judge. It would seem that qualitative researchers could benefit from extended consideration of such issues of technique together with experts in statistics, perhaps in summer institutes or working conferences in which there would be adequate time to learn more about each other's expertise. That dialogue is long overdue.

NOTES

1. I am indebted for this point and for the discussion that follows to Robert Herriot, personal communication, July 1, 1976.

2. Several recent writers on qualitative methods who have emphasized the role of conscious inquiry in fieldwork are Denzin (1970), McCall and Simmons (1969), Pelto (1970), Schatzman and Strauss (1974), and Runcie (1976).

3. For additional expositions of this position see Wallace, 1970:1-45, and the introductory essay in Spradley (1972).

4. The recent work of Kendon (1967), Duncan (1972), and Mayo and La France (1975) also deal with contextualization-cuing processes (under different names), as does my recent work on functions of postural positions and of speech and body motion rhythms in the regulation of interaction in school counseling interviews (Erickson, 1975, 1976a, 1976b).

5. For a review of additional related studies and recommended directions for research, see N. L. Gage (ed.), *NIE Conference on Studies in Teaching: Panel 5*, "Teaching as a Linguistic Process in a Cultural Setting," December, 1974.

6. The work of Duncan (1972) is instructive in this regard. In his analysis of the functions of nonverbal cues in conversational turn taking, he finds chi-square values at the .0001 level of statistical significance.

3

*ETHNOGRAPHY OF BILINGUAL EDUCATION**

Hugh Mehan

Correlational studies, those which employ an input-output research design, have been the predominant research strategy used in the study of the effects of schooling. Aspects of people's lives, social and historical contexts, are treated as social and cognitive "factors" or variables in this design. Some factors, such as social class, age, sex of teachers, abilities of students, attitudes of teachers, and size of classrooms, are treated as input variables. Other factors, such as pupil achievement, economic opportunity, and subsequent career patterns, are treated as output variables. The research task of correlational studies is to test the strength of the relationship between the input and the output variables.

LaBelle, Moll, and Weisner (in press) point out that the correlational model has been predominant in the evaluation of bilingual education programs. For example, the American Institute for Research (1977) evaluation of major Title VII (bilingual) programs used aggregated data from several sites, with a variety of instructional approaches, different levels of implementation, and students with varying language ability, to reach conclusions about the effectiveness and ineffectiveness of bilingual education.

*This is an expanded version of a paper with the same title which appeared in *Bilingual Education: Current Perspectives, Volume 1: Social Science*. I [the author] wish to express my appreciation to the Center for Applied Linguistics of Arlington, Virginia, whose grant from the Carnegie Corporation of New York City made possible both the writing of the original paper and the provision of a forum for its discussion through a series of conferences on various perspectives of bilingual education, including those of linguistics, education, the social sciences, and the law. Reprinted by permission of the Center for Applied Linguistics, copyright©1977.

This evaluation has been criticized for not explaining how bilingual education affects children, and for not showing which educational interventions will optimally promote desired outcomes (Intercultural Development Research Association, 1977; Center for Applied Linguistics, 1977). It is also the case that input-output studies do not capture the actual processes of bilingual education in educational contexts. The process of education that takes place *within* schools has been overlooked when comparisons *between* schools have been made.

Fishman (1977), in his extensive and comprehensive review of social science research in bilingual education, stated that "there is little or no data presently available about bilingual education in bilingual classrooms." In fact, the only reference that Fishman makes to a classroom study (U.S. Commission on Civil Rights, 1973) is not actually about bilingual classrooms *per se*. It is really about Mexican-American students in monolingual classrooms taught by Anglo or Mexican-American teachers.

While I agree with Fishman (1977) that research into the dynamics of bilingual classrooms is desperately needed, I do not recommend following the lead of the USCCR study. There are serious difficulties inherent in the research method used in that study which preclude an examination of classroom dynamics. The research technique employed for the USCCR study was a variation of the Flanders technique (Amidon and Flanders, 1963; Flanders, 1970). The Flanders system is one of the most widely used techniques for making classroom observations (see Dunkin and Biddle, 1974, for a review of many such systems). It involves on-the-spot coding of teacher and student behavior. Observers provided with a set of categories sit in the classroom and tally the action occurring around them at frequent and recurrent intervals. The technique produces a tabulation of the occurrence of certain teacher and student verbal behaviors. The Flanders categories and their definitions are reproduced in Figure 3.1.

The USCCR study modified the Flanders system. The basic Flanders system treats students as a group. No distinction is made between individuals. In the USCCR study, each behavior was coded with reference to the ethnicity of the students. Observers sat in a corner of the target classrooms for approximately one hour. Once every three seconds, for ten minutes in each classroom, the observers marked a tally in a box which most appropriately indicated the behavior that was occurring and the ethnicity of the students. The Flanders scoring sheet, as modified by the USCCR, appears in Figure 3.2.

The purpose of the USCCR study was to determine whether Mexican-American and Anglo students in the same classrooms received different treatment from teachers. Classroom observation was conducted in 494 classrooms in 52 schools in California, New Mexico, and Texas where there was a representative number of Mexican-American and Anglo students. The Commission reported differences in teachers' treatments of these two groups of students; teachers gave Anglos more praise and encouragement and used Anglo students' ideas more often. In addition, the Commission reported that Mexican-Americans speak significantly less often in classrooms than Anglos do.

The issue in bilingual classrooms is the development of skills that students need for success in two languages in school and in society. Current legislation in

INDIRECT INFLUENCE

TEACHER

1 ACCEPTS FEELING: accepts and clarifies the feeling tone of the students in a nonthreatening manner. Feelings may be positive or negative. Predicting and recalling feelings are included.

2 PRAISES OR ENCOURAGES: praises or encourages student action or behavior. Jokes that release tension, not at the expense of another individual, nodding head or saying "uhhuh?" or "go on" are included.

3 ACCEPTS OR USES IDEAS OF STUDENT: clarifying, building, or developing ideas or suggestions by a student. As teacher brings more of his own ideas into play, shift to category five.

4 ASKS QUESTIONS: asking a question about content or procedure with the intent that a student answer.

TALK

DIRECT INFLUENCE

5 LECTURING: giving facts or opinions about content or procedure; expressing his own idea; asking rhetorical questions.

6 GIVING DIRECTIONS: directions, commands, or orders with which a student is expected to comply.

7 CRITICIZING OR JUSTIFYING AUTHORITY: statements intended to change student behavior from nonacceptable to acceptable pattern; bawling someone out; stating why the teacher is doing what he is doing, extreme self-reference.

STUDENT

8 STUDENT TALK-RESPONSE: talk by students in response to teacher. Teacher initiates the contact or solicits student statement.

TALK

9 STUDENT TALK-INITIATION: talk by students, which they initiate. If "calling on" student is only to indicate who may talk next, observer must decide whether student wanted to talk. If he did, use this category.

10 SILENCE OR CONFUSION: pauses, short periods of silence, and periods of confusion in which communication cannot be understood by the observer.

Source: Edmund J. Amidon and Ned Flanders, *The Role of the Teacher in the Classroom: A Manual for Understanding and Improving Teachers' Classroom Behavior*, Minneapolis: Paul S. Amidon Associates, 1963, p. 12.

FIGURE 3.1   SUMMARY OF THE FLANDERS CATEGORIES FOR INTERACTION ANALYSIS

bilingual education dictates that schools must determine the numbers of students with limited English speaking ability, determine the most effective means of instruction, and devise the most effective means of classroom participation. This means that students' language must be described so that educators can strengthen students' linguistic and literacy skills and reasoning in two languages.

School and District Code No.   Date

Access No.   Classroom No.

District Name   Grade   Period

School Name   Subject

Teacher Name   Ability group level

Observer's Initials

	MA	A	B	O	C	TOTAL
1						
2						
3						
4						
5						
6						
7						
8						
9						
10						

FIGURE 3.2   MODIFIED FLANDERS INTERACTION FORM (USCCR, 1973)

A Critique of the Quantitative Approach to Classroom Interaction

In this section, I will illustrate some of the reasons why the quantification approach to observation in classrooms (such as the Flanders system, even as modified by the USCCR) does not provide the kinds of information necessary to meet the goals of bilingual education. There are serious drawbacks to an approach which limits its domain to behavior tabulated into discrete categories. The fundamental consequence is that the contingent nature of interaction is obscured. More specifically, (1) students' contributions to classroom interaction, (2) the interrelationship of verbal and nonverbal behavior, (3) the relationship of behavior to context, (4) the functions of language, and (5) the relationship of the classroom context to the community are not captured when quantification schemes are employed in the classroom.

1. Student contributions. Quantification schemes are useful for tabulating aspects of classroom behavior, but because they focus almost exclusively on the *teacher*, they minimize the contributions of *students* to the organization of classroom events. The classroom is socially organized. Teachers *and* students work in concert to create this organization.

The traditional conception of the classroom places the teacher at the front of the room and students in neat rows of desks facing the teacher. The students' responsibility in this configuration is said to be "responding when called upon" (Dunkin and Biddle, 1974:178). This view is reinforced in a scheme such as that of Flanders which provides only two coding categories for students' behavior (student response-category #8 and student initiation-category #9 in Figure 3.1.)

Let us assume for a moment that classroom life *is* a simple matter of teachers asking questions and students providing answers. A system that merely tabulates the number of teacher questions and student replies will not be able to capture classroom interaction, because even "simple" question-answer exchanges are complex interactional productions. In order for interaction in teacher-directed lessons to proceed smoothly, a question asked by a teacher must be answered both correctly and appropriately by students. And, in order to provide an answer that is consistent with a question, the student must recognize the form of the teacher's initiation act, and interpret the turn-allocation procedure in use. The initiation of action by teacher or student requires synchronization of behavior. Just as a compelling speaker requires an effective listener (Erickson and Shultz, 1977), a successful questioner requires an appropriate respondent. The introduction of a topic into a lesson requires precise timing, including making turn-taking coincide with a previous speaker's turn-leaving.

In addition, student action in a classroom is not limited to responding when called upon. Even in teacher-directed lessons, students do more than respond to teacher-initiated acts. They greet others, provide information to the teacher and each other, give directives, evaluate others' work, comment on the course of events, and work to achieve their objectives in the context of the teacher's objectives. This wide range of student contribution is far more complex than a Flanders-type system is equipped to handle.

The situation is even more complex in student-centered classrooms, team-teaching arrangements, and learning centers. There, students often have some responsibility for organizing their course of study and deciding their length of study time, and influence techniques of discipline. This means that students have to be particularly well attuned to demands that shift with different classroom arrangements. And in bilingual classrooms, shifting situational demands are compounded by code switching. As a result, a methodology that captures the mutual synchronization of behavior, not one that simply tabulates frequencies, is required to answer questions about students' competence, especially in bilingual classrooms.

2. The interrelationship of verbal and nonverbal behavior. Quantification schemes are useful for tabulating *verbal* behavior in the classroom, but because they code only talk, they do not include nonverbal contributions to the organization of classroom events. Verbal *and* nonverbal behavior are interactionally connected in classrooms (Byers and Byers, 1972; McDermott, 1976; Erickson and Shultz, 1977), as in other naturally occurring situations. Students bid for the floor by raising their hand and leaning forward; teachers identify the next speaker with a head nod, and hold the floor for particular students by eye contact and body orientation. A teacher can quiet a child with a touch while simultaneously asking another student a question. Body positioning in conjunction with changes in voice pitch and rhythm provides cues which "contextualize" behavior (Gumperz, 1971) and orient participants to what is happening in different classroom circumstances.

An example from McDermott's (1976) insightful analysis of a videotape of students in a "top" and "bottom" reading group in a school near New York City illustrates this point. In his description of the organization of teaching and learning, some of the strategies that students employed to avoid being called upon by the teacher are revealed. Just prior to the completion of one student's turn at reading, another student began to bid aggressively for the floor. But as the teacher scanned the group for a next reader, this student withdrew her hand, broke eye contact, and avoided being called upon.

Tabulation schemes like Flanders would not record any of these subtleties because they do not treat verbal and nonverbal behavior as interactionally connected. A description of the interconnected nature of teacher-student interaction in verbal and nonverbal modalities is required in order to capture the full range of activities that teachers and students engage in while coping with the complexities of life in bilingual classrooms.

The ethnographic approach that I am recommending for the study of education in bilingual situations avoids simplistic explanations of students' school performance. Instead of placing blame for school failure on either the student or the teacher, the ethnographic approach finds that "school success" and "school failure" are collaborative productions, not the personal property of any one individual. Teachers and students work together to construct the role of successful or unsuccessful student.

3. The contingent nature of interaction. Time sampling may be useful for tabulating the frequency of behavior occurrences, but because teacher and student behaviors are treated as isolated acts, the sequential flow of classroom activity is obscured. Marking tallies at regular time intervals does not reveal the contingent nature of behavior in the classroom. "Student responses" (Flanders category #8) and "giving praise" (Flanders category #2), for example, are not random occurrences in the classroom but are tied together in sequences of interaction. If a teacher's action is coded as "gives praise to a student," it is important to know what that student did immediately before that entry, and what other students who did not receive praise were doing. Or, if "student talks in response to a teacher" (Flanders category #8), did the teacher call on a student who had been seeking the teacher's attention, or did the teacher select one who had not bid for the floor? Are those students who bid for the floor ignored, those who did not, encouraged? There is no way to recover the sequential flow of interaction from a Flanders chart in order to answer such important questions about classroom behavior. As a result, the overall organization of classroom events is lost.

Furthermore, tabulations based on time samplings do not show the context surrounding a tabulated entry. The social organization of the classroom can be divided into events, i.e., "academic lessons," "procedural meetings" (e.g., "circles on the rug"), recess, snack time, etc. Each of these events is informed by normative rules, and different rules apply to different events. These rules are "tacit," seldom formulated, listed or stated in so many words at the beginning of the school year or school day. As a result, students must learn the rules that apply in each situation, be able to recognize differences between situations, and be able to produce behavior that is appropriate to each situation. For example, they should learn that running and shouting is acceptable during recess but not during reading, that calling out an answer is acceptable during "student's time at the rug" but not during "teacher's time at the rug" (Bremme and Erickson, 1977).

The social organization of the classroom also includes a set of procedures for insuring that the flow of communication among classroom participants is orderly and systematic. In addition to eliciting information, providing information or giving directions, teachers allocate turns to students during lessons. Under normal classroom circumstances, the teacher allocates turns by nominating individual students by verbal and nonverbal means (such as head nods, eye contact), by inviting them to bid for the floor ("Raise your hand if you know the answer") and by inviting direct replies ("Anybody, what is this?"). Each of these procedures elicits different behavior. On some occasions, pupils can reply directly, while on others, they must receive permission to reply. To contribute successfully to classroom lessons, students must decide which of these subtle normative procedures is in effect. When one particular student has been awarded the floor by name or nonverbal means, other students must know to be silent. When the teacher invites bids for the floor, students must know to raise their hands and not shout out the answers. When the teacher invites replies, students must realize they can contribute directly. Those who misinterpret an "invitation to reply" as an "invitation to bid" and raise their hands instead of answering, lose the opportunity to display what they know. Those who misinterpret an invitation to bid as an invitation to reply and call out an answer can be sanctioned. A history of lost opportunities can lead a teacher to believe a student is inattentive, unexpressive, and the like.

A particularly telling example of this appears on a videotape I made in a San Diego school. Anyone viewing the lesson on the tape without sound sees one student, Juan, actively bidding for the floor by raising his hand at regular intervals and receives the impression that this student is actively involved. When the same sequence is viewed with sound added, it is evident that this student is seldom called on by the teacher. It turns out that the teacher was employing a turn allocation procedure that invited students to reply directly. It was not necessary to bid for the floor before speaking. Juan had apparently not made the distinction between these two ways of gaining access to the floor. As a result, he was not participating fully in this classroom activity.

Thus, students must not only distinguish *between* events in the classroom and produce behavior appropriate to each; they must also produce behavior that is appropriate to momentary shifts in procedures within events. The relationship of action to these increasingly general concentric circles of context is important, for actions take on different meanings in different phases of an event, in different events, and at different times of the year. As a result of the need to answer the "when is a context" question (Erickson and Shultz, 1977), a simple tabulation of teacher and student behavior would not reflect the moment-to-moment shifts in normative procedures that provide the background for the "involvement" or "noninvolvement" of certain students. We need to know more about the "interpretive abilities" (Cicourel, 1973) that enable students to go beyond the information given in ambiguous utterances and decode tacit classroom rules in order to act appropriately in changing classroom situations.

4. Language functions. The type of summary data produced by a quantification system such as Flanders' ignores issues regarding the functions of language in the classroom (Cazden, et al., 1972; Shuy and Griffin, 1978). A particular language function (e.g., giving a directive, making an elicitation, making a promise) can be realized by many forms of speech. For example, a teacher could say any of the following to a student:

(a) "Can you shut the door?"
(b) "Would you mind shutting the door?"
(c) "I wonder if you could shut the door?"
(d) "The door is still open."
(e) "The door . . ."
(based on an example from Sinclair and Coulthard, 1975:33)

Depending on the context in which they are used, these utterances can take on different meanings. Utterances (a) and (c) could either be a question about a student's physical strength or be a directive; (d) could either be an existential statement or a directive; (e) could either be an elliptical utterance or a command.

Students need to be able to decide the meaning of these utterances by interpreting them in the context of their use. Tabulating how many times a teacher "asks a question" (Flanders category #4 in Figure 3.1) does not reveal what students need to know about language and social context in order to interpret questions and respond appropriately to them.

The simple quantification of classroom behavior also ignores the *multiple* functions that any speech act can serve simultaneously. The following are typical of utterances offered by a teacher to students:

Namecards, good. Ernesto?

Right, Albany is the capital of New York. Sondra?

The red one. Audrey?

In each of these utterances, the teacher is praising one student and eliciting new information from another student. Both of these functions of language typically associated with the classroom occur in one turn of teacher talk.

The teacher who says to a student, "I like the way Brian raised his hand," is simultaneously complimenting that student on his adherence to classroom rules and indexing the existence of such rules for all students. The teacher's statement, "Wait a minute, raise your hand if you know the answer," also serves two functions simultaneously. Retrospectively, it sanctions a past transgression of classroom turn allocation procedures, and prospectively, it instructs students on how to act in the future in order to gain access to the floor.

An utterance can serve an evaluation function and an elicitation function at the same time:

1. Teacher: What color should we paint the sky?
2. Student: Yellow yellow!!
3. Teacher: Yellow?
4. Student: Yellow!
5. Teacher: Yellow, all right.

The teacher's question after the student's first reply (line 3) served not only to evaluate the previous reply (line 2), but also to encourage a clarification of the previous reply.

Quantification schemes, by forcing observers to make discrete choices among categories, and by not presenting the materials upon which coding decisions were based, do not accurately reflect the multiple, often simultaneous, functions that language serves in the classroom. In order to meet the needs of both monolingual and bilingual students in classrooms, we need to know more about how students develop mastery of the multiple ways in which language functions can be realized, and how they make the fit between strategies for using language at home and in school.

5. The culture of the classroom in the context of the community. Taxonomic approaches to classroom behavior seldom relate the culture of the classroom to the community context of which the classroom is a part. Virtually every observer of multicultural classrooms has cited instances in which Puerto Rican and Mexican-American children are criticized by Anglo teachers for being disrespectful when they avert their eyes (especially when being chastised). Such anecdotes are cited as evidence for cross-cultural miscommunication, since eye aversion is a preferred mode of showing respect in certain Hispanic homes, while a sign of disrespect for certain Anglos. More importantly, perhaps, these stories remind us that *all* students (not just students from different cultural traditions) enter classrooms with a background of tacit cultural knowledge. This knowledge is acquired in everyday interaction with teachers, peers and family members. As students employ their culturally provided knowledge to make sense of school situations, they sometimes find themselves cutting against the grain of the tacit and ambiguous cultural demands of the classroom.

Patterns of action learned in daily life can and do clash with patterns of action for the classroom. Isolated clashes can be linked together into chains that lock students into ability groups and onto tracks. These "clashes" should not be used to suggest that students lack knowledge or culture, however; they are a consequence of interaction of different tacit normative systems such as classroom and home.

As educators, we need to become more aware of the norms, values, skills and abilities that members of the community use in their daily lives. We then need to assemble descriptions at the same level of the academic and interactional skills reported in classrooms and other school situations, and make linkages between the community and the school so that the actions required in the classroom are not in conflict with those required in the community.

Especially in the Southwest, the traditional response of United States schools to the presence of students who speak a language other than English has been to "change the child." Children have been told to leave their home language, customs, and values at the door along with lunch pails and hats. Changing children to conform to the norms of the classroom is perhaps the most damaging way to make life in the classroom continuous with life in the community. But there have been equally disastrous attempts to redesign the structure of the classroom to conform to the life style of the community. It is too simplistic to think that making the classroom into a carbon copy of the home can resolve the problem of discontinuity.

There is some evidence of a third way — designing learning environments which activate students' energies, competencies and preferences, yet meet other school goals. The Kamehameha Early Education Program (Jordon, Weisner, Tharp, Gallimore, and Au, 1978; Au and Jordan, this volume) provides a powerful example of how this strategy can work. Native Hawaiian children have a notorious reputation for poor school performance. Yet the Kamehameha project was able to raise the reading scores of native Hawaiians from the 19th to above the 50th percentile in four years. More importantly, perhaps, the children came to enjoy reading. This improvement in performance was obtained by emphasizing a comprehension rather than phonics approach to reading and by capitalizing on the presence of a unique speech event that occurs naturally in native Hawaiian communities. "Talk story" is a narrative which is jointly produced. Instead of a single person telling a story, as is common in mainland speech communities, native Hawaiians contribute bits and pieces of a story as it unfolds.

The teachers of the students who showed rapid improvement in reading incorporated this speech event into their classroom routines. For example, in a lesson concerning pineapples, the teacher might start by asking the native Hawaiians to tell about what they knew about pineapples from personal experience. The context for telling about this topic resembled talk story — any and all who wanted to, contributed; those who did not want to were not compelled to do so. After a suitable interval, the teacher introduced some reading material in which pineapples were prominent. The students read this material *to themselves*. This "sustained silent reading" approach contrasts sharply with conventional reading circles in which each student takes turns and mistakes and successes are public (McDermott, 1976; Griffin and Humphrey, 1978). After the stories were read, another round of discussion took place. This time, the teacher guided the discussion to incorporate comprehension of the story as well as real world knowledge.

Obviously, I am not recommending that talk story be adopted in mainland classrooms. But there is a "recipe" here for structuring a classroom environment that is responsive to children's culturally provided ways of acting.

If the process of bilingual education is to be understood, we need to look through wider lenses to measure students' competence. It is not sufficient to consider the frequencies with which single teacher and student behaviors occur. To obtain these wider measures, the researcher cannot do "quick and dirty" studies (i.e., enter the classroom, tabulate frequencies for a few minutes and then leave) and honestly say that the dynamics of the classroom have been described. To describe student abilities, the researcher must participate in classroom life for an extended period of time and gain a sense of the tempo, rhythm, pace of the class, and the demands and expectations of the teacher. The researcher must describe the structure of classroom events and the language used by teachers and students in these events, and then tie this description to a similar description of the community of which the school is a part.

Summary. The quantification approach to classroom observation is useful for certain purposes, namely, comparing the frequency of teacher talk with the frequency of students' talk, and tabulating the overall frequency of certain acts of speech. However, because this approach minimizes the contribution of students, neglects the relationship of verbal to nonverbal behavior, obscures the contingent nature of interaction, ignores the often multiple functions of language, and does not place classroom life in the community context, it has limited utility for the study of classroom dynamics in bilingual situations.

Although frequency distributions from a study such as USCCR (1973) may be helpful to point out problems in bilingual classrooms for the purposes of initiating legal action, such data are not helpful when improvements, alternatives, and remedies are being considered. In order to change a social organization such as the school, its internal workings and organizational practices must be understood. A description of the interactional mechanisms that generate educational arrangements can be effective in this regard. A detailed description of actual daily educational practices can become the information that educators at the local level need when they consider actual changes and concrete improvements.

An ethnographic approach is recommended as an alternative to the correlational approach for the study of classroom dynamics. This approach is discussed in the following section.

The Ethnographic Approach

"Ethnography" is a term that has been used to mean many things. For some, it is any study conducted outside a laboratory or without an opinion poll. For others, it involves some version of participant observation "in the field." For the purposes of discussion here, I will use the term ethnography to refer to a description of the culture of a community or society,[1] where "culture" implies "members' knowledge" — what people need to know to do in order to act acceptably in a society or community (Goodenough, 1964; cf.: Schutz, 1962; Garfinkel, 1967; Cicourel, 1973).

Description from within the community. An ethnography of this kind is a description generated from within the community or society. Ethnographers try not to impose categories or structures of description which are foreign to the situation being described. Instead, they look for meanings to emerge from within the situation, allowing the categories for description to be determined by the scene itself. The goal of the ethnography is to provide a description that resonates with the members' point of view.

Such descriptions can only be made by careful observations over an extended period of time. There is a shared belief among ethnographers that a cultural description requires a long period of intimate study and residence among members of the community being studied. Since ethnography has been traditionally conducted in communities that are foreign to the researcher, a knowledge of the spoken language and subtle patterns of behavior of the community members has been a prerequisite. This aspect of ethnography places a special burden on researchers studying scenes in their own culture. The ethnographer working in a foreign land is attempting to make the strange familiar, while the ethnographer in local scenes must reverse the process and make the familiar strange in order to understand it.

A changing data base. Traditionally, ethnographers have used field notes as their data base. The resulting narrative accounts are richly detailed and fine-grained. More recently, ethnographers have taken advantage of technological developments in the audiovisual field. Most notably, audiotape and film have been used for data collection and data analysis. Videotape and film are particularly helpful research tools because they enable researchers to come to grips with some of the problems resulting from the use of written field notes. Film and videotape serve as an external memory. Since tape can be viewed repeatedly, different interpretations can be considered as new knowledge about the community emerges. In addition, it is possible to retrieve the grounds of an analysis when audiovisual materials are the data source.

Audiovisual materials have also contributed to a cooperative approach to research. Instead of the researcher's independently defining research problems, gathering data, and communicating results only to professional colleagues, tape from interactional situations can be viewed with participants to obtain their interpretation, which can then be compared to the researcher's interpretation (Cicourel et al., 1974a; Florio, 1978; Erickson and Shultz, 1977; Mehan, 1979). These "viewing sessions" can lead to participant-generated research ideas that are collaboratively pursued (Florio and Walsh, this volume; Shuy and Griffin, 1978; Au and Jordan, this volume) or which participants pursue independently.

The use of audiovisual materials in the research process has also contributed to the study of new topics. Since accurate transcripts of talk and other behavior can be made from tapes, the study of language use in naturally occurring and institutional settings has been enhanced. Audiovisual materials have also been used to examine the interactional work that assembles the structure of routine events. These "constitutive" (Mehan 1978, 1979) or "micro" (Erickson and Shultz, 1977; McDermott, 1976; McDermott et al., 1978) ethnographies have been conducted primarily in educational settings.

Ethnographies of the classroom community. In some of these ethnographies, the school in general and the classroom in particular have been described as analogous to a community. This parallel has been drawn in the following way (Waller, 1932; Philips, 1972; Mehan, 1979). The classroom is like a community in that there are a number of participants who meet regularly in the same location for the ostensive purpose of achieving certain goals and objectives which are academic in nature. Although there is not a system of sexual reproduction in the school as in other communities, there are myths, traditions, taboos, magic rites, complex rituals of personal relationships, folkways, mores, and sanctions (Waller, 1932). As in other communities nested within the larger society, there are preferred patterns of behavior proscribed for members. Some of these patterns of behavior are carried over from the general society. Others are generated within the organization. Both the external and locally generated patterns of behavior are influenced by rules or norms. These rules do not automatically impose constraints on action. They are established by convention (Lewis, 1976), which means that they are co-operatively maintained and must be acquired by the members of the classroom community and interpreted in the context of their use. Classroom rules, like other normative rules, are "tacit" (Polanyi, 1962; Garfinkel, 1967; Cicourel, 1973). They are seldom formulated, listed, or stated in so many words at the beginning of the lesson, school day, or school year (Cicourel et al., 1974a; Mehan, 1979).

Membership in the Classroom Community

Extending the metaphor of culture as "competent membership in a society or community," a number of ethnographers studying education have begun to ask: "What do teachers and students (especially students) need to know to operate effectively in classroom context?" And: "What is the relationship between the skills required in the school and those required at home, work, or play?"

Competent membership in the classroom community obviously involves *academic* skills and abilities. To be successful in the classroom, students must, indeed, master academic subject matter. They must learn to read, write and compute. They must learn the content of such subjects as history, social studies and science. But recent ethnographies of the classroom have shown that classroom competence involves matters of *form* as well as *content, interactional* skills as well as *academic* skills.

To be competent members of the classroom community, students must not only know what to do, but when and where to do it. Inasmuch as the classroom is a socially organized community, participants must be able to act appropriately within its normative constraints. In order to produce behavior appropriate for a given classroom situation, students must interpret classroom rules and procedures that are often implicitly stated and which vary from situation to situation. Such competence constitutes part of the common sense knowledge students use, which ethnographers need to discover and describe.

To date, no study with the express purpose of describing the cultural knowledge that classroom participants use in bilingual classrooms has been conducted.[2] However, constitutive and microethnographies have been conducted in monolingual classrooms (including those that are ethnically mixed). These studies can be heuristic for the study of the process of bilingual education in bilingual classrooms.

Ethnographies of Classroom Organization

The microethnographic approach treats the classroom as a community whose social organization is collaboratively constructed by the interactional "work" of both teachers and students. This approach to ethnography describes the events that routinely occur in the classroom in terms of the practices and strategies which its participants employ to assemble the events. Some of the more recurrent classroom events are: whole class academic lessons (in math, science, reading, art, etc.); class meetings ("circles on the rug," etc.); small group lessons (in learning centers, for example) and lunch and recess. Each of these events is socially organized, and is conducted for certain purposes (although the definition of these purposes might be different when teachers and students' points of view are compared, as Lancey (1976) did). There are preferred patterns of action for the participants in each of these events involving ways of talking and acting that are considered appropriate to each occasion. To be competent classroom members, students must generate the behavior that is considered appropriate for each event.

Circles on the rug and work time. In one such ethnography, Bremme and Erickson (1977) analyzed the procedural meetings ("circles on the rug") in a K-1 classroom that took place throughout an academic year. Upon repeated videotape viewings of these events, they found that these circles were organized into distinct phases. These included the call to the circle, warm up, students' time, teacher's time, and wrap up. The shift to students' time was announced by those at the edge of the circle rising to their knees and facing into the center of the group of children, by the commencement of a long, student-speaking turn dealing with a personal experience or concern, and by the teacher's ceasing to scan the group with her face and eyes and focusing instead on one student (the speaker). Teacher's time was marked by students' rearranging themselves into a sitting position, turning their faces and eyes toward the teacher, and by the commencement of the teacher's scannings as she initiated a topic of discourse dealing with organizational or "teaching" content. Transition times were signaled by the breaking up of either of these verbal-nonverbal patterns (i.e., by the individualization of students' gaze orientation, body positions and conversational topics) along with increased body movement by both teacher and students.

In a related study, Florio (1978) found that work time in the same K-1 classroom was composed of three constituent parts: "getting ready," "focused time," and "wind up." Work time as an event was set off from the flow of ongoing classroom activity by the assembly of participants in a single part of the classroom. Activities within this focused event were also marked posturally and spatially. During "focused time" the teacher and students were oriented in toward the center of activity. Their focus was on the task before them. The teacher verbally discouraged children from talking with each other (e.g., "I just don't want to hear you now") while not maintaining eye contact with students. This centered focus of orientation contrasts with both "getting ready" and "wind up." At these times, participants adopted a more decentralized focus. Florio reports that the task at hand was not a central focus during these phases but was more of a sidelight.

These configurations in the circle and in work time had practical consequences for the organization of behavior during specific phases of time. Certain behavior was acceptable during certain phases, but not others. During circle time, for example, talking without the teacher's specific permission was acceptable during teacher's time, and received her acknowledgement if the utterance met specific (though tacit) criteria of topical relevance. But this behavior was prohibited during student's time; then, students had to raise their hand or call the teacher's name and be acknowledged before the teacher would respond to their talk. In this situation, topical relevance did not matter, which means that the student had to decide which phase (teacher time or student time) of the lesson(s) he was in. This also means that the "same" behavior (e.g., talking) takes on a different meaning in different circumstances. To interact successfully in the circle, students had to coordinate certain behavioral displays with certain phases of the event. A lack of coordination led to negative evaluations. As a result, students had to read the subtle cues that signaled shifts in the phase of the circle, or find their behavior in disfavor.

This system of organization is implicit. Although shifts between phases of the circle were regular and recurrent and marked by the teacher's verbal and nonverbal behavior, this system of organization was by no means obvious. It only became apparent to Bremme after repeated videotape viewings of these events. Because the norms constraining action in classroom events such as the "circle" are often tacit and implicit, students must engage in dynamic interpretive work to produce behavior that is appropriate for different social situations.

Reading groups. In an exceedingly fine-grained analysis, McDermott (1976; McDermott, et al., 1978) has located the constituent components that teacher and students in first grade reading groups employ to hold each other accountable to the ongoing course of interaction. The "top" reading group was organized into three "rounds" of interaction. The first round was a quick discussion and organization period in which the teacher told the children to open their reading books and called on volunteers to start to read. The second round was a long session in which each child in the group had the opportunity to read once. In the third round, the teacher asked the children questions, and the children answered in chorus; then, the students left the reading table and prepared for lunch. These rounds were marked off from each other and surrounding classroom activity in a number of ways. Bodies were oriented and "props" were used differently in each round. In the first round, the students handled the books while looking at the teacher. In the second round, the children all focused on the books. In the third round, the books were ignored, while all attended to the teacher. At the end of a speaker's turn, students shifted their bodies toward the teacher or toward the next person to read. In addition each round was marked by different procedures for sequencing activities. In the first round students vied for turns, in the second they were nominated by the teacher, and in the third they responded in a chorus.

McDermott demonstrates that, within the apparent disorder of the bottom reading group, there was social order equivalent to the order of the top group, and explains the social function of the apparent disorder. At the level of the lesson the groups were basically alike, but the bottom group had four rounds instead of three. This reading group started with the teacher at the chalkboard, inviting children to underline words. Then the teacher passed out books. "Taking turns to read" was the third round to appear and took up one-third of the time. In the fourth round, children wrote words from the board on their work papers. As in the top group, each round was marked by different bodily orientations, use of props, and procedures for sequencing activities.

McDermott and Gospodinoff (this volume) examined what happened when forms of behavior which may be appropriate in an everyday life situation are applied in the classroom. At one point during the school day, a Puerto Rican first-grade student got the attention of his (Anglo) teacher by touching her buttocks. The teacher responded negatively. McDermott and Gospodinoff asked why this student would engage in this behavior with this teacher nine months into the school year, no matter how acceptable that behavior might be for a youngster in Puerto Rican culture. These authors dismiss explanations which focus on conflicts in communicative codes (tactile Hispanic child vs. distant Anglo teacher) as too simplistic, and engage in a context analysis to locate the organizing principles of this incident. An analysis of the action surrounding this incident revealed that the student also broke a number of other rules at the same time, one a general rule (he called the teacher by her last name without the appropriate title), another specific to that classroom (he broke into a small group lesson to get the teacher's attention). McDermott says that the boy showed considerable respect for these rules at other times. A further analysis suggests that the boy picked his behavioral repertoire effectively, in that he not only got the teacher's attention, but (after a slight scolding) got the teacher to scold a child with whom he had been fighting. These authors imply that the boy's action was a strategic manipulation of available social resources. By importing behavior from one situation and using it in another, the boy accomplished a piece of interaction important to him. McDermott and Gospodinoff also suggest that this incident could be seen as functional for the teacher; although she spent time away from the bottom reading group, she engaged in behavior that could be seen as important for the class as a whole.

Whole group lessons. I suggested earlier that classroom competence involves the integration of form and content. I know the importance of this integration in my analysis of nine "whole class" academic lessons taught in an ethnically mixed, cross-age classroom (Mehan, 1979). To be successful in classroom lessons, students must not only know the *content* of academic subjects, they must know the appropriate *form* in which to cast their academic knowledge. Although it is incumbent upon students to display *what* they know during lessons, they also must know *how* to display it.

In this analysis, classroom lessons are described as a series of Initiation-Reply-Evaluation sequences between teachers and students. Most of these sequences (81 percent) are teacher-initiated. The teacher provides information to the students, elicits information from them and directs their actions. Certain replies are called for and others are denied by these initiation acts. To be competent respondents in classroom lessons, students must be able to identify the instructional function implied from the often implicit form of the teacher's speech act, and provide appropriate replies. For example, students must know that "your book is on the desk" is an instruction to clean up, even though it takes the linguistic form of a statement. "This is a _____" is a request for information even though it does not have the appearance of a standard question.

Although teacher-initiated action predominates in classroom lessons, the student's role is not limited to replying when called on. Students can also initiate action during lessons. In my examination of such action, I found that students used language in more complex ways than a quantitative analysis such as Flanders' would reveal. Students elicited information from the teacher and other students in a number of ways, gave procedural instructions, provided information about a wide variety of topics, commented on the course of action, and evaluated the form and content of other students' work.

In order to initiate action in teacher-dominated lessons, students had to gain access to the floor. Gaining access to the floor was a complex process. Students could not talk at random in classroom conversation. They had to locate the appropriate junctures in the flow of talk in which to introduce their ideas. This involved recognizing the completion of previous interactional sequences between teacher and students, and not introjecting new topics in the middle of an ongoing sequence. Once students gained access to the floor, they had to know what to do with it. Many first graders, especially in the fall of the year when they were still learning the classroom turn-allocation rules, raised their hands whenever the teacher asked a question. However, when they were called on, they had nothing to say. At such times it appeared that these students had learned that bidding for the floor was an important aspect of classroom participation, but they had not yet learned that supplying information was an integral accompaniment to that activity.

A similar lack of congruence occurred when students bid for the floor before the teacher had completed a question. Some students raised their hands at each pause in the teacher's talk. This action, in addition to showing what can happen when a student has not learned the classroom turn-taking procedures, can antagonize the teacher.

Once students had learned to gain access to the floor, they needed to maintain control over it. This involved sensitivity to topical relevance. Having recognized appropriate junctures, students had to connect information they wished to introduce with previous topics. If they did not make their comments topically relevant, they were ignored completely by others. If students initiated action at the appropriate juncture and tied their action to previous topics, their information was picked up by other classroom participants. However, if their information was merely a comment on past activities, its life on the floor was short. In order to have their topics incorporated into the course of the lesson, students had to provide topics that were both relevant to previous topics and new and interesting.

In sum, while students are expected to provide substantially correct academic information during lessons, they must employ interactional skills to display that academic knowledge. These ethnographies of the social organization of the classroom describe some of the communicative and interactional skills of students in (predominantly) monolingual classrooms. They portray a wider range of student skills and abilities than quantification studies which are limited to tabulations of students' replies to teachers' questions. These skills include the production and comprehension of functional language, the interpretation of implicit normative rules, and the production of behavior that is appropriate to a number of different classroom situations.

Ethnography for Bilingual Education

This ethnographic approach would be heuristic if applied to the study of the education process in bilingual situations. An ethnographic approach to bilingual classrooms would locate the structure of classroom events and describe what students and teachers do and say in each event. Such a description would focus on the functions of language used in each situation and would not be limited to the grammatical aspects of language. The students' performance would be judged in terms of communicative acceptability, not grammaticality.

The ethnographic approach would compare the language that students use in various classroom situations. These comparisons would show the situations in which students use their first and second language, the degree of skill they exhibited, and the occasions during which they switch between languages (Bruck and Shultz, 1977; Carrasco, Vera, and Cazden, this volume). It could also show how students use language for greeting, taking leave, joking, insulting, and other communicative routines.

This comparison would not be limited to the classroom, however. A comparison of students' language use in the classroom, in educational tests, at recess, and at lunch would shed even more light on the range of students' abilities. These contrasts are important because sociolinguistic studies consistently show that students display different skills and abilities in different social situations. Because of our reliance on educational tests, we seem to know students only psychometrically, i.e., when they answer questions posed by an adult about predetermined topics in a prescribed (and often random) order. While students' performances in their circumstances provide one view of their skills and abilities, we cannot fall into the trap of equating their performance in special events with their overall competence. Indeed, no single assessment of students' performances is an adequate measure of their competence.

This ethnography of the school could not be done in isolation. An understanding of the language used in the community in relation to that used in the school is required. An important dimension of an ethnography would be a comparison of the language used in the school with that used in the home, on the street, in the stores and other speech situations *within* the community, as well as at work, in banks, hospitals, and other places *outside* the community.

This contrast would be important because a working premise of bilingual education seems to be that of incorporating the language of the children into their education. Indeed, the very expression *bi*lingual education implies that the language of the community will be used in conjunction with the dominant language (English in the United States) for the purposes of instruction. However, it is not at all clear what "the language of the community" is, and therefore, what the language of instruction in bilingual education should be.

Contrary to traditional accounts which treat the Southwest as linguistically and culturally homogeneous, the few existing ethnographies of speaking in bilingual communities of the area (Sánchez, 1972; Ornstein, 1974; Elías-Olivares, 1975) reveal a linguistic and cultural heterogeneity. There are many varieties of language spoken by members of a given community. As a result, references to *the* "Chicano community" gloss over important differences that have significant educational implications.

In the relatively small speech community of East Austin, Texas, for example, speakers possess a linguistic repertoire that includes English and at least four varieties of Spanish: (a) a standard Northern Mexican Spanish, (b) popular Spanish, (c) *Español Mixtureado* (a local term for Spanish influenced by English in a variety of ways) and (d) *Caló* or *Pachuco* (Elías-Olivares, 1975). American formal variety is often the one utilized in most language texts for the teaching of Spanish. The popular Spanish of the Southwest shares many characteristics with the popular varieties used in Latin America. *Español Mixtureado* reflects a borrowing of syntactic constructions (e.g., English noun-adjective order), but primarily an influence of English on the lexicon. *Caló* shares phonology and syntax with the other varieties but has its own unique vocabulary. Young Chicanos use *Caló* for intragroup interaction and switch between codes regularly.

What implications does the sociolinguistic situation in the one particular community have for bilingual education in general? The answer to that question concerns the "language of the community" issue, i.e., the variety which should occupy the Spanish portion of bilingual education programs. Should it be the formal Spanish favored by older or better educated community members? Or should it be the "popular Spanish" recommended by first generation speakers? Or should it be the "code switching variety" favored by young Chicanos who see no need for the standard variety? Or should *several* varieties be employed? This last alternative implies that teachers in bilingual situations should be able to shift from one Spanish and/or English variety to another as the situation requires.

In recommending ethnography to bilingual education, I am not offering specific solutions for the structuring of particular bilingual programs. Rather, I am proposing that ethnography be used in order to find out what the structure might be. I am arguing for bilingual programs that are ethnographically based, and which seriously consider what one needs to know about language, communicating and interaction in order to get along in a particular community. No matter which language (or languages) is ultimately chosen for instruction in a particular bilingual program, it is important for educators, researchers, and community members to be aware of linguistic diversity in the community, and to understand how people feel about the use of different language varieties, especially as a medium for academic instruction.

Before implementing a bilingual program in a particular community, we need basic ethnographic research on the linguistic situation of the community in relation to that of the school. Educational programs that are built on the basis of such concrete research can then be made sensitive to the community's needs.

NOTES

1. See the articles by Brice-Heath, Hymes, and Sanday in Gillmore (1979) for a review of various approaches to ethnography from an anthropological perspective. Smith (1979) reviews the field-based studies in education.

2. But see Bruck and Shultz (1977) for a precursor. Carrasco et al. (1979 and this volume) have done a careful analysis of one bilingual student's interaction in a peer-teaching classroom situation. And I am aware that work presently underway by La Belle et al. (1979), and in Chicago and San Diego, will soon make this statement obsolete.

4

ETHNOGRAPHIC MONITORING*

Dell Hymes

I want to consider the contribution of ethnography to bilingual education, and to argue, indeed, that ethnography is essential to the success of bilingual education.

One contribution of ethnography has to do with the planning of programs, and the need for knowledge of the initial state of affairs. This contribution of ethnography (*initial knowledge*) is perhaps familiar, though neglected. There are two other kinds of contribution as well. One has to do with the conduct of programs, the need to recognize and understand patterns and meanings that may emerge during the course of a program, perhaps outside the classroom. The other has to do with evaluation and justification of programs, and ultimately, evaluation and justification of bilingual education itself. These second and third contributions can be thought of as *ethnographic monitoring*, the one of ongoing operation, the other of effects and consequences. I want to argue for attention to both.

To start, let me say a word about the notion of ethnography. It might be thought of as something purely descriptive and objective, done by someone who comes from outside. This is not the view I hold. Ethnography must be descriptive and objective, yes, but not only that. It must be conscious of values and goals, and relate description to analysis, objectivity to critical evaluation. Bilingual education involves social change in the light of certain goals. As a matter of law, it is defined in terms of the goal of equality of educational opportunity. As a matter of social

*Prepared for the symposium, "Language Development in a Bilingual Setting," March 19-21, 1976, sponsored by the Multilingual/Multicultural Materials Development Center, California State Polytechnic University, Pomona, California. Still awaiting distribution and/or publication as of May, 1979.

change, clearly it involves much more — personal goals and commitments, what people take their life chances and identities to be, what they want them to become. Not everyone may agree on the goals of change, or how much and what kind of change is desirable. An ethnographer must come to understand the values involved, and the validity of those values for those who hold them, as well as come to understand his own attitudes (perhaps attitudes that emerge in the course of his work) and the reasons for them. Only explicit concern with values, in short, will allow ethnography to overcome hidden sources of bias. And to be truly useful, the ethnography must relate what is described to goals. It may be that certain goals and certain situations are not compatible, or that certain goals and certain means are not, or that an unwitting inconsistency exists among goals or means. Ethnography is a way of discovering what is the case, an essential way, and social programs that ignore it are blind; but ethnography that ignores values and goals is sterile.

Ethnography might be thought of as something done by someone from without, a hired professional. It does require training and talent; not just anyone can do it. But of all forms of scientific knowledge, ethnography is the most open, the most compatible with a democratic way of life, the least likely to produce a world in which experts control knowledge at the expense of those who are studied. The skills of ethnography are enhancements of skills all normal persons employ in everyday life; its discoveries can usually be conveyed, sometimes best conveyed, in forms of language that nonspecialists can read. It comes to know more of a way of life than those that live that way are consciously aware of, but must take crucial account of what they consciously, and unconsciously, know. A crucial ingredient of ethnography is what in a sense is already known to members of a community: what they must know, consciously and unconsciously, in order to be normal members of the community. As a discipline, ethnography adds a body of concepts and techniques that direct attention, relate observations, more systematically than community members would normally have occasion for doing; that provide for making explicit relationships and patterns that members leave implicit; that provide for interpreting patterns in the light of a comparative knowledge of other ways of life to which a community member would not usually have access. Ethnography, in short, is a disciplined way of looking, asking, recording, reflecting, comparing and reporting. It mediates between what members of a given community know and do, and accumulates comparative understanding of what members of communities generally have known and done.

A member of a given community, then, need not be merely a source of data, an object at the other end of a scientific instrument. He or she already possesses some of the local knowledge and access to knowledge that is essential to successful ethnography, and may have a talent for sifting and synthesizing it, special insight into some part of it. What he or she needs is the other part of disciplined ethnography, the comparative insight distilled over the decades. This can come in a variety of idioms, and does not require a graduate degree. Indeed, one might argue that an educational system devoted to a democratic way of life would provide this other part to every student, as a right and as a basis for citizenship. Not to do so is to withhold from citizens the best that we have to offer for the understanding of social experience, for coming to terms with it or changing it.

When I refer to ethnography in this paper, then, I assume that the person doing the ethnography may be from the community in question. Indeed, I think it is highly desirable that this be the case in a large proportion of cases (cf. Hymes 1972, 1974a for the line of reasoning just presented).

The contribution of ethnography to initial knowledge may be familiar. Still, when I suggested ethnography to the director of a language program in a large city, the response was, "What would you want to know?" The only elaboration of the answer was that the people in the community wouldn't want it to be known that so many of them were illiterate.

Such a response suggests that the idea of sociolinguistic description, of ethnography of speaking, has not gone very far beyond academic halls. Indeed, it has not gone very far within them, so far as educational settings are concerned. One repeatedly cites Susan Philips's study (1972, 1974) of the relation between Madras, Oregon classrooms and Warm Springs Indian reservation culture, not only because it is good, but also because it remains almost unique.

Most educators would agree with the principle that teaching should start where the child is. Few appear to recognize that to do so requires knowledge of the community from which the child comes. Many teachers would agree with the Office of Civil Rights that formal tests do not adequately show the abilities and needs of children. They may not recognize that their own observation may be skewed, confounding impressions of voice and visual appearance (Seligman et al., 1972). Observation needs to be systematic observation across a range of settings and activities, in class, on the playground, at home. The interdependence between specific settings and display of abilities and skills is indeed coming to be recognized as a crucial focus for research.

To start where the child is, then, one needs systematic knowledge of the childs *verbal repertoire* in relation to the verbal repertoire of his or her community: the range of varieties of language, the circumstances, purposes, and meanings of their use. That can differ from one community or district to another; local knowledge is needed. One needs as well to know the role of speaking, hearing, writing, reading, in a given variety, what it means to do each of these activities. That can differ from one place to another too, and local knowledge again is needed. One needs to know, in short, the locally relevant *ways of speaking* (using "speaking" as a shorthand expression for all modes of language use). The organization of language use in a classroom is but part of a systematic whole, from the vantage point of the student, and from that vantage point, classroom norms may take on a meaning not intended nor comprehended by school personnel. (On "ways of speaking," see Hymes 1974c).

It is common to think of choice of one language or another, one variety or style or another, one genre or another, a mode or occasion of use of language, as appropriate or inappropriate, right or wrong. Certainly teachers in classrooms seem often to think that way. An essential ethnographic point is to remember that one may have to do with elements in a system of signs. One has to do with more than right and wrong. It is not only the elements within a language that are to be understood as signs, as uniting form and meaning, as showing their status by contrast with other signs. Every choice within a way of speaking — of language, variety, style, genre, mode, occasion — conveys meaning through contrast with other choices not made, quite in addition to the meaning conveyed by what is written or said. The same is true for the manner of managing use of language, what Goffman (1956) has called *deverence* (what one conveys about one's attitude toward onself). Too often one thinks that one choice represents order, any other disorder, lack of order. This assumption can keep one from discovering the true order that is present, the system of sociolinguistic signs implicit in students' communicative conduct. One may wish to change that conduct, to change that system. One has to recognize it, be able to interpret accurately what is communicated, in order to know what one wishes to change. (This is an example of the relation between the descriptive and critical aspects of ethnography).

The point applies both to rules of language and to rules of the use of language. Let me say a little more about the latter first in order to highlight their importance.

A teacher or curriculum may make an assumption about the role of language in learning, about the etiquette of speaking, listening, writing, reading, or getting and giving information, of getting and giving attention in talk, that is at variance with what students experience elsewhere. Variance in itself of course is simply a fact. Whether or not it is a problem depends on the definition of the situation. If a classroom pattern is accepted and respected by all concerned, it may succeed, at least as success is defined by those concerned. (Their goals of course may not include equality or social change). The pattern may also stamp what is learned in the classroom as appropriate only in similar settings.

Schools have long been aware of cultural differences, and in recent years have attempted to address them, rather than punish them. Too often the differences of which the school is aware, of which even the community is aware, are only the most visible, "high" culture symbols and the most stereotyped conventions. What may be slighted is the "invisible" culture (to use Philips's title), the culture of everyday etiquette and interaction, and its expression of rights and duties, values and aspirations, through norms of communication. Classrooms may be respectful of religious belief and national custom, yet profane an implicit ceremonial order having to do with relations between persons. One can honor cultural pride on the walls of a room yet inhibit learning within them.

One may find children fitting classroom expectations, but in a way that defeats the purpose of their being there. Some Anglo teachers in Philadelphia schools have been delighted to have Spanish-speaking children in their classes, because the children are so well behaved, that is, quiet. The reason for the quietness is that the children do not understand what is being said. When they do understand (after being placed in a bilingual classroom, for example), they participate actively. The equation of being good with being quiet implies a further equation with being dumb (both senses of the word). Communities of course may differ in the meanings and normal occasions of silence, something that needs to be known in the individual case.

Knowledge of the local repertoire of varieties of language is obviously essential. In terms of the descriptive contribution of ethnography, a salient concern is the local meaning and interpretation of the joint use of both Spanish and English forms. Of course instances of the occurrence of elements of one language in the context of another may be quite *ad hoc*, due to the familiarity or the forgetting of particular words. But some may consider mixing of any sort reprehensible, and especially if it is extensive. Others may recognize in extensive mixing a special style of speech, appropriate to certain people and situations. They may find, not a failure to keep languages apart, but a skill in mingling them, one that has to be learned. Someone who knows Spanish and knows English may not know how to mingle them in the special style. From one standpoint, then, error and confusion, are something to be stamped out; from another, a skill with social meaning to be enjoyed.

The significance of mixing cannot be judged without knowledge of community and individual norms, but the knowledge is not an end to the matter. The temptation of descriptive ethnography is to let understanding imply acceptance, but ethnography can be used critically. In a given case, a community may not have been conscious of some aspects of its pattern of language use, and wish to reject some part when brought to its attention. Or a community may decide that a change of pattern is desirable, even necessary. Or it may decide to accept and value a pattern previously little noted. Whatever the case, the goals of bilingual education should be informed by ethnography, but set by those affected. The most difficult issue may be to analyze and assess information bearing on choice of *linguistic norm*, and on its implementation.

It is clear that there is an issue. There have been classrooms in which the native speakers of Spanish were in the back of the Spanish class, the Anglo students doing best and in front. There is a school in West Chester, Pennsylvania, whose Spanish-speaking Colombian teachers are certain that their Spanish-speaking Puerto Rican students need to be taught correct (Columbian-flavored) Spanish, ignoring a demonstration that the students are able to read newspapers published in Madrid. (I owe this observation to Elizabeth Smith). In both types of case, a different classroom norm would yield different results.

There well may be a genuine problem of inadequacy of competence in certain cases. Puerto Rican children raised in New York City may be disadvantaged in schools in Puerto Rico. Children growing up in a particular community may not acquire the full range of varieties and levels of Spanish, especially if Spanish has been part of a stable multilingual situation as a language of the home, rather than of education. Ethnography can help discover the facts of local situations in this regard. Whatever the facts, difficult matters of analysis and assessment remain. At this point the critical, comparative use of ethnographic knowledge becomes essential. One has to look at history and comparative experience, as well as at videotapes, reflect as well as record.

Let me address the issue of linguistic norms — of which to use, accept, reject, and how to use them in terms of English, in the hope that the analysis will be useful in considering analogous questions with regard to Spanish. Some leaders in bilingual education have been heard to say there might be a danger of perpetuating through Spanish the failures of schools in English. We are indeed familiar with the kinds of misperception and misconception of ability that can be fostered by prejudicial attitudes towards varieties of English different from the variety assumed in the classroom. Is the problem of attaining equality then simply one of such differences? Could the problem be solved by eliminating the differences, either by stamping out all but the preferred norm, or by substituting or adding one common norm in the repertoires of everyone?

For myself, I think that such an approach fails, and fails necessarily, in the United States, if the problem is indeed defined as one of eliminating linguistically-defined inequality. If every user of English in the United States used certifiably standard English, in recognizably middle-class ways, little would change. (Except for the cultural impoverishment, the loss of diversity and interest in American ways of life). Fault would continue to be found. People who do not double negatives may be found redundant in their adjectives. People who do not misuse tenses can be faulted for their use of adverbs and conjunctions.

Variability and evaluation of usage are indeed universal in human life, but the issue here is not one of individual differences, of the variation in personal ability inevitable in any group. That is a matter of talent; this is a matter of shibboleths. If linguistic discrimination is a culturally deep-seated way of maintaining social distinctions, then discrimination is likely to continue. If not English as against other languages, then one dialect of English as against others, or one style of standard English as against others, or certain niceties in style as against others. What Barth has shown for ethnic boundaries holds for class boundaries as well: even slight and infrequent features will serve as boundary markers, if boundaries there must be (see Barth 1969a).

One can further suggest that the United States is culturally organized to produce continually the appearance of a "falling rate of correctness," of a "law of increasing illiteracy." There is not only the constant reproduction of linguistic inferiority, the constant renewal of markers of it. There is also the constant projection of decline. This last draws on a disposition to interpret change in language (itself inevitable) as inevitably for the worse. From this standpoint, necessary distinctions are always being lost, never gained; etymology condemns vitality; intelligibility is so often found wanting, in one party to a dispute in a leading journal or paper, by an opponent, that one must infer that for the vast majority of people, talk is nothing better than a verbal blind man's bluff.

It is indeed a curious thing that a country whose civic ideology has been so committed to "progress" should so despair of language. I suspect two complementary attitudes and interests to be at work: a widespread popular distrust of verbal skill, as something associated with personal unmanliness and institutional exploitation, on the one hand, and as elite's definition of verbal skill as something only it can have and so control. It is perhaps an interaction between these two forces that produces such a phenomenon as a president careful to explain to his audience that he didn't know a word he used and had to look it up in a dictionary, while expecting to be trusted to manage a vast bureaucracy that lives and breathes with the manufacture and manipulation of esoteric discourse.

These are only suggestions. The role of language in the maintenance of cultural hegemony in the United States has been little explored. The main point — and this brings us back to the role of schools — is that the United States would seem to have a culture in which discrimination on the basis of language is endemic. To achieve equality within a given language, it would never be enough to change the way people speak. One would have to change what the way people speak is taken to mean.

In this regard, one can hardly avoid the thought that a latent function of schools has been to define a certain proportion of people as inferior, even to convince them that they are so, and to do this *on the seemingly neutral ground of language*. Language seems a neutral ground, so long as one can maintain that there is just one proper norm, and that the schools do their duty if they provide everyone access to that norm. The language of the norm is necessary, and everyone has a chance to acquire it — so one can imagine the reasoning to run. Any inequality of outcome cannot be the fault of the school or system, but must be fair, must reflect differences in ability, effort or desire on the part of students. If it is pointed out that some students begin unequally, relative to the norm assumed in the school, the responsibility is assigned to the student or student's community, for lack of proper language or even virtual lack of language at all.

Bilingual education challenges the very fabric of schooling, insofar as it adheres to the goal of overcoming linguistic inequality, by changing what happens in schools themselves. Yet if linguistic discrimination is a culturally deep-seated way of maintaining social distinctions, deeply embedded in educational institutions, is bilingual education likely to escape its influence? I have suggested that the form of attention to language in schools serves to maintain social stratification, and that so long as the society requires such stratification, it is likely to find ways to reproduce it linguistically. The society is defined as one of opportunity, yet the relative distribution of wealth and class position hardly changes year after year, decade after decade; language is likely to play some part in accomplishing and legitimizing that result. Is success for bilingual education then to mean that the accusation, "That's not Spanish" will be heard as widely as the accusation, "That's not English?" That children who know varieties of Spanish other than the norm adopted for a classroom will bear the stigma of not knowing *two* languages? (One hears reports of teachers who say to a child, "I thought your problem was that your language was Spanish instead of English; now I find out that you have no language at all.")

The issue of linguistic norms is inescapable within the level of an established standard itself, because of the distinctness of Cuban, Puerto Rican, Mexican and other national standards represented in the United States. It is inescapable as well with regard to the relation between national and regional standards, on the one hand, and the other components of the verbal repertoires of Spanish speakers in this country. The issue of norms involves the verbal repertoire as a whole. What is to be the desired role of each component of the repertoire, and what is to be the attitude toward each? As I have indicated, ethnography can assist in obtaining the initial knowledge needed to determine the present state of affairs. Clearly ethnography is needed, instead of questionnaires and surveys. What to make of the knowledge provided by ethnography is a matter for the bilingual community to decide. Perhaps in a given case it may be decided that an insistence on standard Spanish is necessary in order to maintain the language. It is also entirely possible that some may decide to reject bilingual education and Spanish as necessary ingredients of, say, Puerto Rican identity, spurred in their decision perhaps by elitist decisions as to the norm within Spanish. (See the question of the relation between political policy, class, and language policy, as discussed in a paper by members of the Centro de Estudios Puertorriqueños.)

Let me make clear that I do not mean to imply that all evaluation of language and usage is merely social bias. The point is that social bias infects evaluation. It is not the case that "anything goes," but it is also not the case that there is a single, homogeneous, unquestionable norm. The existence of a norm is a social fact, but not a fact beyond critical analysis in the light of knowledge of other norms, of the effects of the norm in question as it is implemented, of alternative relations between linguistic norms and ways of life.

There are indeed normative criteria that apply to languages and their uses, criteria of clarity, elegance, pithiness, musicality, simplicity, vigor, and the like. The difficulty is that people differ in the criteria to which they give most weight, even within the same community, let alone between communities. And people may differ in what they count as satisfying a norm on whose importance they agree. Much of the history of language policy and attitude, indeed much of the history of linguistic research itself, can be related to alternate attitudes towards the existence and character of two broad classes of norm, "standard" and "vernacular." In general, social bias affects willingness to recognize the presence and legitimacy of a norm in the first place, and the interpretation placed upon meeting or failing to meet it. Is adherence to a "standard" elegance or pretentiousness? logical regularity or empty form? Is adherence to a "vernacular" revitalizing or corrupting? natural or uncouth? an expression of the spirit of the folk or of the spawn of the uneducated?

Differences in pronunciation are stigmatized as stupidity the world over; absence of features of grammar is taken as absence of logic, propriety of diction identified with virtue. Such interpretations of the speech of others are frequently arbitrary. The association between a feature of language and a feature of intelligence or character is generally not inherent and universal, but local, secondary, projected.

Within one's own linguistic tradition, one may be on surer ground, assessing the speech of those who share it, but it is ground that cannot be made more secure than the tradition itself. One can judge others (and oneself) in relation to known norms, but not withhold the norms themselves from scrutiny, if their consequences cause them to come into question. Despite their pervasiveness and familiarity, the norms may be secondary and projective. We may honor them because through them we have experienced so much that is inseparable from our own naming and knowing of life, satisfactions and illuminations even that mastery of a norm may sometimes permit. Even so, we have to accept that similar experience may occur in relation to norms we can hardly recognize as such. There must be norms, if there is to be mastery, whether of interactional wit or composed art. But the norms themselves are not fundamental, I think. What is fundamental is what the norms make possible, the functions served in creative, resourceful, adaptive and expressive uses of language. Many norms can serve those functions, and a given norm can be made into an enemy of them.

We want to ask, then, not whether the norm is observed, but what is accomplished through observance of the norm? Is it desirable to spend a term insisting that a child be perfect in a minor grammatical feature, if the result is to teach that child that the norm of which the feature is a part is a torture chamber? If the child is inhibited from ever attempting to use that norm resourcefully?

We recognize that there are universal capacities for the structures and functions of language shared by all normal human beings; that a degree of individual variation in ability is inescapable; that a degree of normative stability is essential to the possibility of reliable communication and expressive mastery; that mastery of features may facilitate their resourceful use, but that the same features, treated as shibboleths, may inhibit resourceful use of language. The functions of language are fundamental, the forms instrumental. Quite literally, the letter killeth, but the spirit giveth life.

The goals of a community, of course, may not be to encourage creative and resourceful use of language. The goals may be to ensure that persons can be placed by the way they speak and write. Or to ensure that persons can perform useful work, reading instructions, newspapers, and other communications from those who direct things. (It is perhaps instructive that our society defines reading, a receptive ability, as its main concern, not the productive ability to write). Insofar as a community both says and means that resourceful, creative use of language is a goal for all its citizens, then questions of norms, and questions of pedagogy, too, must be decided in favor of an emphasis on function as primary, form as instrumental. This is not to ignore the one in favor of the other but to recognize which of the two will bring the other in its train.

If this view is accepted, then the task of ethnography is both indispensable and difficult. It is not enough to discover what varieties of language are in use, when and where and by whom, and what features of language vary according to what parameters. One has also to discover what varieties of language, features of language, are being used *for*, and to what effect. Is the choice of one norm over another the choice as well of certain functional possibilities as against others? Let me cite the circumstances of many Native American communities, which have acquired English, but not the literary glories that English departments like to cite, while having lost rich literary traditions of their own. These communities have English instead of some Native American language, insofar as it is a question of language alone. They have been impoverished insofar as it is a question of the functions of language.

The issues and choices are difficult. I only hope to have shown that the knowledge one needs in order to deal with them is ethnographic in nature. This is true, not only with regard to initial knowledge, but with regard to the monitoring of ongoing programs and of outcomes. Let me now say a little about each.

Whatever the strategy of a program, those who direct it obviously benefit from feedback during its course. Test scores and other classroom results may give some indication of the progress of students. Even with regard to what is learned alone, observation is desirable as well. Students may show abilities in peer-group interaction and other settings that do not appear on tests. Insofar as the program is concerned with the general development of the students, and with the success of bilingualism itself, ethnographic observation is essential. A central question will be: what does it come to mean to succeed, or to fail, in the program? what does it come to mean to do well or poorly?

Perhaps some of the meaning will have been assigned through the assignment of students to locations in the classroom or to other groupings. Studies by Ray Rist, Ray McDermott and others have shown the importance for success and failure, and for social meaning of success and failure, of teacher-assigned groupings.

Some of the meaning of the program to its students, and to the community from which they come to school, will emerge in interaction outside of school. Peer-group discussions and judgments, family discussions and judgments, community perception of the purposes and consequences of the program, need to be known, and taken into account. While the program is teaching language, it will also be creating social definitions and judgments. These definitions and judgments may be as important to success for bilingualism in the country as formal instruction.

A great deal can be accomplished by establishing regular community participation in the guidance of the program. However since none of us is a perfect (or even adequate) ethnographer of ourself if engaged in observation, comparison, and inference only *ad hoc*, it would be a valuable element of the monitoring of a program during its operation to have one or more persons formally responsible for ethnographic observation and inquiry. What groupings emerge in classrooms, on playgrounds, elsewhere? Does use of language change outside the class during the course of the program, and if so, in what ways? Does conversation about language change? What is said about the program, about those who succeed better than others, about those who do less well? Even more meaningful is discovery of what is *presupposed* in which is said — what comes to be taken as shared assumption in terms of which specific remarks are to be understood. (e.g., that a student who does well is a teacher's pet, that a student who does poorly is stupid, that only students from a certain class or neighborhood or kind of family do well, or do poorly, etc.).

Ethnographic monitoring need not be conceived as an isolated task. The staff of the program and representatives of the community could participate, if one or a few people were responsible for coordinating information, providing initial orientation as to the kinds of observation needed, and, indeed, for listening to learn of kinds of observation that might not have been initially thought of. A much higher degree of validity might be possible through cooperation. Since the purpose of the ethnography is to aid the program, its results must be communicated to the participants in the program. Far better to have the communication an ongoing process throughout the program. An additional benefit may be to share ethnographic skills that participants in the program will be able to use in other circumstances.

The greatest value of cooperative ethnographic monitoring is that the participants in the program will have the firmest grasp possible of the working of the program, of its successes and failures, strengths and weaknesses, in relation to their hopes for it. They will not be in the position of being confronted by an outside evaluator's charts and tables, and being told a rating for their program, with nothing to say, or nothing, at least, that such an evaluator feels required to heed. The participants will not have been bystanders. They will have concrete knowledge of the process of the program, and be able to address the processes that have produced whatever statistics and graphs a formal evaluation process may yield. An evaluation in terms of gross numbers can only guess at what produced the numbers, and indeed, can only guess as to whether its numbers were obtained with measures appropriate to what is being evaluated. The participants in cooperative ethnography may benefit from having their cumulative observations and interpretations compared with independently obtained measures. Both kinds of information could be combined to provide a deeper understanding. But if measures are to mean anything, especially in relation to bilingual education as a process of social change, the ethnography is essential.

All this is the more important, if we look ahead, and think of the monitoring and assessment of individual programs as contributing to judgments likely to be made a few years from now as to the success or failure of bilingual education as a national policy.

A few years from now the charge is likely to be made that bilingual education has failed. Money was spent, little was accomplished — it is easy enough to predict what will be said, if bilingual classrooms join bussing and poverty programs as targets of resentment.

The political strength of those who support bilingual education may be great enough to offset the pressure of those who will make such charges, once the first wave of support and funding has crested. And much can be said to deflate the prejudice that may lie behind such charges. From the standpoint of what is known about languages and their uses, it is clear that bilingualism can be an entirely taken-for-granted aspect of a society, something entirely within the normal capacity of individuals. The list of flourishing bilingual, even multilingual, situations throughout the world is long indeed. The evidence that human beings can readily acquire a range of varieties of language is so clear that the question must be, not, is it possible, but where it does not happen, what prevents it?

Arguments based on suspicion of bilingualism in general, then, can be won. Arguments based on the situation of bilingualism in the United States may be more difficult. Arguments will likely raise two issues: educational success, and political consequences. As to educational success, it can be pointed out that the consequences of generations of effort to impose monolingualism in schools can hardly be overcome in a few years' time. And insofar as successful programs require research, there has been little accumulated knowledge on which to build. Most linguists have been as blind to the importance of the linguistic diversity of the country as anyone. They, too, have proceeded as if knowledge of English alone would be sufficient. Far too few scholars of other disciplines have been helpful. Only in recent years has any substantial number of anthropologists thought ethnographic research in their own country legitimate. As we know, bilingualism has been made a vital issue through social, political, and legal processes. Research, by and large, has only begun to follow. Insofar as successful programs require accurate initial knowledge of the situations in which they operate and appropriate methods for assessing the communicative competence of students, they have had little on which to draw. Bilingual education may be accused of having failed before it has been fairly tried, if to be fairly tried means to have the support of the kinds of knowledge and methods indicated.

In this regard, the ethnographic monitoring of programs can be of great importance. The circumstances and characteristics of successful results can be documented in ways that carry conviction. Unsuccessful efforts can be interpreted in the light of the conditions found with success. Attempts to argue that bilingual education as a whole has been a failure in the United States can be countered by getting down to cases, and knowing well what the cases are. To do this, I realize, requires confidence in the kind of knowledge that ethnography provides, a willingness to accept the legitimacy of the conclusions arrived at by cooperative ethnographic observations and analysis, if such conclusions differ from formal tests and measurements. I think we do frequently accept the legitimacy of understandings of our own that are ethnographic in nature, as against statistics that run counter to our personal knowledge. I think we should do so, that to do so is essential to a democratic way of life, but that it is necessary to admit that we do; only by admitting that we do can we proceed to go beyond impressions and attain the validity of which an ethnographic approach is capable.

Some will argue against the political consequences of bilingual education, claiming that it is divisive. (A New York Times editorial not too long ago pointed to dispute in Quebec as evidence of the danger of carrying bilingualism too far). There is a general answer for this, of course; the social meaning of languages is not inherent in them, but a consequence of the uses to which they are put. Where languages are symbols of division, it is because of social forces that divide and pit people against each other along lines that coincide with language boundaries. Difference of languages is hardly necessary, a single sound will suffice, as the Biblical example of the killing of those who said *shibboleth* instead of *sibboleth* indicates. The greatest internal conflict in the history of the United States, the Civil War, was not fought in terms of language boundaries. On the other hand, there are many areas in which multiplicity of language is in no way a part of social mobilization and conflict. In sum, small differences can become symbols of hostility, and large differences can be accepted and ignored. The causes are outside of language.

To be sure, a given language policy may favor some interests as against others. Bilingualism may be experienced as a burden by people who have been able to assume that theirs was the only language that counted, that their convenience and the public interest were the same. But to argue that bilingualism is divisive is really to argue that it makes visible what one had preferred to ignore, an unequal distribution of rights and benefits. It is common to call "political" and "divisive" the raising of an issue that one had been able to ignore, and to ignore the political and oppressive implications of ignoring it. In this regard, the ethnographic monitoring of programs can also be of great importance. The ethnographic approach can go beyond tests and surveys to document and interpret the social meaning of success and failure in bilingual education.

It may be that some years from now those who work for bilingual education will not themselves be of one mind about its role. One view of the relation between such movements and general social processes is that they represent a phase of the interdependence between an expanding world economy and locally exploited groups. It may not be presently clear to what extent the movement for bilingual education is a recognition of sheer educational necessity; an expression of a phase in the relation between a minority group and forces dominant in the society; an expression of a growing commitment to the ideal of a multilingual, multicultural society. It may be that some sectors of the Spanish-speaking community will argue for intensive English training as a preferable route to economic opportunity, while others argue for Spanish maintenance programs on the grounds of cultural identity. Class differences may appear in this regard.

My own belief is that a multilingual society is something to be desired and maintained; but it is for others to decide their own interests. Whatever the ultimate policies decided upon, the wisdom of those choices will be greatly enhanced if ethnographic monitoring has been an integral part of bilingual education.

5

*CULTURALLY RESPONSIVE EDUCATION: RECOMMENDATIONS FOR ACHIEVING LAU REMEDIES II**

Courtney B. Cazden
Ellen L. Leggett

According to Section II of the "Task Force Findings Specifying Remedies Available for Eliminating Past Educational Practices Ruled Unlawful Under *Lau* v. *Nichols*" (Office of Civil Rights, 1975; hereafter referred to as the *Lau* Remedies):

> The second part of a plan must describe the diagnostic/prescriptive measures to be used to identify the nature and extent of each student's educational needs and then prescribe an educational program utilizing the most effective teaching style to satisfy the diagnosed educational needs. The determination of which teaching style(s) are to be used should be based on a careful review of both the cognitive and affective domains and should include an assessment of the responsiveness of students to different types of cognitive learning styles and incentive motivational styles — e.g., competitive vs. co-operative learning patterns. . . .

*Revised version of a paper presented for the National Conference on Research and Policy Implications of the Task Force Report of the United States Office of Civil Rights: *Findings Specifying Remedies for Eliminating Past Educational Practices Ruled Unlawful Under Lau vs. Nichols*, Southwest Educational Development Laboratory, Austin, Texas, June 17-18, 1976.

We are grateful to the following people who responded generously and quickly to requests for documents for this review: Carter Collins of the National Institute of Education, Steven Diaz of the Harvard Graduate School of Education, Roger Rice of the Center for Law and Education, Rudolph Troike of the Center for Applied Linguistics, and Herman Witkin of the Educational Testing Service. Responsibility for the views expressed here, however, are ours alone.

While this paper was being revised for publication, word was received of the death of Herman Witkin (*N.Y. Times* 7/11/79). Dr. Witkin's important research on the cognitive style dimension of field dependence is discussed at some length, and he was particularly helpful during our work on the original version of this paper. I am grateful for this opportunity to express public appreciation for his generous spirit as both scientist and human being — CBC.

Complying with this section of the *Lau* Remedies requires a decision about what, in addition to language, must be changed to create bilingual/bicultural education (BBE) that will be more responsive to cultural differences among children. Specifically, school systems are asked to consider cognitive and affective aspects of how different children learn so that appropriate teaching styles and learning environments can be provided that will maximize their educational achievement. Whatever the legal purposes that prompted this Office of Civil Rights document, it can be used more broadly to focus attention on issues fundamental to improved education for all children. In rejecting the District Court's previous approval of the Cardenas Plan for Denver (1974) that was based on a "theory of incompatibilities" between the characteristics of minority children and the characteristics of typical instructional programs, the Court of Appeals stated:

> The clear implication of arguments in support of the courts' adoption of the Cardenas Plan is that minority students are entitled under the fourteenth amendment to an educational experience tailored to their unique cultural and developmental needs. Although enlightened educational theory may well demand as much, the Constitution does not. (Center for Law and Education, 1975, p. 55)

While legal arguments continue about what the Constitution demands, we address ourselves to issues of "enlightened educational theory."

The assertion in the *Lau* Remedies that how we teach should be adapted to how children learn is supported by fundamental concepts in anthropology and psychology, which speak to differences among groups and individuals. In anthropology, the concept of culture includes not only language and a catalogue of visible objects and events but also the tacit knowledge that the members of any community share (Hymes, this volume):

> Schools have long been aware of cultural differences, and in recent years have attempted to address them, rather than punish them. Too often the differences of which the school is aware of which even the community is aware, are only the most visible, "high" culture symbols and the most stereotyped conventions. What may be slighted is the "invisible" culture (to use Philips's 1974 title), the culture of everyday etiquette and interaction, and its expression of rights and duties, values and aspirations, through norms of communication. Classrooms may respect religious belief and national custom, yet profane an implicit ceremonial order having to do with relations between persons. One can honor cultural pride on the walls of a room yet inhibit learning within them.

In psychology, the concept of intelligence:

> . . . postulates diverse mental abilities and proposes that intelligent behavior can be manifested in a wide variety of forms, with each individual displaying certain areas of intellectual strength and other forms of intellectual weakness. (Stodolsky and Lesser, 1967, p. 562)

In their widely cited article, Stodolsky and Lesser (1967) report research on cultural differences in patterns of mental abilities among first-grade children and hold out a vision of eventually being able to maximize children's learning by matching instructional practice to such differences.

How far have we come toward a realization of that vision? Expansion of this section of the *Lau* Remedies into more detailed recommendations should ideally rest on the following:

1. We know how to describe accurately how individual children learn because
   a. There is valid research data that children from identifiable cultural groups overwhelmingly exhibit certain learning styles, and/or
   b. We know how to make valid individual diagnoses of individual children in each classroom.
2. Having that information on children, by group and/or by individual, we know how to vary how we teach in relevant ways, that is,
   a. We have a repertoire of teaching styles, and
   b. We have research evidence that a match between characteristics of children and characteristics of teaching environments will significantly increase their achievement.

Educational psychological research on these issues has focused on the *aptitude-treatment interaction (ATI)*. Typically, *aptitude* refers to a test score, for example intelligence or previous achievement as measured with standardized instruments, while *treatment* often means curricular content or the pace at which material is presented. A much broader view of aptitude-treatment interaction is taken here, following Cronbach and Snow (1977). They define aptitude as

> . . . any characteristic of a person that forecasts his probability of success under a given treatment. We emphatically do not confine our interest to "aptitude tests." Personality as well as ability influences response to a given kind of instruction. Nontest variables (social class, ethnic background, educational history) may serve as proxies for characteristics of the learner that are not directly measurable. (p. 6)

Similarly, treatments may include many dimensions, such as the manner in which the teacher manages interaction between herself and the students.

During the past decade, considerable research has been done in this area, and reviews of the field are available (Berliner and Cahen, 1973; Tobias, 1976; Cronbach and Snow, 1977). In general, Tobias speaks for the field:

> (T)he bulk of the work remains to be done, and the visibility of the ATI construct for the illumination of our understanding of instructional events, as well as for advancing practice to the point where instructional prescriptions can be made, is still to be demonstrated. (1976, p. 63)

But while it is probably true that findings to date have not provided us with a great deal of prescriptive information, the ATI concept appears to be a useful one for consideration of instructional problems. Cronbach and Snow (1977) conclude:

> ATI has come of age. Research on instruction will need to incorporate its implications in theory and practice, regardless of how one ultimately proceeds with instructional adaptation. ATI methods and ideas have a fundamental role to play in educational evaluation as well as in educational design, and in psychological science generally. (p. 524)

Some attention is given to work on cognitive style, but the emphasis will be on studies of what has been termed interactional style, and on the possible relationships between cognitive and interactional style. While the former has been assessed with tests, the latter has not. In both domains, discussion is limited to discussions of differences among children where:

1. Evidence exists that individual differences are correlated with membership in particular cultural groups, and
2. Suggestions have been made for how instruction might be adapted to these differences.

Where evaluation data are available on the effects of adaptations on educational achievement, they are presented. Because this paper focuses on implications for formal, school-based education, environmental antecedents of the cultural differences are not discussed. This paper suggests how school systems may comply with *Lau* Remedies to create more culturally responsive education.

At the outset it is important to keep in mind a distinction between universal and particular goals of education. Universal goals are those that we expect all children to achieve and that we demand all schools teach. Literacy and mathematical competence are certainly such universal goals, whatever else one might want to include. Particular goals, by contrast, are both more optional and more varied — skilled performance in sports or the arts, for example. This discussion of the *Lau* Remedies is limited to its application to universal goals where:

> . . . the implication of recognizing individual [and cultural] differences is that different instructional strategies must be found which will optimally promote each child's achievement of basic, universal skills. (Lesser, 1971, p. 533)

Any complete educational program should also provide rich options for instruction toward more particular and optional goals, but they will not be considered here.

This paper does not discuss diagnostic/prescriptive measures themselves. It should be noted, however, that certain aspects of some management systems for diagnosing and prescribing children's educational needs (for instance, in reading and mathematics) may make culturally responsive education more difficult. In particular, thoughtful attention should be given to these aspects of whatever system is used:

1. The amount and frequency of testing required
2. The extent to which instruction is excessively individualized, in the literal sense of each child working alone
3. Cultural bias, or at best cultural meaninglessness, in the materials themselves, especially if they have been produced for a large-scale use over a wide geographical area.

Cultural Differences in Cognitive Style

The term *cognitive style* is used by psychologists to refer to ". . . individual variation in *modes* of perceiving, remembering, and thinking, or as distinctive ways of apprehending, storing, transforming, and utilizing information" (Kogan, 1971, p. 244). There is no theoretically based set of methods to describe such variations. There is only a list of labels for variations that psychologists have studied. One such variation is the contrast in sensory modalities between visual and auditory strength that may underlie the findings reported by Stodolsky and Lesser (1967). Kogan (1971) lists nine other cognitive style dimensions:

1. field independence vs. field dependence
2. scanning — a measure of how attention is focused
3. breadth of categorizing
4. conceptualizing styles — e.g., analytic vs. thematic categories
5. cognitive complexity vs. simplicity
6. reflectiveness vs. impulsivity
7. leveling vs. sharpening — a measure of assimilation in memory
8. constricted vs. flexible control — susceptibility to distraction
9. tolerance for incongruous or unrealistic experience (p. 246).

Of these nine dimensions, field dependence/independence is the most thoroughly researched. To our knowledge, differences in sensory modality strength and in field dependence are the only two dimensions of cognitive style in which evidence of cultural differences have so far been found. In these two areas, individual differences in cognitive styles do seem to be correlated with membership in particular cultural groups. In addition, suggestions have been made as to how instruction might be adapted to these differences, and in a few cases, evaluation data on attempted adaptations are available.

Visual vs. Auditory Sensory Modality Strength. Many teachers observe informally that some children seem to learn more through their eyes while other children learn more through their ears. My own experience is probably typical. In 1974-1975 I taught a combined first-second-third grade in San Diego. Two of the six first-graders were Mexican-American boys who did very well in beginning reading but seemed to learn in strikingly different ways. Rafael seemed to learn more through his eyes, remembering with remarkable accuracy how a word looked and where he had seen it. For example, in the game of *Concentration*, in which pairs of word cards are scattered face down on the table and players take turns trying to find the pairs, Rafael could beat anyone in the class, child or adult. Alberto, on the other hand, although an exceptional artist, was not particulary good at *Concentration*. He had a much easier time with the sounds that words are made of, and daily wrote stories with invented spelling to match his Spanish accent, e.g., "An tis coner is drragn" (In this corner is dragon.) (See Cazden, 1976, for two of Alberto's pictures and accompanying captions.)

Beyond such informal observations, which may reflect within-group differences, there is considerable research evidence, both experimental and ethnographic, for differences in sensory modality strength between cultural groups. *Strength* refers to some combination of ability and preference, which are often hard to separate. Stodolsky and Lesser (1967) gave four "mental ability tests" to middle- and lower-class children from four cultural groups in New York City (Chinese, Jewish, Black, and Puerto Rican) and three groups in a replication study in Boston (Chinese, Irish, and Black). On space conceptualization, a visual strength, the Chinese ranked first; and this superiority found originally in New York was completely replicated in Boston. Social class differences within each group affected absolute scores but not the overall pattern, and differences among the groups were greater among lower-class children than among middle-class children.

Cazden and John (1971) report extensive observations on the visual strengths of Native American children from many tribes; and Philips (1974) adds observations from the Warm Springs Reservation in Oregon. Kleinfield (1973) reviews comparable evidence for Alaskan Eskimos for the same sensory modality strength, which she calls "figural." John-Steiner and Osterreich (1975) report visual strengths in a study of learning styles among Pueblo children.

It is easy to imagine how relative visual strength could be exploited in instruction in reading or mathematics, but the evaluation of controlled experiments so far presents a mixed picture. Bissell, White, and Zivin (1971) review two studies in which individual children's modality strength was matched with types of reading instruction. Modality strength was assessed by tests of visual discrimination of letter combinations and auditory discrimination of letter sounds. The relationship between the children's relative scores and sight vs. phonic method of instruction was then analyzed. The results are inconclusive; one study reports that matching helped and the other reports that it did not. Whether the weakness is in the assessment of individual differences or instructional design is unclear.

Lesser (1971) reports similar attempts to match instruction in mathematics to modality strength. Certain mathematical concepts can be portrayed either by visual means such as graphs or Venn diagrams, or by equivalent words or numerical symbols. Lesser concludes from the few studies to date that:

> [T]his research . . . is clearer about the destructive [effects] of mismatching than it is about the constructive effects of matching . . . The inhibiting effects of mismatching seem well documented; the rational bases for arranging uniformly successful matches remain to be clarified. (1971, pp. 541-542)

It is likely that the educational effects of differences in sensory modality strengths are most significant in the early school years. Whereas adults usually can readily transmit information learned in one modality to the other modalities, children's sensory modalities are not as highly correlated (Bissell, White, and Zivin, 1971). Because of the inconclusive results from attempts at an instructional match and the dangers of mismatching, our best strategy presently seems to be a deliberately multisensory curriculum. A detailed example of multisensory teaching of the mathematical concept of set is given by Bissell, White and Zivin (1971).

As they point out:

> By teaching the concept of a set or any other concept with a multisensory approach, one is not only more likely to reach all the children in a class but also more likely to make each child's learning experience a richer thing. (p. 150)

Their recommendation applies to all children, but it applies with greatest force to the children to whom the *Lau* Remedies apply. Schools in general rely too heavily on verbal presentations by teachers and on demands to children for verbal expressions of what they have learned. But this over-reliance on words for the representation and communication of information is especially unfortunate in classrooms where the ability of children to comprehend or produce the language of instruction is in question or where children feel conflicts and pressures about their language use.

Our first recommendation, therefore, is that enforcement of the Lau *Remedies include attention to rich and diverse multisensory modes of instruction.*

Field Dependence vs. Field Independence. Because ". . . the field independence-dependence dimension is unquestionably the most widely known and thoroughly researched" (Kogan, 1971, p. 247) and because there is some evidence that relative field dependence is a characteristic of at least some Mexican-American children, the largest single group to whom the *Lau* Remedies apply, it is important to consider this research in some detail.

Research on the dimension of cognitive style called field dependence/field independence began in the 1950s when Witkin conducted a series of studies investigating individuals' ability to locate their bodies vertically in space when seated in an experimental room that was tilted at an angle (Body Adjustment Test — BAT). Some people were more influenced by the position of the room and located themselves "vertically" along the axis of the room's inclination. Witkin termed this greater reliance on the surrounding context as field dependency. Other people relied on bodily cues more than visual cues to determine "vertically" and were thus less influenced by the position of the room; they were labeled field independent. This work promoted further studies investigating aspects of perception other than bodily awareness. Tests include the now well-known Embedded Figures Test (EFT), which requires subjects to find a simple design within a more complex one, and the Rod and Frame Test (RFT), which requires subjects to adjust a rod to a position perceived as vertical within a square frame that is tilted, much like the tilted room task. From these three tests, it is possible to obtain quantitative measures of the extent to which an individual's perception is influenced by, or is more sensitive to, the surrounding field.

Around the core of scores on these three perceptual tests, researchers have attempted to describe broader personality characteristics of individuals with more field dependent or field independent cognitive styles. (For a review, see Witkin and Goodenough, 1976.) This research has been welcomed by Witkin as showing that the field dependent/field independent dimension of cognitive style pervades many aspects of behavior. In a review Witkin et al. (1977) state that "cognitive styles . . . cut across the boundaries traditionally . . . used in compartmentalizing the human psyche and so help restore [it] to its proper status as a holistic entity" (p. 15). In evaluating this claim, it is important to remember that data relating personality and social behavior to perceptual and intellectual functioning are correlational data. Even when the correlation is statistically significant, it is never perfect or even close to perfect. Any sample of people will include field-dependent individuals who score high on social characteristics measured in the particular study as well as field-dependent individuals who score low.

Besides the dangers of invalidly stereotyping perceptual and social behavior under one field-dependent or field-independent label, application of the labels themselves represents a misconstrual of what the test scores signify. Throughout the research literature, people are classified into two groups on the basis of their tendency to use one mode of functioning more than the other on the perceptual tests. It must be remembered that the scores form a continuum from very low to very high. Although the scores at the far ends of the continuum may be clear examples of one or the other cognitive style, we must question the accuracy of these labels for individuals (or, more accurately, for scores) in the middle ranges of the continuum. In studies in which two groups of subjects are contrasted by sex, social class, or ethnicity, the tendency to label one group as field dependent and the other as field independent is even more suspect. The scores for one group can only be considered more field dependent or field independent in relation to the scores of the other group; there is no absolute measure of field dependence or independence.

Witkin (1974) himself has warned against the danger of stereotyping and has stressed the importance of considering individuals as unique even more strongly. Witkin et al. (1977) later stated:

> Because scores from any test of field dependence-independence form a continuous distribution, these labels reflect a tendency, in varying degrees of strength, toward one mode of perception or the other. There is no implication that there exist two distinct types of human beings. (p. 7)

Despite these cautions, the danger continues to exist that each new study will strengthen the stereotypes with the addition of another distinction between "two types of people."

The dangers of stereotyping become compounded by tendencies to consider field-independent cognitive style inherently better. Ramírez and Castañeda (1974) criticize Witkin for placing a higher value on field-independent than field-dependent style. This criticism applies to Witkin's book (1974) in which he stresses the positive aspects of field independence; but those views have since been changed (Witkin et al., 1977). The original higher valuation of a field-independent style probably resulted from data that showed a developmental trend toward field independence and thus provided justification for the widespread view that field independence is a more mature and adaptive mode of functioning. The changed valuation comes from the realization that the perceptual tests rank individuals on their degree of articulation and differentiation in apprehending the physical world, while subsequent research on personality correlates can be interpreted as showing greater development of social sensitivity and social skills by relatively more field-dependent individuals.

To understand more about cognitive styles of language-minority children, De Avila and Duncan (1978) have undertaken a large study comparing children from different cultural groups on nine cognitive styles measures. So far, only pilot analyses have been completed. To date, the characterization of Mexican-American children as more field dependent than Anglo children rests on two studies. Ramírez and Price-Williams (1974) compared the scores on a portable Rod and Frame Test of fourth-grade children in Houston, Texas, from three cultural groups: Mexican-American children who were Spanish/English bilinguals, Black children in bilingual French/English families from Louisiana, and Anglo children. Scores of both the Mexican-American and Black children were more field dependent than the Anglo children. More specifically, degrees of error in their estimation of verticality were about twice as great. There were smaller but still statistically significant sex differences (girls were more field dependent than boys), and no differences in social class within each cultural group. In a larger comparison in Riverside, California, by Caravan (reported by Ramírez and Casteñeda, 1974), Mexican-American children in grades K-6 were significantly more field dependent in the Man-in-the-Box Test (an instrument similar to the portable Rod and Frame Test).

Ramírez et al. (1974) report considerable variability on the field-dependence/field-independence dimension among Mexican-American children and relate that variability to different socialization practices in traditional, dualistic, and atraditional communities. Although scores for children in even the atraditional community are more field dependent than Anglo children, Ramírez et al. (1974) wisely suggest that ". . . implementation of experimental model programs for Mexican Americans in settings different from those in which they were originally developed must be carried out with great caution" (p. 431).

Research on the educational implications of the field-dependence/field independence dimension is summarized by Kogan (1971):

> Witkin's analytical-global dimension would appear to be ideally suited for research on the interaction between variables of cognitive style and instructional treatment. Both ends of Witkin's dimension have adaptive properties, though of a distinctly different kind, and it is feasible that educational programs could be devised to profit each of the polar types. Unfortunately, no work of this sort has as yet been carried out. (p. 253)

In a review of more recent studies of the educational implications of the field-dependence/field independence dimension, Witkin et al. (1977) categorize the studies according to three questions: how students learn, how teachers teach, and how students and teachers interact. Although these studies deal with education, few took place in regular classrooms.

While the findings reported are of interest, they do not address the most important question: does matching the cognitive style of teachers and students result not only in greater interpersonal attraction but also in improved student academic achievement, especially in relation to some universal goal of education? There is no evidence to answer this question. Witkin reports a study of his own in which students of field-dependent and field-independent teachers did not differ significantly in their test scores at the end of an experimental "mini-course." Although this result does not address the central question, it does suggest that when students are grouped heterogeneously by cognitive style, the cognitive style of the teacher does not affect average group achievement. The data as presented do not give information on the students' cognitive styles, and it would be of interest to know whether the achievement of individual students who matched their teacher in cognitive style was significantly higher than the achievement of students who did not.

Some suggestions for educational practices that should enhance learning for field-dependent children are simply suggestions for better education in general, e.g., providing more structure in curriculum tasks and creating more learning situations that allow for interpersonal interaction. They would be generally considered aspects of good teaching. More specific and prescriptive recommendations go beyond the present state of our knowledge.

Ramírez and Casteñeda (1974) put forward an important proposal for "bicognitive development and educational policy":

> Our research on *bicultural* children led us to the discovery that children who could cope effectively with the demands of *two* cultures were those children who exhibited some capacity to be able to perform within both field-sensitive and field-independent cognitive styles. This finding led us to posit a concept of bicognition or bicognitive development . . . The goal that children become more versatile and adaptable to the increasingly complex demands of life in a postindustrial society may be reached by helping them develop the ability to switch cognitive styles — to be cognitive "switch-hitters" — or to draw upon both styles at any given time. (pp. 153-154)

In implementing this proposal, the cognitive style of each child is assessed through several Child Behavior Observation Instruments designed by Ramírez and Castañeda. Students are grouped within each classroom according to their cognitive profile: into either an extreme field-dependent group, a middle group, or an extreme field-independent group. In addition, the preferred teaching style of each teacher is assessed by means of two Teaching Strategies Observation Instruments. Teachers are then trained in the unfamiliar teaching style so that they will be proficient in using both styles in the classroom. They also learn to recognize characteristics of each cognitive style in children. Children begin in one group matched to their cognitive style and move to another group when the teacher decides they are ready, moving from one extreme group to the middle group and finally to the opposite extreme group. Ramírez and Castañeda (1974) suggest that as both teachers and students become more flexible in their use of both styles, groupings may become less rigidly defined. It is not clear what proportion of each school day children would spend in these groups. Ramírez and Castañeda say their approach is ". . . most effective in implementing the cognitive-styles component of culturally democratic educational environments and for encouraging development of bicognition in children" (p. 146), but no actual evaluation data are presented.

Our second recommendation, therefore, is that the program developed by Ramírez and Castañeda, and the many other research ideas in Ramírez (1975), be tried and evaluated; but until we have more research evidence, it does not seem advisable to make specific recommendations for educational policy on this dimension of cognitive style.

Cultural Difference in Interactional Style

Cultural differences exist not only in cognitive information processing habits but also in the interactional contexts in which people prefer to learn and demonstrate what they have learned in some kind of performance. These latter differences we call *interactional style*. This label can include some of the social correlates of the field-dependent style discussed above. It includes different reactions to cooperative vs. competitive situations mentioned in the *Lau* Remedies, and it includes considerable ethnographic evidence on children's responses to different interactional situations in school and in their home community.

One experimental study (Kagan and Madsen, 1971) has supplemented ethnographic observations that rural Mexican and Mexican-American children are more cooperative and less competitive than Anglo children. Anglo and Mexican-American children 4-5 and 7-9 years old in Los Angeles and Mexican children 7-9 years old in Baja California were taught to play a game in which only cooperative play allowed pairs of players to win a toy reward. All the younger children were overwhelmingly cooperative. But among the older children, Mexican children were by far the most effective cooperators, Anglo children least cooperative, and Mexican-American children in the middle. For example, in frequencies of trials labeled "completely cooperative," Mexican children had 63 percent, Mexican-American children had 29 percent, and Anglo children had only 10 percent.

The most detailed ethnographic research on the discontinuities that children from minority cultures face in public school classrooms has been done by Philips (1972, 1974) on the Warm Springs Reservation in Oregon. In the public school classrooms on the Warm Springs Reservation, teachers use four participant structures (1974):

> In the first type of participant structure the teacher interacts with all of the students. . . And it is always the teacher who determines whether she talks to one or to all, receives responses individually or in chorus, and voluntarily or without choice. In a second type of participant structure, the teacher interacts with only some of the students in the class at once, as in reading groups. In such contexts, participation is usually mandatory, and each student is expected to participate or perform verbally, for the main purpose of such smaller groups is to provide the teacher with the opportunity to assess the knowledge acquired by each individual student . . .
>
> A third participant structure consists of all students working independently at their desks, but with the teacher explicitly available for student-initiated verbal interaction, in which the child indicates he wants to communicate with the teacher by raising his hand, or by approaching the teacher at her desk. In either case, the interaction between student and teacher is not witnessed by the other students in that they do not hear what is said.
>
> A fourth participant structure, and one which occurs infrequently in the upper primary grades, and rarely, if ever, in the lower grades, consists of the students being divided into small groups, which they run themselves though always with the distant super-

vision of the teacher, and usually for the purpose of so-called "group projects." (pp. 377-378)

By contrast with non-Indian children, Philips found the Indian children reluctant to participate in the first two structures, large group and small group recitations, which were the most frequent in the classrooms; but Indian children were more talkative than non-Indian children in the last two contexts of student-initiated talk with the teacher and student-led group projects.

Philips (1972) explains these cultural differences as caused by sociolinguistic interference between participant structures in the school and in the children's home and community. In their homes Indian children learn by a combination of ". . . observation, which of course includes listening; . . . supervised participation, and . . . private, self-initiated self-testing" (p. 387):

> In summary, the Indian social activities to which children are early exposed outside the home generally have the following properties: (1) they are community-wide, in the sense that they are open to all Warm Springs Indians; (2) there is no single individual directing and controlling all activity, and, to the extent that there are "leaders," their leadership is based on the choice to follow [which is] made by each person; (3) participation in some form is accessible to everyone who attends. No one need be exclusively an observer or audience, and there is consequently no sharp distinction between audience and performer. And each individual chooses for himself the degree of his participation during the activity. (p. 390)

> This process of Indian acquisition of competence may help to explain, in part, Indian children's reluctance to speak in front of their classmates. In the classroom, the process of *acquisition* of knowledge and *demonstration* of knowledge are collapsed into the single act of answering questions or reciting when called upon to do so by the teacher, particularly in the lower grades. (pp. 387-388)

Other ethnographic reports suggest that the difficulties felt by the Warm Springs Reservation children in teacher-dominated recitations are felt by other minority-group children as well. Boggs (1972) reports that Hawaiian children participate volubly in choral responses and individually volunteer information to teachers when they sense receptivity but become silent if called on by name. Dumont (1972) contrasts two Cherokee classrooms — one in which children are silent and one in which children talk excitedly and productively about all their learning tasks. In the silent classroom, teacher-dominated recitations fail. In the other classroom, children have choices of when and how to participate, and small group projects not directed by the teacher are encouraged.

These observations suggest that children from several minority groups are less apt to perform on demand when asked a question individually in a large group and more apt to participate actively and verbally in group projects and in situations where they can volunteer. In Philips's (1974) terms, there is an incompatibility between the children's communicative competence and what is entailed in "getting the floor" in most classrooms. More accurate differentiation among the interactional styles of children in various cultural groups must wait for:

> . . . closer examination of the extent to which Blacks, Chicanos, etc. differ and/or are the same in their classroom behavior, of the ways in which their behavior is or is not in

some way related to different and/or similar experiences outside the classroom, and of the extent to which they are as different from one another as all of them are from the white middle class. (p. 122)

Even in a more multisensory curriculum, verbal participation in classrooms is important for all children as one indicator of engagement as well as one kind of demonstration to the teacher of what has been learned. For bilingual children, verbal participation in either language is also important as a learning activity in itself. Classroom environments should be designed to maximize that participation on educationally relevant topics. These generalizations about cultural differences in interactional style also underlie our concern about the excessive amount of testing and degree of individualization in some management systems for diagnosing and prescribing children's educational needs.

The problem of cultural differences is highlighted by Report V of the Mexican American Education Study of the United States Commission on Civil Rights (1972) and Jackson and Cosca (1974), which report observations of teacher/student interaction in 494 elementary and secondary school classrooms (not BBE programs) in California, New Mexico, and Texas. The report is a damning document:

Teachers praised or encouraged Anglos 35% more than they did Chicanos, accepted or used Anglos' ideas 40% more than they did those of Chicanos, and directed 21% more questions to Anglos than to Chicanos. Thus, Chicanos in the Southwest receive substantially less of those types of teacher behavior presently known to be most strongly related to gains in student achievement. (Jackson and Cosca, 1974, p. 227)

And this was observed in classrooms that had been selected from only those schools with no previous record of civil rights violations or investigations and in which teachers were aware that an observer from a federal civil rights agency was present. Clearly this situation, probably all too typical of schools with minority-group children, must be changed; and it is unlikely, in view of all the above research, that simply trying to change teacher reinforcement patterns will suffice. In the conclusion of her study of Warm Springs Reservation children, Philips (1974) comments on the Commission on Civil Rights report:

The orientation of the Commission Report is such that cultural differences of the sort considered [here] are not dealt with in attempting to account for the disparities discussed. The impression is given that the disparities are due to what is typically referred to as discrimination. *But* even where teachers are well-intentioned, the results are similar, because the minority students' efforts to communicate are often incomprehensible to the teacher and cannot be assimilated into the framework within which she operates. The teacher, then, must be seen as uncomprehending, just as the students are. And it is primarily by virtue of her position and her authority that the students and not the teacher come to be defined as the ones who do not understand. (pp. 311-312)

We agree that the teachers in those Southwest classrooms are not discriminatory in intent, but their teaching style becomes discriminatory in effect.

Consideration of cultural differences requires that the concepts of diagnosis and prescription be applied not only to children but to classroom learning environments themselves. This is being done in the Kamehameha Early Education Program (KEEP) in Honolulu (Jordan et al., 1977; Gallimore et al., 1978; Au and Jordan, this volume), and their experience is extremely important for all such efforts. In designing an educational program that would foster school success in "educationally-at-risk" Hawaiian children, Jordan et al. found that applying information on children's out-of-school life was a complex process. Some cultural patterns turned out to be positively applicable, notably similarities between a successful reading program emphasizing comprehension rather than phonics and the Hawaiian narrative style of "talk story." Some cultural patterns seemed neutral in their effects on education; for example, instruction did not have to be "Creolized" to match the children's dialect. And some cultural patterns had to be reversed so that children reared in peer-affiliation milieu would become attentive to the adult teacher. Jordan et al. conclude:

> The question is, which cultural data will be relevant for what kinds of classroom situation — and if relevant, should familial/cultural behavioral patterns be encouraged, ignored, or reversed? Anthropologists are not yet at a point where predictions and situations can be specified in enough detail to provide such advice; and classroom teachers and educators are similarly not certain enough about teaching and learning situations to specify what from the cultural/community settings may be effective in helping children learn. The answers to person-by-situation issues such as these can only come from an interaction between classroom experiments, and ethnographic interpretations and question-generation between educators and cultural and behavioral researchers. (p. 14)

Monitoring cultural as well as individual differences in children's participation should be a continuous part of the formative evaluation component of all BBE programs. This is what Hymes (this volume) calls "ethnographic monitoring," and there is probably no more powerful way to create culturally responsive education.

In a simple and general way, such monitoring can be done in any school system right now. Where children's participation is low, teachers and supporting personnel (both professional and community) can examine the classroom learning environment, try alternative participant structures in the light of research findings such as those reviewed above, and monitor the results. A more complex version, in which a trained ethnographer studies interaction patterns in a particular community and then works with the school staff and advisory community group in planning change, should be supported as widely as possible. [See Sherzer (1975) for extensive discussion.]

Research projects funded by the National Institute of Education include a few such efforts. Coburn (1975) promises to incorporate ideas on the social context of speech from Philips's research into the teacher's manual that will accompany reading and language arts materials created in and for Indian communities in the Pacific Northwest. And at least four related projects were funded in 1978: by Attinas, Poplack, and Pedraza (Center for Puerto Rican Studies) in East Harlem; Simons and Gumperz (UC Berkeley); Erickson (Michigan State University) and

Cazden (Harvard) in Chicago; and Tenenberg and Morine-Dershimer (California State University, Hayward).

Our third recommendation is thus for both shorter- and longer-range efforts to change interaction patterns in BBE classrooms to maximize children's engagement and thereby their learning: effective immediately, classroom monitoring; and wherever possible, community-specific ethnographic research and application.

Staff Selection and Training

The most important factor in achieving culturally responsive education is the school staff. It creates the learning environments in which children succeed or fail. Because culture is largely a matter of implicit knowledge, it is not sufficient for Anglo teachers to take formal courses on non-Anglo language and culture. The *Proposed Approach to Implement Bilingual Programs* prepared by the National Puerto Rican Development and Training Institute (Undated) is very clear on this point. Accepting the importance of ethnic foods, festivals, and courses on cultural history, the Institute states:

> But this is a limited interpretation of the concept of culture. What seems to be forgotten is that culture is acquired by direct, frequent, varied participation and experience in *all* aspects of the life of a group of people. A very large part of this acquisition occurs outside of the learner's awareness. It follows that culture in this deep sense cannot be taught in culture classes.
>
> Culture can only be "taught" or transmitted if special efforts are made to incorporate into the school, its curriculum, its staff and activities as many aspects as possible of the life of the cultural group to which the learner belongs. (p. 30; also quoted in *Aspira* v. *Board of Education of the City of New York*, 1974, p. 15)

Teachers as well as children can learn only in this way.

Three changes in staffing patterns can each contribute to bringing the minority child's culture into the school. First, parents and other community members can participate in all aspects of the school program, including direct work with children. B. Cardenas (1972) gives an example from the Edgewood School District in San Antonio:

> A cultural responsiveness permeates the Edgewood project. You may not see the Aztec sign in every classroom, but you do see the relationship between child and teacher as a very culturally relevant thing. You do see a culturally oriented learning style being respected. You do see parents in the classroom, and parents are transmitters of culture. (p. 21)

John-Steiner and Osterreich (1975) give many examples of parent, grandparent, and other community participation in Pueblo classrooms.

Second, there must be a plan for hiring and promoting school personnel who are members of the child's cultural group. As the Cardenas (1974) plan for Denver states:

> . . . at least a portion of this staff must be reflective of the characteristics of the minority child. Teachers who are members of the minority groups have the highest propen-

sity for understanding and responding to the characteristics of minority children. (p. 25)

It can be argued that this "propensity" may not be automatically reflected in classroom performance. For instance, in the United States Commission on Civil Rights study (1972), the disparity between the praise and encouragement given to Anglos vs. Chicano students was greater for Spanish-surnamed teachers than for Anglo teachers (Jackson and Cosca, 1974). But this observation was made in programs that didn't pretend to be either bilingual or bicultural, and name alone is an imperfect indicator of cultural identification. (Note that here we are arguing for the hiring of minority-group staff on grounds of educational relevance. Such arguments are separate from, and in addition to, other arguments on grounds of affirmative action.)

Third, there must be in-service education. Staff development needs will be different for teachers according to whether they are or are not members of the child's culture. Our discussion is focused on the needs of Anglo staff. (See the *Handbook for Staff Development Workshops in Indian Education*, Center for Applied Linguistics, 1976, for detailed suggestions for staff development of Native American personnel that could be adapted for other groups.)

For Anglo teachers, inservice education must include firsthand experience in the child's community and with the child's home culture, and the nature of that experience must be designed and implemented by a joint group of professional and community people. More than ten years ago, Landes (1965) described an "anthropology and education program for training teachers" at Claremont Graduate School that was based on *knowing* as well as *knowing about*:

> In American schools, emphasis is laid primarily on words to represent all the reality comprehended by men: ideas, values, skills, creations, details of knowledge, teachers, and the beneficiaries of teaching — that is, the pupils and the community. But heavy use of this prime tool can fail educators in their goal of attuning instruction to actual processes of learning. This happens when educators talk more *about* pupils than *with* them and their families. Separateness from the objects of discussion forfeits the experiences words should mirror. (p. 64)

This is not to say that *knowing about* is of no value, rather that it must be integrated with experiential forms of more direct *knowing* as well.

Such a requirement of direct experience is included in the *Recommendations for the Implementation of the Guidelines for the Preparation and Certification of Teachers of BBE Through Inservice Training* (Center for Applied Linguistics, 1974). It states, in part:

> That various "cultural" activities or experiences be included as sessions in any inservice course . . .
>
> That teachers be involved in community affairs where they interact with persons of the "other" cultures . . .
>
> That during inservice training teachers be provided with genuine experiences within the community, especially with minority groups of the same origin as the students.
>
> Opportunities for voluntary natural interaction in community activities are to be provided on an ongoing basis, with follow-up sessions for discussion of observations and questions . . .

The most detailed plan to date for what a school system must do to conform to the *Lau* decision is the *Master Plan for Bilingual-Bicultural Education in San Francisco* developed by the Center for Applied Linguistics and the Citizens' Task Force on Bilingual Education (1975). Part 4 of that plan discusses Training Program Development. The modes of training described include "Action Training" such as observation and community visitation, and "Formal Training Types" such as workshops and seminars that include explicit requirements for the participation of community members. One sample module of training session development is given in detail (see pp. 23-28). The overall goal of the module is:

> To increase the competency of fifth grade classroom staff to teach the interdisciplinary curriculum unit on "Politeness in language and society in the Phillipines and the U.S." and to integrate the unit into the total development of the child. (p. 32)

This training module is related to general cultural differences in interactional styles as well as to specific curriculum content particularly important feature is the participation of community members (e.g., one for every 15 participants for certain workshops), who provide the teacher participants with both information and opportunities to practice the appropriate verbal and nonverbal behavior. Griffin (1978), one of the Center for Applied Linguistics staff members who worked on the San Francisco plan, proposes a combination of research, inservice education, and curriculum development:

> If we take as given that the above three kinds of social factors [sociology of language, ethnography of speaking, and pragmatics] need to be taken into account in consideration of language in a BBE program, how can it be done? . . . The answer seems to be to generate a subject area in the curriculum that is "bilingualism" . . . A cooperative effort by teachers, parents and researchers can prepare the course content during a unique type of adult education. Such an educational setting is about the only chance that most of the adults will have ever had to experience the bilingual-bicultural learning that they plan for the children. (We at CAL were surprised that the San Franciscans had not considered that choice and combination of language in staff training and community meetings could be a matter of "practicing" what the program was "preaching" for the children).

If a reminder is needed about what happens when a well-intentioned school administrator tries to do some inservice education on his own, *Pickets at the Gates* (Fuchs, 1966) reports a true story. A principal of a largely Black and Puerto Rican school, who ". . . had been reading a great deal concerning the characteristics of children in depressed areas" (p. 6), found out that he would have 15 new White teachers in the fall. Hoping to help them, he wrote a letter to the faculty, with a copy to the PTA president, sharing his "facts" about the children and their families. As we would now expect, the parents reacted strongly, demanding his removal. Thus, symbolically at least, the "pickets at the gates."

This story dates from the mid-1960s, and we may feel sure we have grown in cultural sensitivity in the intervening 10 years. But we still sorely need case studies of successful models of inservice bicultural education.

Our fourth and final recommendation is that inservice education along these lines be required, and that case studies of successful models be accumulated and widely distributed.

Summary

The concept of culturally responsive education rests on fundamental concepts of the nature of culture and the nature of intelligence and is a very important part of the *Lau* Remedies. Four recommendations for research and educational policy to achieve culturally responsive education have been made:

1. Because children differ in sensory modality strength and the learning of all children in BBE schools may be depressed in overly verbal environments, all such schools should deliberately plan more multisensory instruction.

2. Because the educational implications of differences in field dependence/ independence have not yet been evaluated, this is an important topic for research.

3. Because classroom participation is an indicator of children's engagement and thereby of their learning, and is also a valuable learning activity in itself in BBE programs, monitoring of that participation and subsequent planning for change where needed should immediately become part of formative evaluation procedures in all BBE schools. In a few communities, longer-range field research projects should be supported in which an ethnographer works with staff and community members on a specific diagnosis of incompatibilities between the interactional styles of community and school, suggests directions for change, and then helps to monitor the results.

4. All school systems should bring the invisible culture of the community into the school through parent participation, hiring and promotion of minority-group personnel, and inservice training for the school staff. This inservice training should include both experiential and formal education components along the lines described in the *Master Plan for San Francisco*. Case study descriptions of successful inservice programs should be accumulated and distributed widely.

6

THE TEACHER AS COLLEAGUE
IN CLASSROOM RESEARCH*

Susan Florio
Martha Walsh

Introduction

Classrooms are social places. During the school day — at play, during lessons, while cleaning up, at lunch — teachers and children engage in talk and movement that is subject to interpretation from moment to moment. Such interpretations of talk and movement are the basis for the teacher's decision-making about the children's social and academic growth and readiness. It is important to study these interpretive procedures, because of the impact they have on children's lives in school.

Typically, people do not need to plan their interpretive procedures in advance or put them into words. Nor do they necessarily share these procedures, particularly with others from different cultural and linguistic traditions. Because interpretive procedures differ from group to group, this state of affairs can complicate life in a pluralistic society in general. In particular, it can complicate

*Paper originally presented as part of a symposium on Studies of the Social Organization of the Classroom at the annual meeting of the American Educational Research Association in San Francisco, California, April 21, 1976.

The research reported here was supported in part by a Spencer Foundation grant awarded to Frederick Erickson. The authors also wish to acknowledge the cooperation of the Institute for Research on Teaching at Michigan State University and the Newton, Massachusetts, Public Schools. The authors accept sole responsibility for the ideas expressed in this paper.

teacher decision-making in culturally diverse classrooms, where teacher and students may not share the same interpretive procedures.

One of the aims of ethnography is to describe the interpretive procedures of members of particular social groups, by means of observation and participation in the ways of life of those groups. In this process, group members can become informants as they are called upon to step outside the ebb and flow of life and comment upon it. This process is of interest to researchers because they can come to understand the interpretive procedures used by the informant, which are likely to be quite different from their own. The process can also be revealing for the informant, because interpretive procedures are not usually explicitly and consciously known to group members, despite the frequency of their use.

When the social setting is a classroom and the informant a teacher, the teacher may reflect upon usually taken-for-granted practices of daily classroom life. This paper traces the evolving relationship of a teacher and a researcher who shared life in a kindergarten/first-grade classroom for an academic year. Their relationship became the basis for new ways of thinking about the social and academic competencies of children in the class and for new ways of thinking about the aims and conduct of classroom research.

Setting the Scene

The evolution of colleagueship between teacher and researcher reported in this paper was embedded within the context of a pilot study of classroom interaction. In the 1974-75 academic year, researchers at the Harvard Graduate School of Education initiated a study of which the history reflects several years of thinking about — and trying out — methods for producing ethnographically valid accounts of classroom communication. In many ways, therefore, it is a history of trial and error — and of insights that could not be anticipated. The researchers sought an experienced primary school teacher to join them in a study of the socialization of young children to the ways of behaving and making sense operant in the classroom. They hoped that the teacher would be willing to have graduate students videotape periodically in her classroom and to watch and discuss the tapes with the research team during the school year. A kindergarten/first-grade teacher, Martha Walsh, was recommended by the principal not only because she had taught successfully at his suburban Boston Title I school for seven years, but because she was particularly open about the operation of her classroom and had a reputation of willingness to try new things. Ms. Walsh typically taught the K/1 class, and the majority of her students came from blue collar, Italian-American families.

From the outset, the study was intended to depart from traditional studies of teaching. The data to be analyzed would be videotaped samples of naturally occurring classroom activities. The samples were taken at the beginning, middle, and end of the school year. The study was an ethnographic one in that its purpose was to learn about the social organization of Ms. Walsh's classroom and the process by which kindergartners became accustomed to it through analysis of taped talk and movement. As such, it resembled other more traditional ethnographies. Theory about face-to-face interaction guided the formation of initial research questions and data collection, but extensive viewing of the tapes was required to discover what the functionally relevant ways of behaving might be for those involved in the scene. As a result of this early work, subsequent major modifications were made in research questions and data collection procedures.

The first year of the study in Ms. Walsh's room provided for the careful recording of retrievable slices of classroom life for detailed analysis. However, it only scratched the surface in obtaining a sense of the shared understandings guiding the interactions of the teacher and class members. The study did not provide for long term, systematic observation of and participation in classroom activity by a field worker. Although it was possible to construct models of the organization of activities in the classroom on the basis of videotape analysis and conversations with the teacher, the researchers lacked a sense of the school and neighborhood as they impinge on life in the classroom and, most significantly, the researchers had little direct experience of the everyday classroom life they had so faithfully recorded on tape.

In an attempt to gain closer access to the general patterns of life to which kindergartners become accustomed upon joining Ms. Walsh's class, participant observation was an obvious addition to the study. In the fall of the second year of the study, Susan Florio joined Ms. Walsh's class as a field worker. She was an advanced doctoral student who, prior to entering graduate school, had been a middle school teacher of language arts. With the added perspective that fieldwork made possible, the research team acquired an enriched ethnographic framework in which to view and analyze the videotapes. Also, because of the colleagueship that developed between Martha Walsh and Susan Florio during this phase of the study, it was possible to consider seriously ways in which classroom interaction research can articulate with and be used in the service of the daily needs and goals of teachers and children.

Beginning the Fieldwork

Both teacher and fieldworker held several unanalyzed and preconceived assumptions about the nature and purposes of classroom research at the outset of the pilot study. Before the classroom videotapings began, the research project was not seen as a learning experience by the teacher. She initially volunteered to participate feeling that she would not be changed in the least by the experience. However, among her unstated assumptions were that teachers often do things wrong and that outsiders — researchers — come in to fix or criticize them; and that educational research is carried out typically where and when a setting is in need of altering. She was confused about the actual purpose of the study. Her initial questions were, "How did they find *me*?" and "What can I do for them that someone else couldn't do better?" Her decision regarding the study was that she would do what she had done for the past seven years in her classroom, and that the researchers were welcome to observe. If they learned from her or liked what they saw, great! But she was not going to worry about any negative implications of her involvement.

The fledgling fieldworker entered the classroom setting with assumptions about educational research which had arisen from her introduction to the study of teaching. Although attempting classroom participant observation, she assumed, for example, the following:

> 1. that educational research is typically conducted in the context of "proof," or that outsiders observe phenomena in order to evaluate needs, prescribe treatments, and then to measure the effectiveness of those treatments;
>
> 2. that it is possible to observe a setting as complex as a classroom easily, systematically, and "objectively" and thereby to arrive at a description and understanding of the setting;
>
> 3. that the needs and questions of a classroom researcher probably do not overlap or articulate with those of a classroom teacher.

Changes of Perspective

In the first year of the study, classroom videotaping without participant observation left little time for communication between teacher and researcher(s). Data collection took on the aspect of traditional classroom observational research. The researchers gathered data — eyes glued to cameras or ears tuned to headphones. They would tape, take notes, pack up, and leave. Though not put off by them, the teacher did not feel particularly included in or informed about what they were looking for.

The sessions held at the university, in which the teacher was invited to view and discuss tapes collected in her classroom, gave the teacher and researcher(s) their first chance to get involved with each other. It was through these sessions and small group discussions that the teacher's perspective began to change; she began to see herself as a member of the team. Naturally the process took time. At first, although told to watch and comment freely, she was not clear about what was expected of her. The sessions were very open-ended, but the teacher still saw herself as an object of investigation, unable to generate any of the questions and capable of providing only "right" and "wrong" answers to the researchers. Although the tapes began to be valuable to her at this time as an awakening tool for thinking about her classroom and students, the teacher was unsure of what others wanted to get from them or in what light she should comment while viewing.

A great deal of the teacher's discomfort was occasioned by the researchers' own vague ideas of how to proceed at this point. Unlike many scientists, they had not generated explicit *a priori* hypotheses about Ms. Walsh's classroom. Instead, they generated guiding questions or "working hypotheses" as they went (Geer, 1969). They attempted to ground these hypotheses in what they were seeing in the classroom tapes. Having chosen to adopt an ethnographic stance, they seriously intended their open-ended questions. Yet asking questions such as "What's happening here?" and "What do *you* see in the tapes?" despite their roles as university "experts" and researchers, served to communicate an uncomfortable double message to the teacher.

Gradually the teacher and researchers developed a sense of trust, a personal rapport, and — not surprisingly — a more clearly defined set of research questions. They came to know one another as individuals, in the classroom, at the viewing sessions in university offices, and at informal dinners. They came in the process to know a great deal more about classroom interaction research as well.

Research in the Context of Discovery —
The Joint Enterprise of the "Participant Observer"
and the "Observant Participant"

In the second year of the study the participant observer entered the classroom with the rather vague and naive idea that by means of various research strategies she could learn something about what went on in the classroom, share her insights with the teacher, and thereby leave the teacher with something that would "make a difference" in the confrontation and solution of her day-to-day classroom problems. This process was to be only a by-product of the fieldwork research process, a way of repaying Ms. Walsh for her participation: it was not to be the heart of the participant observer's study.

As a result of her initial experiences as both participant and observer in the classroom, however, the fieldworker was forced both to reconsider the complexity of the classroom phenomena she had hoped to document and perhaps influence, and to make explicit and question critically her assumptions about how and why one engages in classroom research. Despite a background in the literature of classroom interaction and experience as a nonparticipant classroom observer, the researcher found herself "just teaching" as she spent more and more time with the children in this class. Her awareness of sociolinguistic issues did not automatically change anything that she could see or feel in her own behavior as she engaged in daily activities with the children. She was not very different in this role than she had been as a teacher in her own classroom several years before.

What was different, however, was the kind of disciplined reflection she forced herself to engage in after each school day was over. Having adopted the stance of a field researcher, she was inclined to think through the day's events in light of what she was reading and thinking about the functions of language and nonverbal behavior in social contexts. She also had the added available resource of videotapes of typical daily activities, and thus she was able to step out of the thick of events and take a second (and often a third) look at the kinds of events that transpired in the room and the roles that people played in them.

Gradually, the researcher realized that if her experience as a participant observer was different at all from what it had been as a teacher in her own classroom a few years ago, it was in that she was becoming more sensitive to the dynamics of everyday life in classrooms. She also had more time and tools available for reflection about classroom events — the formation and disbanding of groups, the eruption of arguments, the management of interruptions, the demonstration of the mastery of academic skills.

The following anecdote reported in the early field notes illustrates the experience (Field Notes, 9/9/75):

> I was playing Candyland, a board game, with a group of students. It was the fourth day of school and the first where I was not preoccupied with videotaping. During the taping of the first three days of school and in conversation with the research team that had been there for the taping, and now — most noticeably — during the game, I was unable to refrain from forming strong impressions of most of the children. One of the boys in the group (Harry) seemed to me to be manipulative. At cleanup time, he did not join in, and I attempted to get him to help in the effort. Uncertain of my authority in a room where I was not the teacher, and therefore hesitant to issue an imperative, I deliberately said instead, "Harry, will you help us put away the game now?" He replied simply, "No." At that point the teacher, having overheard the exchange, said, "Alright, Harry, go over and help them clean up."
>
> This incident can be thought about in a number of ways. It may be that, in fact, Harry, being new both to me and to the kindergarten, misunderstood the discourse function of my utterance and responded to it as a yes/no question rather than a command. However, it is also possible (and something in my teacher's intuition says more likely) that he fully understood what I had meant but was quite able to take advantage of my uncertain position of authority (expressed especially in my linguistic choice) and was almost successful in opting out of the cleanup job.
>
> In any case, thinking about the event and about the intuitions that I already have about Harry and where they may have come from, it occurs to me that my theoretical perspective and field methods may not be able to alter the way people act in social encounters, but they may at least put some extra steps between those social encounters and the ways we think and feel about students. If teaching is largely a matter of forming and testing hypotheses about children, then it seems like a good idea to have as much data available as possible — to have many ways of thinking about and accounting for what we observe, experience, and do with children.

The researcher began to speculate that the change of perspective she was experiencing might also happen to the teacher if she were invited to become more intimately engaged in the research process. The early insight was critical for the researcher in defining, with the teacher, both what the nature of their relationship and the goals of the research might be.

As the researcher spent more time in the classroom, the teacher felt more comfortable and better informed. The teacher felt that she was beginning to have a definite hand in the research. She realized that, although teachers do not have time to be ethnographers in their own classrooms, they can become more observant participants. New insights and questions generated by the teacher and researcher could be checked out by the teacher by means of observation during and reflection after teaching. These activities enabled her to become a part of the process, not just a source of data.

The participant observer put great effort into incorporating the teacher into the research plan. Constant contact with the research process helped the teacher to see herself as a relevant member. During the second year of the project the teacher also received a salary. This was a tangible demonstration of her membership and provided additional motivation for her to take an active role. Also, during the second year of the project, the teacher's views were actively sought. Classroom participation by the researcher allowed more time for conversations than had been previously provided by viewing sessions. While in contact with the children during the school day, the distinction between teacher and researcher was often blurred. Observations and questions could be shared on the spot or during release time and lunch. However, there still remained days when, busy with tasks specific to their separate roles, all that teacher and researcher could manage were a "Hello" and a "Good-bye."

The Blending of Roles

One of the first areas of joint discovery for teacher and researcher as they began to experience the blending of their respective roles concerned the idea of educational "change." The issue of whether the research intended to change anything in the classroom was a problem for both teacher and researcher. Since so many strangers enter classrooms to engage in some sort of intervention, the role of participant observer implied that change might be one goal of the project. However, ideas about the complexity of behavior and about what might be meant by "change" grew and were refined in the teacher/researcher dialogue almost from the outset. In fact, thoughts about change became more modest during the course of the study than they had been at the beginning. The teacher was not seen as someone in need of a "treatment;" and the researcher, who became in time less an outsider, was not seen as a conventional agent of change.

Like any teacher, this one had particular classroom problems; and the participant observer, of course, had a personal agenda of research questions. However, it was interesting to discover just how much these two problem domains overlapped. Since each hoped to be helped with her individual concerns by sharing the diverse perspectives and kinds of expertise brought to the experience, both the teacher and the researcher could be said to have been in some sense "changed" by the other during the course of the research experience.

An example of how the teacher's thinking was affected by her involvement with the research effort is demonstrated in the following anecdote taken from field notes (Field Notes, 2/4/76):

> There are specific problems which might be addressed with videotapes and analysis. One of these is the question of Jerry and the issue of whether he is suffering or benefiting from his remedial, bilingual tutorial help.
>
> The issue of interruption and speculation about the pros and cons of taking children out of the classroom for extra help has been discussed before by the teacher and the researcher. Some children clearly benefit from the help, and it seems worthwhile to sacrifice their classroom time and place them in a new social setting with yet another adult/evaluator in the interest of mastery of some fundamental skill. However, for other students, like Jerry, the added social complications of special help may, in fact, interfere with the mastery of those skills.
>
> In Jerry's case, the tutorial help doesn't seem to be working. The tutor manifests a different style than the teacher. It appears that the tutor encourages Jerry's dependence on her. He can't function when he returns to the regular class.

The teacher has raised the problem in conversation with the researcher. They have noted that the ethnic identity of Jerry and the Italian teacher, combined with the tutor's lack of experience in classrooms, and finally combined with her obvious temperamental differences from the regular classroom teacher may make learning with the tutor a very different kind of experience than learning with the regular classroom teacher.

The teacher has suggested that an examination of the ways in which tutor and classroom teacher *behave differently* might be useful in both understanding and creatively solving the problem. She has suggested that each professional observe and/or view videotapes of the other in an attempt to discover how their own behaviors differ and how Jerry works differently with them.

The task for the researcher, on the other hand, was to become more and more a part of the scene. She was continually asking, looking, and being with the children. Yet, it was important for her to be both "stranger and friend" (Powdermaker, 1966), preserving a kind of "double vision" that enabled her to account in some larger arena for how and why things made sense to those members in the ways they did.

For the teacher, the task was curiously reversed. She was continually immersed in the fray, and, like many other teachers, experienced loneliness and frustration in that immersion. The teacher learned gradually to look at her classroom problems not only in the company of her researcher colleague, but to reflect on those problems using more of the perspective and techniques demonstrated by the new colleague. She reflected on what she thought, did, and absolutely *knew* about her class. She was an insider gaining some internal distance from her role. She was thus able, at certain moments, to see the familiar in a fresh new way.

Procedure for Research

Concretely, this curious blend of roles engendered a procedure for classroom research in which both teacher and researcher worked closely in the posing of researchable questions, the formulation of hypotheses, and the gathering and analysis of data. The teacher and fieldworker agreed early on that classroom research ought to address the daily concerns of teacher and children and not merely be descriptive or proscriptive. The way of working which they devised came out of this shared point of view. They were interested not only in addressing questions about classroom interaction, but in examining as a phenomenon in its own right the process of change of perspective and consciousness that occurred for both of them as they engaged in joint research.

The procedure had four components that were carried out jointly by teacher and researcher. They were organized chiefly by the researcher. The components were participant observation, selective videotaping of classroom activity, joint viewing sessions, and some microanalysis of taped segments.[1]

There was ongoing generation of questions for research. Questions could come from many sources: the problems of individual children, the effects of room organization, the disruptions that occurred and their possible causes. Once a question of mutual interest was selected, the investigation proceeded by going back through videotapes and field notes previously collected and by collecting new tapes and observations. The team tried to find instances of the particular problem raised and then began to generate hypotheses that might answer the question. Finally, by means of viewing and microanalysis of segments as well as focused classroom observation, they attempted to locate *in actual behavior* the sources of the issues raised and thereby test their informed hunches. They discovered that working this way served both to provide a rich ethnographic context for microanalysis and to diffuse the anxiety usually associated with self-analysis by means of videotape.

In making the collaborative process a subject for study as well, the team carefully documented meetings trying to keep track of their insights, their unique approaches and analyses, and the ways their perspectives were modified as a result of dialogue and joint inquiry.

As a final component, the team attempted to think about and monitor instances of behavioral change — spontaneous and/or deliberate — that occurred in the classroom as a result of the joint study.

A Case Study

This case study is intended as an illustration of the research method. The teacher and the researcher arrived at the problem for study in several ways. The teacher had mentioned one day over coffee that she was curious about why one first-grader student (Arthur) was able to "get to her" in a way that another student (Louise) was not. The researcher recorded this comment in field notes.

About a month later the teacher and researcher were again engaged in casual conversation about the classroom when the teacher repeated her question about Arthur and Louise. The teacher was surprised to learn that the researcher had previously noted it as one of the teacher's concerns. They decided to pursue the question since it had emerged as salient for both of them — Arthur and Louise being children frequently discussed by the teacher and appearing often in the researcher's field notes.

The research process began with a directed conversation about the two children. The team of teacher and researcher discussed similarities and differences between Louise and Arthur. They were both first-graders who tended to talk a great deal, yet they seemed to be treated very differently by their peers. Arthur was a leader among them, and Louise was an object of teasing and exclusion. They also had differential success in gaining the floor as they attempted to talk in large class meetings called "circles" (see Figure 6.1).

With these observations in mind the team went back through videotapes collected during the very first weeks of school. They chose to look at circles because they were contexts in which both of the children appeared and in which teacher and peers were also visible. The team noted the following regularities as they viewed these tapes:

> Louise and Arthur tended to dominate the circle times. They talked and moved a great deal and were "noticed" often by the teacher.

> Louise and Arthur seemed to be "doing the same things" in their attempts to gain the floor, but Arthur clearly had a great deal more success than Louise.

The similar behaviors of Arthur and Louise included sitting on the outer edge of the group, raising hands, shifting from sitting to kneeling positions, moving toward and away from the teacher, and verbalizing a great deal.

The team then selectively taped the entire class during another typical circle in order to determine whether these regularities were still occurring some six months into the school year. The team watched the tape without sound, hoping thus to pay primary attention to the large scale movements of Louise and Arthur and not to be distracted for the moment by theirs or the teacher's speech. Even without microanalysis, certain behaviors again emerged as common to both of the children, including kneeling/sitting, raising/waving of hands, and leaning forward or away from the teacher. These behaviors were chosen for microanalysis for no other reason than that they seemed to "jump out" at the viewers from the tape. They seemed to be the major ways in which the children of interest were expending energy in attempting to get a turn to talk (Pike, 1967).

For the purposes of microanalysis the team carefully watched a four minute segment at the beginning of the circle, noting variation in the behaviors mentioned. They looked for beginnings, endings, and changes of intensity. A fourth category — presence or absence of talk — was added to the analysis, but the content of that talk was excluded for the purposes of this analysis.

Upon charting variations in these behaviors, the team discovered that, indeed, there were similarities between the behaviors of Louise and Arthur. How-

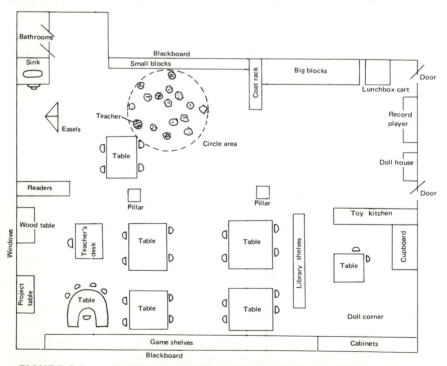

FIGURE 6.1   FLOOR PLAN OF KINDERGARTEN/FIRST-GRADE CLASSROOM DURING CIRCLE (2/27/76)

ever, there were some important differences in what might be called the efficiency with which the two children manifested those behaviors (see Figure 6.2). It appeared from the charts that when Arthur wanted to talk he employed all four of the noted behaviors almost precisely at once. He presented a unified front to the teacher, making it clear that he intended to get the floor. This picture of his behavior seemed to be consistent with the teacher's characterization of him as a "leader" among the children and as an active participant in the circle.

Louise, on the other hand, had been enigmatic to the teacher. She was of large physical size, and the teacher described feeling that Louise "crept up on her" during circles. When looking at the graphic representation of Louise, it was clear that she often moved up and down and in and out simultaneously. Since no hand movement or verbalization generally accompanied such movement, it was difficult to tell if Louise was attempting to gain the floor or not. What did emerge, however, was a snake-like pattern of movement in which Louise seemed to be, indeed, "creeping up" on the teacher.

Arthur talked in quick bursts and moved more often during the four minutes analyzed. Louise, on the other hand, held the floor only once. She talked for a very long time and was eventually cut off by the teacher. She did not move a great deal while talking.

Leaving Louise and Arthur briefly, the team looked at the teacher's behavior during those first four minutes. Again, they chose to chart salient movements — head and hand movements, gaze direction, and the presence or absence of talk. The class group seemed to divide naturally into thirds — left, center, and right — in receiving the teacher's gaze. However, the teacher looked at the center section almost half of the time and at the right hand section (containing Louise and Arthur) nearly all of the rest of the time (see Figure 6.3).

For the purposes of contrast, therefore, the team decided to take a microanalytical look at one of the students from the third of the group receiving least of the teacher's gaze. The team quickly found that this student (Lee) showed few of the behaviors of Arthur and Louise. He was chosen in part because he shared some traits with the other two students: he was of large physical size, a firstgrader, and a student who often sat on the outer rim of the circle. However, he differed from both of them in that he was very quiet and did not move quickly. Although Lee was quiet, however, the teacher never seemed to doubt that he was paying attention. She referred to him as "academic" and felt no need to "check up on him" by calling on him. In charting his behaviors, the team realized that most of the behaviors selected for Arthur and Louise simply did not apply for Lee. He did not speak alone at all and never raised his hand, but he did move his head and move in and out slightly. It is interesting that he moved most while the teacher was talking, perhaps behaviorally demonstrating to her that, although virtually silent, he was a person who listened and paid attention during circles (see Figure 6.2).

The implication of this brief and cursory look at how some simple microanalytic techniques were applied in addressing a teacher's assessment of, or difficulties with, particular children is that there really seem to be easily spotted behavioral correlates to the ways a teacher feels about children. Per-

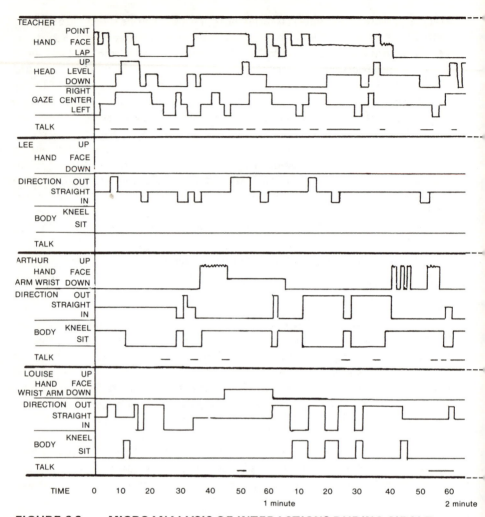

FIGURE 6.2   MICROANALYSIS OF INTERACTIONS DURING CIRCLE

haps these kinds of data are important ingredients in the teacher's assessments of children or in her decisions about how and why she organizes activities in the way she does. Furthermore, if the teacher wishes to intervene in her own setting, she has the means to document the ways in which that intervention might change actual *behavior* — something more concrete and perhaps less threatening than feelings, and something that is critical to the genesis of those feelings.

The early analytic work on this segment suggested further research. The team hoped to look in more detail, for instance, at the function of gaze direction. They hoped to consider amount of talk, the syntactic and semantic features of that talk (including topical relevance); paralinguistic features such as pitch, loudness and rate of speech; and other nonverbal behaviors that appeared to co-vary with them. Finally, the team hoped to return to the original question, linking

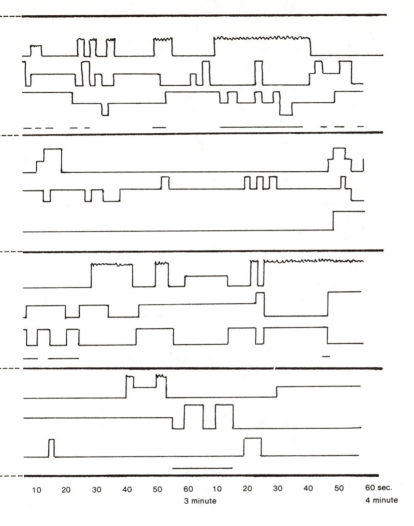

the analysis of behavior that took place at a low level of inference back to the feelings and problems that had initially prompted the question. In this way, the team hoped to discover how the ways in which children used talk and movement helped to create particular impressions of themselves and locate them in their respective places in the larger social order of the classroom.

Rationales for the Method

There are ethical, epistemological, and pragmatic reasons why it is worthwhile and important to adopt such a collegial ethnographic method of research in classrooms. This way of working treats the teacher and children not as the objects of study, but as active participants in the inquiry. The teacher's opinions are valued. She is seen as a vital member of the research team. In fact, her cooperation and

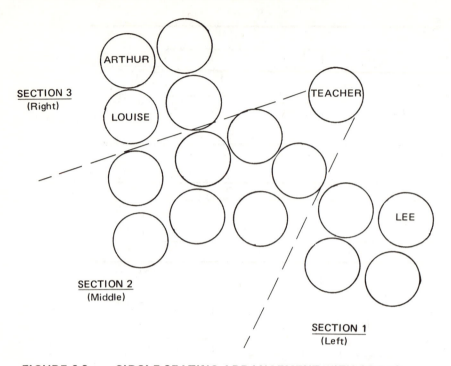

**FIGURE 6.3   CIRCLE SEATING ARRANGEMENT WITH AREAS
RECEIVING THE TEACHER'S GAZE**

insight are essential to the process of inquiry. The entire research operation becomes more congenial and the findings beneficial to all involved. Both parties go
away having gained something of value.

This system essentially delegates the role of change agent not to an outside
consultant, but to the people who possess in many ways the most direct and explicit power and responsibility to do things in the setting. In this study, the ethnographer did not merely acquire data in the setting and depart, nor did she generate
in isolation theories or treatments to apply to manipulate the experience of class
members. She was an integral part of the scene, gathering both information of use
and interest in the development of a unified theory of classroom interaction, and
facilitating by means of her expertise in certain research methods, ways for the
teacher to gain a new kind of perspective on her role and her students.

There is a need for inservice work and continuing education courses which
will help teachers share experiences and solutions and raise individual self-esteem
and awareness. For example, the staff development literature in recent years has
been replete with arguments for revolutionary forms of inservice training that
would give teachers the major role in determining the nature and direction of their
professional development. In this light, this method of field work could be modified to benefit most public school systems on a larger scale. The method proposed
would utilize two resources which are frequently underutilized in schools — the
videotape equipment which almost every school system has and often uses only

minimally and the teaching teams and friendship groups that exist among class-room teachers in any given building.

Faculties have tended to become more stabilized in the past few years. Pre-established familiarity, trust, and a working relationship among small groups have been established on many faculties. The members have a head start in that they already know and share much ethnographic data that an outsider would have to work quite hard to assimilate. Many schools have curricula, grade levels, and class-room settings based upon an established team approach. Rather than having a full time ethnographer follow an individual teacher, the emphasis here would be on helping the members of a team of teachers to become inside change agents, co-operating with their peers in professional development. Teachers working as parti-cipant observers in the classrooms of their peers could constitute a source of energy and impetus for idea exchange and dialogue unusual in many schools.

This method of field work also confronts the problem of the loneliness ex-perienced by self-contained classroom teachers (Sarason, 1971). Teachers have friends among their colleagues but rarely get to share individual professional tech-niques, problems, or experiences with one another. They are assigned, or perhaps confined, to their respective rooms, children, and areas of expertise. They often feel isolated, defeated, and overwhelmed by their own problems, which they tend to internalize or ignore due to their isolation. They often do not admit to difficul-ties or share their innovations and successes, feeling, "Who really cares?" or "It's *me* — with or against these twenty-five children."

In research carried out in the context of discovery rather than proof, social scientists are the instruments putting themselves through changes in order to learn about the phenomena of interest. They do not manipulate the environment but focus rather on isolating, describing, or discovering the dynamics of that environ-ment: what is predictable about it, how it functions, and what kinds of break-downs can and do occur. By making the teacher a co-researcher it is possible for the same thing to happen to him or her. It is in this way that a teacher's behavior can be said to be changeable — by having a new experience in a familiar setting. If teachers were to share in the process of classroom inquiry in the absence of a trained ethnographer, it is not difficult to imagine that they could become eyes and ears for each other on a continuing basis, using both their member knowledge and the techniques of field research. They would work together as peers, avoiding the awkward tendency for researchers from the outside to take or have attributed to them more power or authority than the teachers with whom they work. Teachers working together could become sources of idea exchange and dialogue for one another in creatively thinking about classroom problems.

NOTE

[1] Microanalysis is defined for the purposes of this paper as the careful viewing of selected be-haviors — verbal and/or nonverbal — as they occur across time in an activity. In this paper a sample of microanalysis of social interaction is presented. It is in part by means of micro-analysis that teacher and researcher alike can gain insight into the behavioral sources and cor-relates of the thoughts and feelings that they have about the social situations in which they are participants or observers.

PART II
Microethnographic Studies of Minority Culture Children in the Classroom

7

CULTURAL DIFFERENCES IN TEACHING STYLES
IN AN ODAWA SCHOOL:
A SOCIOLINGUISTIC APPROACH*

Gerald V. Mohatt
Frederick Erickson

For decades persons involved in Indian education have been concerned about the repeated failure of large numbers of Indian students to stay in school and perform on a par with non-Indians (Merian, 1928; United States Congress, 1969; Wax and Dumont, 1964; Bryde, 1970). Researchers developed or outlined theories explaining why Indian students had difficulties in school and suggested appropriate interventions to reverse the situation. In the late sixties and seventies, Indian control of Indian education became the major intervention (McKinley, 1970; United States Congress, 1969). As Indian communities influenced and controlled schools, curricula began to change, and often schools' physical appearance began to reflect local cultural images. Training programs introduced as part of the Career Opportunities program, Teacher Corps, and Head Start and Follow Through increased the number of native teachers. However, despite these efforts, the native schools often remained primarily staffed by non-Indians. Also, statistics indicated that native students were still achieving at lower levels in school than non-native students (Kinsley, 1976; Philips, 1974), in spite of major changes in organizational structure, curricula, and federal program funds.

New efforts to reverse this trend have focused on the need for bilingual education. Such interventions among native children have grown rapidly and have shown encouraging results. The immersion model developed by French Canadians

*Funds for the research reported here were provided by the Ontario Department of Indian Affairs and Northern Development through the sponsorship of the West Bay Band and Ojibwa Cultural Foundation, West Bay, Ontario.

(Lambert, 1967) has brought about dramatic positive changes in learning among minority children, and has been applied to native Canadians with interesting results (Battiste and Mohatt, 1977). The Lau decision and remedies have helped some native groups gain access to bilingual education. However, these remedies are not used in many native communities because the majority of children no longer speak the native language. School boards and government and funding agencies feel that, once the referential language of a tribal youth is gone, the tribal culture ceases to be an important variable influencing Indian children's school performance. The same inference is made by psychologists and special education personnel about the fair assessment of native children under P.L. 93-142. Over and over one hears that native children are identical or very similar to non-native children in their manner of language, dress, and interests. Belief in the "universal child" model is shared by teachers, counselors, psychologists, and administrators, who expect Indian children to act and learn like all other children. Given the appearance of many external similarities between Indian and non-Indian, bicultural and bilingual education tends to lose its attractiveness. Schools look instead to teacher effectiveness training, affective and humanistic education, behaviorial management, etc. All such programs rest on the universal child model and ignore culture as the critical factor in native children's learning.

The findings of the project to be described here show us that culture is, indeed, an important factor in Indian children's school experiences. The methods used, based in part on the detailed analysis of videotape, give us a way of understanding cultural influences in the context of classroom teaching. We will examine, in a case analytic manner, cultural differences in the way two teachers (one Indian, the other non-Indian) organize classroom structures for participation. We will compare classroom participation structures to those typically found in the children's everyday life. Finally, we will describe how the research data was used in teacher training, and look at the response to the data by native and non-native persons involved in the education of Indian children.

The two teachers studied both taught first grade Indian children, but they organized everyday life in their classroom very differently, by their pacing of events and exercise of social control. These differences in teaching style seem not to be just individual differences, but seem to be related to cultural patterns for the conduct of everyday life in community contexts outside school — to definitions of appropriate ways to act and to interpret the acts of others in everyday life at home, in children's play, and in adult life in the community.

Theoretical Background

There seem to be some fundamental differences in the ways people are expected to act face-to-face, between rural Canadian non-Indians and Indians on the particular Odawa reserve studied. Differences exist in what is considered polite or impolite and in what is considered supportive or intrusive. Even though they are fundamentally important in the process of education at school, some of these differences are subtle in surface form. Big, obvious differences between non-Indians and Indians have been reduced somewhat because Indians use non-Indian formal living arrangements and ways of talking and dressing.

The cultural differences that remain, then, are not obvious at first glance. They have been called "invisible" culture, implicit rather than explicit, a "silent" language. They have to do with aspects of social behavior that we do not think about consciously (cf. Hall, 1959); they are patterns that are "transparent." For example, the patterning of turn-taking in everyday life is transparent for speakers and listeners in everyday situations, although, upon reflection, the patterns of social interaction can become consciously known to a participant. Anthropologists have begun only within the last 20 years to study systematically the specific ways in which everyday social life is culturally patterned outside of conscious awareness (Hall, 1959; Goodenough, 1971; Frake, 1964; Wallace, 1970; Blom and Gumperz, 1972; Gumperz, 1976; Erickson, 1976). Until just recently there has been little application of these perspectives to the study of teaching in classrooms (for a review, see Erickson, 1976).

Some of the aspects of teacher and student behavior that seem to be culturally patterned and to have special relevance for Indian education include the following:

1. The overall tempo of teaching — how fast the teacher and the students interact, how quickly classroom "scenes" change from one activity to the next.
2. The overall directiveness of teaching — how much and what kinds of "control" the teacher can appropriately exercise over student behavior in the classroom, how much "leeway" or "elbow room" is provided for students.
   a. The teacher's use of public scrutiny for "singling out," calling attention to the individual child's behavior in front of an audience of other children (the "teacher searchlight" phenomenon) — to what extent the teacher, by questioning, commanding, praising, smiling, looking pointedly, and other means of directing attention to a specific child, focuses on what the child is doing in the presence of an audience of other children. At issue here is not the positive or negative emotional content of the teacher's attention to an individual child (i.e., the function of such attention as "positive" or "negative" reinforcement) but rather the public "audienced" nature of such attention. We discuss its two aspects as *monitoring* and *intervening*.
   b. The way the teacher manages and reinforces children's attentional behavior — what constitutes "paying attention" from the teacher's point of view, and how much attention is appropriate (constant, total attention or partial, periodic attention), attention focused by the child on the teacher or on other children, or on a child's own work.
   c. The amount of time the teacher allows for the children to comply with commands — how long a "grace period" there is between the issuance of a command and its reiteration; the length of pause between the question and either rephrasing or restating it when no answer comes from the students.
3. The types of structures the teacher uses to stimulate speaking in her classroom — teaching to a whole group and demanding answers to questions in

this context to determine whether children were "listening," small group work in which students help each other and the teacher serves as a resource.

Overall we want to determine the rules by which teaching and learning are organized in classrooms and compare these with the rules organizing interaction and learning in Odawa homes and everyday events. Differences among teachers along such dimensions as *overall tempo* and *directiveness*, and differences among students in *attentiveness* and in *doing work on one's own*, are usually thought to be caused by individual differences in factors such as temperament, intelligence, motivation, and, in the case of younger students, developmental level. It seems reasonable to assume that individual differences do have some influence on the social behavior of teachers and students in classroom learning environments. But recent research suggests the *group* differences also influence social behavior in classrooms and in other learning environments in the wider community. These group differences are cultural in origin; they are conventionally shared definitions and expectations of what is appropriate in the conduct of everyday social inter-action.

Since cultural variables have not often been investigated systematically in educational research, it is appropriate to present here a working definition of culture. Goodenough (1971) defined culture in cognitive, ideational terms as "a system of standards for perceiving, believing, evaluating, and acting" (p. 41). This definition asserts that what one has to know in order to act appropriately as a member of a given group includes not only knowing what to do, but also anticipating and judging the actions of others (see also, Wallace, 1970; Spradley, 1972).

Operating from such an orientation, Philips (1972, 1974) investigated life in classrooms and homes on the Warm Springs Indian Reservation in central Oregon. Through careful firsthand observation she identified models for the most common *participation structures* at home and at school (Philips, 1972). These models account for what all parties to an interactional event are doing, for example, not only how the teacher or parent talks to children but how children listen as the adult talks. Philips discovered areas of cultural incongruity between participation structures in homes and at school. This incongruity resulted in conflict and un-comfortableness in face-to-face interaction between Indian children and teachers. A major difference between the participation structures most commonly found in the classroom involved the role of the adult (or other leader, such as an older brother or sister) in the interaction. At school the leader (the teacher) attempted to control all activity, communicative and otherwise. In terms of how children were to speak in school, the teacher functioned as a "switchboard operator"; much talk was addressed to her, and she allocated turns at speaking. In such a participation structure, the Indian students showed much more inappropriate be-havior (silence, failure to answer questions, nervous giggling) than did White students in the classroom. The teacher's way of organizing interaction in the class-room seemed culturally congruent with the White student's expectation for how things should happen, but culturally incongruent with the expectations of Indian students. The school was a rural public school attended by non-Indian and Indian children and staffed almost entirely by non-Indian people. Such schools are comparable to those operated by the Provincial Board of Education.

Evidence for attributing the Indian children's confusion and inappropriate behavior to cultural incongruity rather than to personality characteristics of the individual children came from Philips's observation of their everyday life outside school. On the reservation, Philips reported an absence of participation structures in which one person overtly controlled or attempted to control a great deal of the activity of other people in the interacting group. From this Philips concluded, "The notion of a single individual being structurally set apart from all others, in anything other than an observer role, and yet still a part of the group organization, is one that Indian children probably encounter for the first time in school" (Philips, 1972, p. 391).

If the findings and interpretations that Philips, Wax and Thomas (1966), John-Steiner (1975), and Dumont (1972) report, generalize to other North American Indian communities, we will observe over and over that classroom life is organized according to non-Indian cultural rules. Such findings will have profound implications in understanding the Indian child's dilemma in school. Philips's interpretations explain the often reported phenomenom of the "silent Indian child" in the classroom (cf. Dumont, 1972), and provide at least a partial explanation for the generally low school achievement and high dropout rates among Indian students in Canada and the United States. Such a view shows that the terms "bicultural" and "bilingual" have meaning even when the referential language of the children is English. Repeatedly the research in this area indicates that invisible cultural rules survive and remain quite strong long after the children lose their referential language, although this in no way implies that referential language is unimportant for culture. Systematic cultural differences appear in classroom interaction even when everyone speaks English.

If this view makes sense, we expect cultural differences to become apparent when we examine the way native and non-native persons organize classroom interaction. We can look not only at the differences in the teacher's behavior, but also at how such differences relate to everyday native and non-native ways of organizing social interaction.

Methods

The school chosen for study was an Odawa school. All the students were Indian, and some of the teachers were non-Indian. We identified two teachers for videotaping. One was an experienced Indian first grade teacher, a member of the local reserve community who had taught in a one-room school for 14 years and in a self-contained primary classroom for about seven years. The other first grade teacher, a non-Indian, was an experienced teacher of Indian children who had just come to the school and was teaching children for the first time after a number of years as an administrator.

In planning this work we took care to find two good teachers to observe and compare. Both teachers were experienced, competent, and effective as judged by outcome measures. This point cannot be overemphasized. By comparing the teachers we do not mean to be invidiously "evaluative" in the usual sense of that term in educational practice. The differences we observed did not reside in the teachers' good intent or technical ability as professionals, but in the relative "cultural congruence" of their teaching styles with the children's experience of social life outside school. We did not attempt to determine the impact of cultural congruence on the learning of basic skills.

The procedure was to videotape both teachers in the early fall, in the late fall, in the winter, and in the late spring. One teacher was taped for 11 hours on nine different days, the other for 13 hours on ten different days. The videotaping was done continuously, with a minimum of camera editing, to provide as undistorted a record as possible of the natural flow of interaction. For 16 of the tapes, sound was recorded by a microphone suspended from the classroom ceiling, and for six tapes a Vega wireless lavaliere microphone was worn by the teacher and a few students in the two classrooms. Two children from each of the classrooms were videotaped with their families at home. On four separate occasions, two-hour tapes were made for each child. Analysis of this corpus of tapes was done by the co-investigators, by Indian and non-Indian research assistants, and by Indian and non-Indian teachers from reserve and off-reserve schools in Ontario.

Analysis and Findings

When one looks at and listens to the tapes of the two classrooms, one feels intuitively that they are different. Through systematic analysis of the tapes, it is possible to discover what some of the specific differences in interaction styles are — what the teachers and children are doing differently in each room. Some of these differences are global and are apparent in the relative amounts of time spent by the teachers and children in main classroom activities, such as beginning the school day, recitation, small group instruction, individual seatwork and instruction, and leaving the room to go to recess. More subtle are such things as the overall pacing in each of these classroom scenes and in the sequencing between scenes. We will first report the more global data on the two classrooms and then proceed to more fine-grained data.

Major Classroom Activities. Synoptic charts were made indicating the main activities to be found and the amounts of time spent on these activities. The charts were based on 18 one-hour tapes of classroom interaction, ten for one classroom and eight for the other.

When the amounts of time spent in main activities in the two classrooms are summarized, some similarities and differences between the two rooms are immediately apparent, as seen in Table 7.1. (Classroom I was taught by the Indian teacher, Classroom II by the non-Indian teacher.) Both teachers spend the largest amount of time circulating among the students and giving individual attention (Activity 6), with relatively little time at the blackboard in teacher-focused instruction (Activity 4). For these activities, the percentages of time spent are almost the same.

Some differences between the classrooms are also significant. Activity 12,

TABLE 7.1   Amounts of Time Spent in Major Classroom Activities

Activity	Classroom I			Classroom II		
	Minutes	%	Number of Instances	Minutes	%	Number of Instances
Entering and settling	43.7	7.3	(7)	28.7	5.9	(7)
Prayer	1.7	0.2	(2)	0	0	(0)
Finding the day's date	1.3	0.2	(2)	0	0	(0)
Teacher at blackboard, class reading aloud	10.4	1.7	(2)	8.9	1.9	(2)
Teacher passing out paper	5.3	0.8	(2)	1.2	0.3	(2)
Teacher circulating, giving individual attention	225.0	37.5	(11)	177.5	36.9	(6)
Teacher sitting, giving individual attention	58.7	9.7	(4)	50.3	10.0	(1)
Small group work	66.6	10.1	(3)	15.8	3.3	(1)
Teacher waiting for class	36.2	6.0	(4)	0	0	(0)
Finishing work	15.1	2.5	(1)	15.5	3.2	(3)
Free time playing in class	0	0	(0)	26.3	5.5	(2)
Class leaving	18.7	3.1	(7)	39.1	8.1	(7)
Other	212.3	29.9		116.7	33.9	
TOTAL	600.0	100.0		480.0	100.0	
	(N of tapes - 10 hrs.)			(N of tapes - 8 hrs.)		

class leaving, takes a considerably greater proportion of time in Classroom II, taught by the non-Indian teacher, than in Classroom I, taught by the Indian teacher. Children are given free time (Activity 11) in Classroom II and not in Classroom I. In Classroom I the teacher spends time waiting for students to finish their work (Activity 10), and this does not occur in Classroom II. More small group work (Activity 8) occurs in Classroom I than in Classroom II. In Classroom II there were two instances of free time for play (Activity 11), and none in Classroom I.

In terms of Philips's model, the differences between the two classrooms for Activity 11, free time, are especially significant. *Free time* as distinct from *work time* presupposes a discrete boundary between two loci of social control: activity "belonging" to the students, and activity "belonging" to the teacher. This is the case for Classroom II, taught by the non-Indian teacher, which can be characterized overall as a place in which one thing at a time is supposed to be happening. It is the teacher's time, then the students' time (work time or free time), then time again for everybody to pay attention (or for an individual to pay attention immediately) or for nobody to pay attention. The teacher exercises social control overtly to make clear whose time it is now. When the time belongs to the teacher, the teacher monitors the attention of the children: "John, pay attention"; (looking at a particular child) "sit still."

TABLE 7.2   Mean Duration in Minutes for Selected Classroom Activities

	Classroom I	Classroom II
1. Entering and settling	6.2	4.1
5. Teacher passing out paper	2.7	0.6
6. Teacher circulating, giving individual attention	20.5	28.8
7. Teacher sitting, giving individual attention	14.7	50.3
9. Teacher waiting for class	9.1	0
10. Students finishing work	15.1	5.2
12. Leaving	2.7	5.6

In Classroom I, taught by the Indian teacher, the distinction between teacher's time and students' time is not made so sharply or monitored so overtly. Social control is distributed in Classroom I as a *shared quantity*; leadership by teacher and by students interpenetrates and is not divided into separate compartments. The teacher clearly has "control" of the students, but achieves this partly by paying attention to the rhythms of student activity, and judging when the students are ready for things to change. This is our interpretation of the frequencies for Activity 9 (teacher waiting) and Activity 1 (entering and settling). The teacher in Classroom I is accommodating to the children's rates of beginning, doing, and finishing work at the same time as they accommodate her. Over the year, the teacher in Classroom II also began to allow more student time and to share in it (e.g., Activity 7 typically increased during the second part of the year).

Watching the tapes of Classroom I, one has the impression of slowness and smoothness as classroom events unfold. The sense of pacing — of doing the right things at the right time — has been noted by Smith and Geoffrey (1968) and by Kounin (1970) as a key feature of successful teaching performance. We will argue that a shared sense of pacing between teacher and students (part of their mutually congruent interactional competence, their shared *culture* as defined by Goodenough) is manifested behaviorally in an interactional smoothness which is observable. The overall impression of slowness and smoothness in Classroom I is borne out by the mean durations of activities summarized in Table 7.2.

It is clear that things happen somewhat more slowly in Classroom I than in Classroom II. Activity 1, entering the classroom at the beginning of the day (and coming back into the room after leaving it during the day) occurs at a slower rate. Teacher I passes out papers twice as slowly as Teacher II (Activity 5). Students were given 15 minutes to finish work in Classroom I, and an average of five minutes in Classroom II (Activity 10). At first glance, one might infer that Teacher II just moves more slowly due to age, temperament, etc.; but consideration of further evidence shows clearly that this is not the case. Despite the more gradual pace of starting up activities in Classroom I, it takes the children and the teacher much less time to get organized to leave the room (Activity 12) in Classroom I than in Classroom II (an average of 2.7 minutes contrasted to 5.6 minutes).

There are also differences in the ways in which the teachers give individual attention to the students, either by circulating around the room (Activity 6) or by sitting at a desk with the student (Activity 7). The durations for giving attention are shorter for Teacher I than for Teacher II because, for Teacher I, giving attention to individual students is interspersed with other activities of formal instruction and classroom management such as passing out paper and working in small groups with children. Teacher I handles issues of classroom logistics and works individually with students while she circulates around the room. She does this often in response to the silent request of a student, who will look up from seatwork to ask for help nonverbally. Teacher II's pattern is to give individual attention in larger chunks, to stay in one place longer while working with students individually, and then to move more rapidly around the room. During the latter he does classroom social management and logistical work, and then returns to working with one student at a time.

Directives and Monitoring. A teacher directive can be defined operationally as any utterance or nonverbal act by the teacher of which the function is to get a student to change his/her behavior in compliance with the teacher's wishes. In speech, the directive function can be realized by a variety of linguistic forms: (1) the imperative declarative statement, such as "Sam, sit down"; (2) a "wh- question," such as "Why don't you sit down?"; and (3) an indirect declarative sentence, such as "It's time for people to stop running around," or "Now we're going to get started." Directives can put the spotlight of public attention on children in front of an audience, or they can be accomplished in a more masked, indirect way that does not single individual children out for public scrutiny. Part of the "spotlight effect" in the issuing of directives by the teacher comes from using the name of an individual child. Another part can come from what Hall (1966) terms a *proxemic relationship* — interpersonal distance that carries social meaning. If the teacher calls out a directive to a single individual from all the way across the room, the spotlight effect is heightened, giving the directive the force of a command or rebuke rather than a suggestion.

Thus the frequency of directives and their spatial placement as the teacher moves around the room, "casting" them like a fisherman, provides an index of the teacher's social control. This shows not only how overtly the control is being exercised, but how large the span of control is — whether the teacher is trying to control the behavior of all (or many) of the children at once, or whether the teacher is controlling individuals separately. Teachers can differ in the frequency with which they exercise overt control, and also in the generality or specificity of their directive moves.

Teacher I's movement and directives are highly intercorrelated. She does not call across the room to named individuals. She generally is in face-to-face contact with the child or children she is addressing. She herself follows a clear path to the reading table. Teacher II, on the other hand, moves in and out around the tables and creates a pattern that appears to be less symmetric. He calls across the room to named individuals. He does not establish the same intimate contact with the children in the reading group, either by using their names or by being in closer proximity to them. Later in the year, when he has established more intimate contact, we see a greater economy in his organization: it becomes more sequential and students seem to have a better grasp of his expectations of them.

Another aspect of the spotlight effect is teacher monitoring of children's behavior. During the teaching of a lesson by the two instructors, we counted the number of times either teacher made reference to a child who was not part of the specific group or task in which the teacher was involved. This monitoring and intervening in out-of-group behavior by the teacher was considered interesting, because we had observed in Odawa home situations that parents seldom used it.

The two teachers differ quite strikingly in this area. Table 7.3 shows the amount of verbal and nonverbal monitoring done by Teachers I and II while working with individuals or small groups. The figures are not exactly comparable since

TABLE 7.3	Verbal and Nonverbal Teacher Monitoring	
	Teacher I	Teacher II
Individual		
Verbal	4	27
Nonverbal	0	7
Group		
Verbal	0	9
Nonverbal	8	64

they are based on 720 feet of tape for Teacher I, and 860 for Teacher II. The category "nonverbal to individual" is a physical move toward the offender. "Nonverbal-to-group" is visual scanning of the group. Teacher I does not verbally monitor children's behavior on a continual basis. Rather, she establishes her presence through regular, rhythmic movements. Teacher II more frequently calls names, corrects behaviors or refers to individuals that he is not directly teaching. In order to mark options as important or critical, he will move toward and speak to the student, or physically move him.

The monitoring and intervening of the two teachers also differs when they are working in whole group situations, although the non-native teacher does less monitoring and intervening in this situation than in others. For instance, he less frequently refers to the behavior of individual children. The native teacher, however, seems not to focus on individual children at all during either participation structure. Teacher I uses periods averaging about five minutes in whole group structures, as compared to the 15-minute periods used by the non-native teacher. However, during one time period the native teacher used this participation structure for a much longer time. She related in an interview that she was quite uncomfortable with it, because she did not typically use it. We expect that the children would also be quite unfamiliar with the demands of this situation, and that they might show more misbehavior as a result. This would increase the amount of teacher monitoring necessary. In one analysis of monitoring in whole group teaching, we found that the frequency of this behavior was 1.4 per minute for Teacher I, and 2.2 per minute for Teacher II.

As we have seen, Teacher I seldom calls across the room. She refers in public to the behavior of only two children. She speaks to the majority of the children individually. Although at times she does this in a loud enough voice for others to hear, the situation and her tone clearly indicate that she means the message for only this person. Teacher II singles children out more across all contexts since he uses the "talking across the room" strategy. When he speaks directly to the individual, he will talk while he moves toward the person and also once he arrives. This singles out the individual more since it creates a commotion focusing attention on him. Although the native teacher monitors and intervenes in class activity, she never approaches the amount used by the non-native teacher, who favors across-the-room comments over face-to-face comments. As a "last straw" mechanism, he goes to the individual in a one-to-one context, while the native teacher prefers this as her first option in giving directives to students.

Monitoring relates to the teachers' views of what they are doing as teachers and what they are doing in relation to cultural rules for social interaction. In terms of the former, both teachers say they need to know what the students are doing. However, the non-native teacher stresses more often that he needs to know on a fairly constant basis what each child is doing. The reasons for his vigilance are that he wants to identify those who have trouble with the lesson, to know if they are listening, and to ensure that the student he calls on probably knows the answer. He does not want to embarrass the children by calling on them if they have not been paying attention. A factor he watches for is "confidence" in the child. His monitoring interventions are aimed at establishing the child's attention, giving him help, and ensuring that he or she will listen, work, and have confidence. The teacher looks for relevant cues that a child lacks confidence, is not paying attention, and does not know the answer. Because he will not call on children unless they seem likely to know the answer, some are called on early, others later, and a few seldom. Children called on less than others are typically those who, in his judgment, do not know. He finds that those who know volunteer to come to the board or use their hands to signal readiness. However, the most salient cue is "looking up at you." The soundness of the cues he uses to judge students' readiness to respond must be seen in a cultural context. Are the nonverbal behaviors Odawa children use to signal their desire for the floor the same as the non-native teacher expects?

The native teacher also has reasons for her use of monitoring. Throughout our interviews, she did not state that she needed to know where the children were or what they were doing. She stated that she questions the children directly about their work or watches as she roams throughout the room. She also allows them to come to her to ask questions and to show her what they are doing. She says she chooses these methods because they relate to how children get attention at home (through an interruption); although this may seem rude to Anglos, it is considered appropriate behavior for a child of this age in Odawa culture. Only gradually and later do they learn to wait until the mother is finished with her task. Rather than forcing the students to wait until she questions them, Teacher I allows them to initiate questions. They can monitor their own work and choose the time to interrupt the teacher's activity.

Videotapes showing the way monitoring and intervening are accomplished in Odawa homes provide us with additional data supporting the view that Teacher I's style of interaction is culturally congruent. The tapes show that both monitoring and intervention do occur, but under the following conditions:

1. They occur on request from the children.
2. They are often done by older siblings rather than by adults.
3. They are done periodically by the mother/father, especially in the absence of older siblings.
4. They are done in a one-to-one context.
5. Interventions do not involve raising of the voice, verbal reprimand, or physical moving to the person, unless the deviant action is very serious.
6. Interventions do not involve across-the-room or room-to-room verbal commands.

Pauses. Another significant aspect of the concept of "elbow room" arises when we look at pauses in each teacher's speech. When teachers give a directive or ask a question, they must pause to allow for a response. While quick responses are generally valued, rapid-fire question and answering leaves little room for reflection and implies the answer should deal directly with the question. We compared the two teachers in our project on this dimension because it seemed to be a sensitive cultural issue. Observation of band council meetings, home tapes, and everyday Odawa speech showed us that the people speak slowly and pause often (Fox, 1976). Frequently the pause prior to another person's turn is long and leisurely. We measured the number of seconds each teacher gave students to respond following a question, prior to rephrasing or asking a question of another student, during four periods when each was teaching reading.

The two teachers differ in the amount of time they allow students to answer. Teacher I allowed students an average of 4.6 seconds to respond, as compared to an average of only 2.0 seconds for Teacher II; the native teacher provides a much longer pause than the non-native teacher. The differences in the overall structuring of student control and "elbow room" hold true even when one looks at more micro-events.

Summary. The strategies for accomplishing very ordinary classroom management work, getting a small group started, giving directives and monitoring students, and pausing after a question were quite different for the two teachers. Teacher I's strategies involved proceeding fairly slowly and deliberately, exerting control over the whole class at once, and not singling out individuals in the total classroom group, yet focusing on children in more intimate, private situations, and giving longer pauses for answers. Teacher II moved more rapidly around the whole room, giving directions to the total classroom group and the small reading group at the same time, keeping control of the public arena in the classroom, calling out directions to individual children across the room and over the other children's heads, and giving short pauses for answers. The previous analysis involves only a few examples of classroom management by each teacher abstracted from our 10 hours of videotape, but more detailed analysis of micro-events indicates that these styles of interaction hold up over the entire corpus (Erickson and Mohatt, 1978).

Discussion: Participation Structures
and Cultural Congruence

Both teachers are effective and experienced. In the kinds of classroom scenes we have reviewed, each teacher's strategies for getting organized "worked." The reading group ended up doing reading and the other children ended up practicing reading through individual seatwork. But the two teachers relied on strategies based on different participation structures. These strategies reflected different presuppositions about ways of playing out the same kind of scene — cultural presuppositions of what is appropriate in ordinary social relations between adults and children. Differences in the teachers' styles of interacting seem to be related to characteristic Odawa Indian participation structures, in contrast to non-Indian ones. At issue, then, is not the general effectiveness or efficiency of either style of teaching, in terms of final results, but the cultural congruence of each style with the patterns of interaction customary for Indian children in everyday life.

Hallowell (1955) notes that the pattern of social structure in which no one is in a position to order anyone else around has as its interactional concomitant the avoidance of levels and kinds of social pressure that to non-Indians would seem very trivial. He found this pattern persisting in the 1930s and 1940s even among relatively acculturated Ojibwa in Eastern Manitoba. The Ojibwa, the Huron, and Odawa were neighbors in Ontario in the 17th century (and still are today), and similar traditional patterns of political decentralization and everyday conduct have been reported for the Odawa (Kinietz, 1972). It seems reasonable, then, to infer that the patterns we find in community life on the reserve today represent the persistence of traditional patterns of interactional etiquette.

Because modern dress, cars, outboard motors, television sets, and fluency in English are all in evidence on the reserve, the relatively subtle aspects of interactional etiquette are likely to go unrecognized by non-Indian teachers as they meet Odawa children at school. Ways of avoiding direct commands and not putting people in the spotlight are not considered as a part of culture. From the point of view of school authorities, curriculum developers, and teachers, "culture" apparently is traditional art, beadwork, food, language, and legends. This is a content idea of culture. The process idea, that implicit, informal culture shapes people's ways of acting in everyday life, does not seem generally to be taught to teachers, whether Indian or non-Indian.

The non-Indian teacher we studied, who was teaching Indian children in the classroom for the first time in many years, intuitively adopted during the course of the year some of the ways of acting used by the Indian teacher next door. He was developing a more culturally congruent teaching style by making more use of

Odawa participation structures. He increased the amount of time he spent with individual children and small groups, and decreased the amount of contact he had with children in the public arena of large group instruction. In that participation structure, however, he still used the "spotlight" and issued directives much more frequently and explicitly than did the Indian teacher. It made perfect sense for him to do so, because by classic European and North American pedagogical standards good teaching is providing content focus and maintaining control (Barnett, 1905; Bagley and Keith, 1924). Yet our case analysis suggests, together with the work of Philips and others, that there also exist culturally congruent ways of accomplishing intellectual focus and classroom control, and that it is probably important to attend to them.

Application to Training School Personnel

If educational projects are to make a contribution to native communities, they must involve those to whom education is entrusted. Although we knew that our conclusions were tentative and our methods perhaps lacking in control, we presented our findings to the personnel in the school systems on or near the reserves in which the research took place. We organized undergraduate and graduate courses to introduce both the theory on which the research was based and our results. The judgments of participants in the course would determine whether our approach was a helpful one or merely another ivory tower prescription for change.

The courses were taught during the summers of 1976, 1977, and 1978. They were held three hours a day for four weeks and were accredited through the local university (Nipissing College University or Laurentian University). Teachers, counselors, and administrators attended. All except two of the total of 30 participants taught or worked with Indian students. The majority of the participants were native.

The theory of culture on which the project was based was presented during the first week. Videotapes were analyzed to determine the overall participation structures used by various teachers. Tapes from Erickson's research on interethnic communication were used to show styles of social interaction in other ethnic groups. The other weeks were divided between presenting theory (one hour a day) and analyzing tapes from the Odawa classrooms. In the second week, students looked at specific issues, e.g., the patterning of questioning, control and directives, pauses in teacher speech, turn-taking, exits and entrances, etc. By the middle of the third week, much time was spent identifying everyday situations analogous to classroom interactive events. In the final week we analyzed home and playground tapes, and made field trips to a local Indian public event to analyze turn-taking or speech rules for getting the floor, and how people showed they were attentive. During this last week, we delineated what we considered cultural and noncultural in the way the two teachers taped organized classroom interaction. We also examined how counseling sessions, disciplinary actions, and teaching were influenced by implicit culture.

The response to the course and approach was extremely positive. Native students responded well to the idea of implicit culture; it was an "aha" experience for them. They said that they now saw the cultural patterning of things that they had previously taken for granted. What was implicit had become known and explicit. The students wrote papers in which they analyzed tapes of the two teachers and related specific interactive events in the classroom to their cultural analogues. In 1976, one native woman who was an elementary principal researched how the native teacher's linguistic commands become requests; through voice tone, pacing, and context. Another native woman did a paper outlining how various participation structures were more or less effective, in terms of volubility of student response; learning contexts which were similar to those in everyday Odawa life produced more response. She analyzed how Odawa children learned to swim and fish and related the cultural rules in these events to the participation structures in the classrooms taped. Another student analyzed turn-taking in a band council meeting, and suggested ways teachers could pattern turn-taking in the classroom using similar rules. These student papers helped clarify how knowledge of implicit culture could be used in organizing classroom social interaction. The results of the course confirmed that the approach we were taking could be fruitful for teachers. The course provided school personnel with:

1. A concrete definition of culture that resonated with personal experience in one's own cultural milieu.
2. A way to relate culture to the needs of teachers, counselors, or administrators.
3. A way to think about solving classroom issues, through an analysis of interactional events in relation to the students' and teachers' cultural backgrounds.

The course was meaningful not only for native and non-native teachers of Indian children, but for others who taught Canadian minorities. French Canadian teachers related problems in classroom learning that derived from cultural conflicts between French and English Canadians.

Mohatt has lived and worked on a Sioux reservation since 1968, and his work often involves interaction with teachers of native children. He has had the same positive response to the approach outlined here from teachers involved with other bands and tribes. The board of directors of the native group for whom the research was done recently voted to seek funds to continue and expand the research in order to control variables and to see whether more culturally congruent participant structures will increase achievement among native students.

Clearly, the project outlined here demonstrated its heuristic value. It generated both productive applications and more questions to be researched. If the process of bilingual and bicultural education is to survive, research must relate implicit everyday culture to teaching, assessment and other types of school social interactions. In this manner the field can move to a new level of specificity and show how culture continues to be a critical variable in school contexts, in spite of the loss of referential language.

8

SOCIAL CONTROL AND SOCIAL ORGANIZATION IN AN ALASKAN ATHABASKAN CLASSROOM: A MICROETHNOGRAPHY OF "GETTING READY" FOR READING

Howard Van Ness

This paper presents a microethnographic analysis of the organization of behavior as six Koyukon Athabaskan students, one non-Indian student, and a Koyukon Athabaskan teacher "get ready" for an instructional activity in a rural Alaskan kindergarten classroom. The analysis of getting ready as an event in this classroom provides an example of the ways a Koyukon teacher and her students establish a social organizational structure to accomplish an instruction activity. Of particular importance to the analysis are the demonstration and display of the covert and indirect ways the Indian teacher exercises her classroom authority as she orchestrates the establishment of the whole-groups structure by the class. As the teacher and the students go about getting ready, they complete certain observable tasks, e.g., some of the students move their chairs to new locations in the classroom, the teacher distributes the workbooks containing the material for the coming instructional activity and the students find the page in the workbook containing the exercise to be worked on. The ways in which the teacher and the students go about accomplishing these tasks also establishes the structural configuration of the social organization of the class for the coming instructional activity — the teacher and the students working through the workbook exercise as a whole group.

The study was conceived as a preliminary venture to assess the utility of microethnographic analysis in providing insight into the workings of Alaskan cross-cultural classrooms. This term is conventionally used in Alaska to mean classrooms with students of Eskimo, Indian, or Aleut descent. The analysis was organized around the following questions:

1. What are socially significant structural elements or features of the organization of face-to-face interaction during the segment?
2. How are these elements observable in the students' and teacher's behavior?
3. How are these elements organized together as a system and how can such a system be analytically comprehended?
4. What insights for substance and method in further research are suggested by this preliminary single case analysis?

Several assumptions were made in conducting this research. The first is that the behavior of the teacher and students during the segment is organized around participants' "definition of the situation," i.e., as the definition of the situation changes during the segment, the organization of the teacher's and students' behavior also changes (see Goffman, 1964, Kendon et al., 1975, Erickson, 1975 and Florio, 1976, for discussion of "situations" and "situated behavior"; see Cazden, 1970, Blom and Gumperz, 1972, for discussion of "situated verbal behavior").

The second assumption made is that the definition of the situation is negotiated or jointly elaborated by the participants (in this case the teacher and the students) in a process of continual monitoring and interpreting of the social environment — the setting, the task, and each other's behavior — that seeks discrimination of the context for social activity (Kendon et al., 1975; Cicourel, 1972; Goffman, 1961).

The third assumption made in conducting this research is that, as members monitor and interpret the social environment in face-to-face interaction, behaviors appropriate to the emerging definition of the situation are generated by the participants through a process of "tacit choice-making." Cicourel combines the interpretive capability and tacit choice-making by participants in positing the notion of "interpretive procedures," described as "constitutive of member's sense of social structure or social organization" (Cicourel, 1974a, p. 44). Interpretive procedures serve as the "executive function" for an individual in everyday social life in helping him to interpret the social environment (including the behavior of others) in negotiating a definition of the situation, and in helping him to select social behavior appropriate to the emerging definition of the situation from his communicative repertoire (Cicourel, 1974a; 1974b).

The fourth assumption is that the corpus of tacit knowledge operated on by an individual's interpretive procedures in negotiating the "definition of the situation" and in generating appropriate social behavior is *culturally organized.* Implicit in this assumption is a "cognitive theory of culture," discussed by Goodenough (1964; 1971; 1975) and Spradley (1972). According to this point of view, a society's culture consists of

> . . . whatever it is one has to know or believe in order to operate in a manner acceptable to its members. . . . By this definition, we should note that culture is not a material phenomenon it does not consist of things, people, behavior or emotions. It is rather an organization of these things. It is the forms of things that people have in mind, their models for perceiving, relating, and otherwise interpreting them. (Goodenough, 1964, p. 36)

The fifth assumption is that the organization of behavior is emergent in the conjoint social interaction of the teacher and the students as they individually exercise their interpretive procedures. The teacher and students mutually monitor and interpret the social environment, including one another's behavior, in an active process of achieving or accomplishing the social organization described and analyzed in this paper (see Garfinkel, 1967, for discussion of the social order as members' accomplishment).

Viewing the classroom social order during the segment as an interactional accomplishment by the teacher and students focuses attention on both as active agents in the establishment and maintenance of the classroom order. In adopting this perspective, this study is distinguishable from such efforts as Flanders (1970), those reviewed in Dunkin and Biddle (1974), Grant and Hennings (1971), and Good and Brophy (1973), which focus primarily on the teacher as the active agent in the classroom social order. This view is also distinguishable from the view of the classroom social organization as consisting of sets or relationships and attendant rights, obligations, and duties ascribed to teachers and students by the conventions of the institution (cf. Firth, 1954; Goodenough, 1965). Studies such as Waller (1932), Grambs (1969), Jackson (1968), and Eddy (1969) focus on the regularities of these limits or boundaries across classrooms in describing the classroom (school) as an institution distinct from other institutions as arenas for social life in the society.

Florio reconciles the institutional order of classrooms with the interactional order of everyday classroom life by suggesting that variability of behavior is allowed by the institutionally conventionalized social arrangements: "a teacher can behave in a variety of ways — with students, parents, or cohorts — and still be a teacher" (Florio, 1976, p. 39). While the organization of the teacher's and students' behavior is bounded by institutional conventions for appropriate or expected behavior, these conventions for classroom social arrangements are mediated by Koyukon Athabaskan knowledge of appropriate social behavior. The Koyukon Athabaskan teacher and students "get ready" for an instructional activity in a classroom setting in ways consistent with Koyukon organization of social behavior in face-to-face interaction.

The Exercise of Authority:
Indian vs. Non-Indian Style

Philips (1972), studying non-Indian teachers in Oregon, reported incongruity between the culturally organized ways authority is exercised in the classroom and in the Warm Springs Indian community. Erickson and Mohatt (this volume) considered how a teacher could exercise authority in ways consistent with those of the Indian community. "We would expect more covert ways of exercising social control: less attention directed to individual children in the presence of other children as an "audience," less overt monitoring of the classroom behavior of individual children through verbal and nonverbal sanctions by the teacher (p. 9)." In analyzing their classroom data, they found consistency between the theoretically generated form for the Indian exercise of classroom authority and the ways the Odawa Indian teacher actually exercised authority in her classroom. They also found signs of "adaptive drift," as the year progressed, by the non-Indian teacher (who was characterized as concerned, possessing good intuition and who also benefited from helpful advice from his Indian principal) toward the "Indian general form" in his exercise of classroom authority.

The study presented in this paper pays particular attention to the ways the Athabaskan teacher exercises her authority in the classroom. This aspect of the inquiry explores: (1) the interactional devices manifested by the teacher as she exercises her classroom authority, and (2) the degree of voluntariness and self-determination in participation allowed the students by the teacher.

One of the ways teachers on the Warm Springs Reservation exercised their authority in ways discontinuous with those of the Indian community was in the use, as a pedagogical device, of placing students in the position of committing "public mistakes." Erickson and Mohatt (this volume) investigated "to what extent the teacher, by questioning, commanding, praising, smiling, looking pointedly and other means of directing attention to a specific child, focuses on what that child is doing in the presence of an 'audience' of other children" (p. 4). Their findings indicate that the Indian teacher put students in the public "spot-light" much less than did the non-Indian teacher; additionally the non-Indian teacher seemed to make decreasing use of the "spotlight effect" as the year progressed. The inquiry here combines the insights of both Philips (1972) and Erickson and Mohatt in examining (1) the degree to which the social organization of the lesson is organized around the teacher's placing students "in the spotlight," and (2) the management of "public mistakes" by the teacher and the students.

Analysis of the Lesson

In the lesson analyzed in this paper, initiation-reply exchanges occur throughout the sequence. The initiating may be done by the teacher as in this example:

(21)   T: (S_7's name), where's your book like this?
       S_7: (shrugs)

The initiating may also be done by students.

(30) S_5: Are we here, (teacher's name)?
       T: Yeah.

These initiation-response exchanges are organized in two forms, somewhat analogous to Philips's notion of participant structures. In the first form, the teacher interacts with students individually on a one-at-a-time basis. For example:

(83)   T: You're finished, (S_5's name)?
       S_5: (nods)

This form of teacher-student interaction occurs in two domains of performance, constituted by vertically co-occurring social phenomena: (1) private performance, and (2) public performance. Teacher-student interactions in private performance typically are signified by (1) both teacher and student lowering their voices; (2) decreases in the interpersonal distance between the teacher and the student; and (3) postural orientation by the teacher that more clearly "focuses" on the individual student to the exclusion of others. Other members of the class not involved in the private performance go about their business, manifesting behavior that indicates not only that they are not involved in the interaction, but also that they are not paying attention to the private performance (even though the private performance may be audible and visually accessible to them).

Lines 30-35 of the transcript provide an illustration of teacher-student interactions in private performance. The teacher is standing at the head of Table B (Fig. 8.1). The teacher, S_5 and S_7 are speaking in lower voices than they use in public performance.

(30) S_5: Are we here, (*teacher's name*)?

> The teacher orients her upper trunk, head and gaze to S_5. S_6 and S_7 briefly glance at the teacher and S_5, then return to looking at their books.

T: Yeah.

> S_5 looks at the book.

S_7: Here, (*teacher's name*).

> The teacher shifts her feet, orients her upper trunk, head and gaze to S_7. S_5 and S_6 glance briefly at the teacher and return to their books.

T: Yeah, on this side.

> Teacher points. S_5 and S_6 glance briefly at S_7's book, then return to their own.

S_7: This one?

> Teacher remains oriented to S_7. S_5 and S_6 continue looking at their books.

T: Yeah.

Teacher-student interactions in public performance typically are signified by both teacher and student speaking louder, with greater interpersonal distance between the participants, and a more inclusive postural focus by the teacher. In public performances, it is not necessary for other members of the class to "actively disattend" to the interaction. An example of the teacher interacting with an individual student on a one-at-a-time basis in public performance occurs in lines 83-84 of the transcript. The teacher is sitting on the end of Table A (Fig. 81.); S_5 is in his seat. The teacher's voice is noticeably louder than it was in the example cited above of private performance.

(83) T: You're finished, (S_5's name)?

S_5: (nods affirmatively)

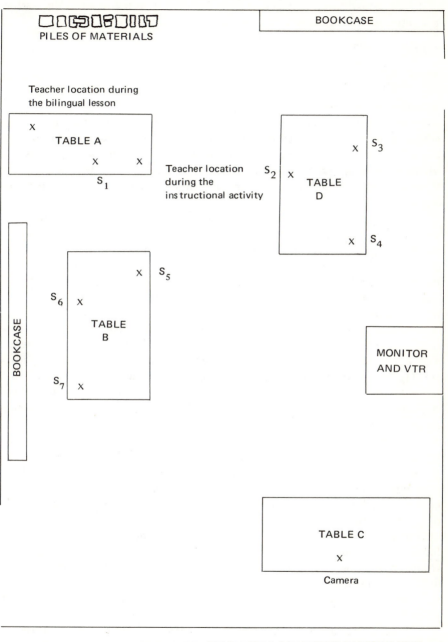

PILES OF MATERIALS

BOOKCASE

Teacher location during the bilingual lesson

X

TABLE A

X   X

S_1

Teacher location during the instructional activity

S_2 X

S_3
X

TABLE D

S_4
X

BOOKCASE

S_5
X

S_6 X

TABLE B

S_7 X

MONITOR AND VTR

TABLE C

X

Camera

FIGURE 8.1   TEACHER AND STUDENT LOCATIONS DURING THE LESSON

The second form of teacher-student interaction in the lesson is the teacher interacting with the class as a whole group:

(47) T: What page are we on?

S$_7$: Ah——

Many: 40.

By definition this form occurs only in public performance.

The teacher interacting with individual students on a one-at-a-time basis in private performance, the teacher interacting with individual students on a one-at-a time basis in public performance, and the teacher interacting with the class as a whole group comprise three social contexts for interaction in the lesson. These three contexts are organized together in a more superordinate level of social organization.

Initially, the videotape behavior record of the lesson was viewed with the sound off. In attending to nonverbal channels of behavior, the lesson seems to be divided into three segments. In the first, the students move their chairs from around Table B to the locations shown in Figure 8.1. The teacher moves around the room, handing out the materials for the lesson. In the second segment, the teacher remains seated on the end of Table A. During the third segment, the teacher again moves around the room interacting with the students.

Erickson (1976b) and Scheflen (1973) demonstrate that locational and postural shifts can be reliable indicators of junctures between behavioral segments. The nonverbal behavioral clues that indicate the junctures of these three segments are: (1) the students relocating and the teacher beginning to circulate around the room; (2) the teacher seating herself on the end of Table A and remaining there throughout the second segment; (3) the teacher getting up and again circulating around the room; and (4) the students handing in their books.

Examination of the verbal behavior of the teacher and students during the entire sequence provides further indication that the lesson can be divided into three distinct social units. In the first segment, the teacher addresses 87.5% of her utterances to individual students and, on these occasions, interacts with students in private performance. In the second segment only 25.9% of her utterances are directed to individual students in private performance. Another 24.1% of her utterances address individual students on a one-at-a-time basis, but in public performance. Fifty percent of her utterances are addressed to the class as a whole group. In the third segment, 89.9% of the teacher's utterances are addressed to individual students in private performance. Her only public utterance in this segment closes the lesson, "OK, hand in your books." These data are summarized in Table 8.1.

Further indication that Segment 1 and Segment 2 are distinct contexts for social interaction is provided by the patterns of "who initiates" the exchanges. In the first segment, the teacher initiates only 28.6% of the exchanges, while in the second segment, she initiates 85% of the exchanges. The third segment does not differ from the second along the "who initiates" dimension with the teacher initiating 85.7% of the exchanges. In the second segment, however, 76% of the ini-

TABLE 8.1   Focus of Teacher Utterances in Public and Private
             Performance

| | Public Performance | | | | |
	Whole Class	Small Group	Individual Student	Other	Subtotal (Public)
Segment 1	0	0	0	1	1
Segment 2	27	0	13	0	40
Segment 3	1	0	0	0	1
Total	28	0	13	1	42

| | Private Performance | | | |
	Individual Student	Total Utterances	% Total Utterances Public	% Total Utterances Private
Segment 1	7	8	12.5	87.5
Segment 2	14	54	74.1	25.9
Segment 3	8	9	11.1	89.9
Total	29	71		

TABLE 8.2   Teacher and Students as Initiators in Verbal
             Exchanges in Public and Private Contexts

	Segment 1	Segment 2	Segment 3
Public			
Teacher initiates exchange	0	30	1
Student initiates exchange	0	8	1
% Public initiation	0	76.0	14.3
Private			
Teacher initiates exchange	2	12	5
Student initiates exchange	5	0	1
% Public initiation	100.0	24.0	85.7
Total			
% Teacher initiates	28.6	84.0	85.7
% Student initiates	71.4	16.0	14.3

tiations are in public performance, compared with 14.3% in the third segment. These data are summarized in Table 8.2.

The data summarized in Tables 8.1 and 8.2 demonstrate coherence of particular patterns in the teacher's and the students' verbal behavior within the junctures suggested by their nonverbal behavior. Tables 8.1 and 8.2 also show the distinctiveness of the patterns of verbal behavior in each segment within the lesson. Figure 8.2 provides schematic orientation to the structural and temporal relationships of the segments in the lesson.

The teacher and the students, however, do not generate this observable interactional order for its own sake. Nadel (1957, p. 158) points out that social organizations "have jobs to do." At the level of focusing on the social organization of the *lesson* as a classroom event, Nadel's observation is relevant. Classroom lessons are organized around topically oriented tasks and activities. The particular

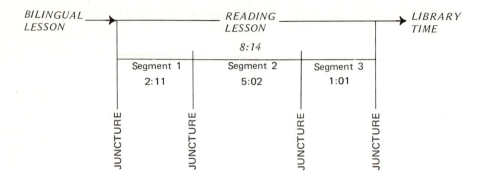

FIGURE 8.2   SEGMENTS IN THE LESSON

task or activity is set by the teacher and constitutes a major element in the "teacher's agenda" for the lesson (Mehan et al., 1976). Another major element of the "teacher's agenda" for a lesson includes establishing the broad structural configuration of the social organization of the lesson in ways that contribute to the "working through" of the task or activity by the students in the allotted time. It is the teacher who establishes whether the class will "work through" the task or activity as a whole group, in small groups, or as individual students. A third major element of the teacher's agenda for a lesson is that the students "work through" the task or activity in orderly ways — ways that do not disrupt the accomplishment of the task or otherwise irritate the teacher. Thus, from a teacher's perspective, at the level of the *lesson* as a classroom event, the "job" of the social organization of the lesson is to facilitate the "working through" of the task or activity by the students in orderly ways within the allotted time.

In this lesson, the task the students work through is a "reading readiness" exercise from a page in a workbook. The broad structural configuration of the social organization of the lesson is that the students work through this exercise as a whole group under the direction of the teacher. The task and the mode for its working through were decided on by the teacher before the beginning of the lesson (personal communication). That this lesson plan was accomplished by the students and the teacher in an orderly way is observable in the behavior record of the lesson. The social order evident in the lesson, however, is not the product of the students following an explicit script written by the teacher. The evident order is "assembled" in the interaction between the teacher and the students during the course of the lesson.

Social Organization and Control
in Segment 1

During Segment 1, the teacher and the students "get ready" for the reading readiness exercise. As they get ready, they conjointly assemble the structural configuration for working through the readiness exercise as a whole group. We now examine aspects of the interactional order evident in Segment 1 for the purposes of gaining insight into its accomplishment by the Koyukon teacher and the students.

Segment 1 occurs between the close of the bilingual lesson and the beginning of the working through of the reading readiness exercise by the class. During the bilingual lesson, the students and the bilingual teacher are clustered around Table B (see Figure 8.3). The instructional activities completed during the lesson are: (1) playing a game with flash cards in which the teacher displays a card and individual students take turns responding to the picture on the card; (2) singing, in unison, a song about birds in the Koyukon language; and (3) singing, in unison, "Good Morning Teacher" in Koyukon and English.

The structural configuration of the social organization of the bilingual lesson is that of a "whole group activity" — during each of the instructional activities, members' involvement and attention are directed toward participation in the efforts of the *group as a whole* to accomplish the task. Students participate verbally in the bilingual lesson as individuals (the flash card game) and as a group in unison (singing the songs). The individual student turns during the game are embedded in the interactional organization of "playing the game" by the class as a group. This is demonstrated by the following:

1. The allocation of turns among members of the group provides for participation by the students in ways that make for an orderly progression of the game, rather than simply the orderly completion of the turn.
2. Students not involved in taking a turn display behavior making it evident they are attending to the turns of others and are thus still part of the group playing the game.
3. The instructional activity is completed when the game ends, rather than when a turn is completed.

The working through of the reading readiness exercise by the class, the episode which follows Segment 1 in the behavior record, also is structured as a whole group activity. Students participate verbally both in individual public performance and in unison as a group. Individual student verbal participation is embedded in the social organization of the instructional activity as a whole group activity. This is indicated in the following ways:

1. Individual student verbal participation is keyed to the rate the class as a group works through the exercise. It is inappropriate for students to attend verbally, in public performance, to parts of the exercise ahead of or behind those being focused on by the group.
2. The students not "doing" an individual public performance during the working through of the exercise display behavior that indicates they are "paying attention" to the person who has the floor.
3. The completion of an individual verbal "turn" in public performance does not complete the instructional activity or absolve the participant from manifesting behavioral signs of ongoing involvement in the group's efforts. The instructional activity is completed when the *group* has worked through the exercise to the teacher's satisfaction.

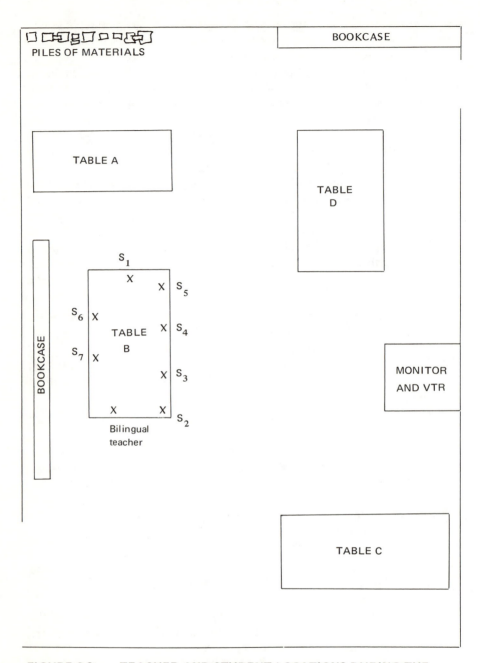

FIGURE 8.3   TEACHER AND STUDENT LOCATIONS DURING THE BILINGUAL LESSON

Segment 1, in occurring between the bilingual lesson and the reading readiness exercise, is not only temporally intermediate between them, but it is structurally intermediate as well. It is the occasion for the restructuring of the class for the reading readiness exercise as a whole group activity after the dissolution of the whole group structure of the bilingual lesson.

The social organizational structure of the bilingual lesson begins to dissolve toward the end of the last instructional activity in the lesson, the singing in unison of "Good Morning Teacher," when the bilingual teacher begins putting materials from directly in front of her on Table B into a cloth bag. After she begins doing this, but before the song is completed, S_5 slides her chair away from Table B.

With the ending of the song, the interactional organization of the bilingual lesson more evidently dissolves. S_2 and S_3 slide their chairs back from Table B and posturally orient themselves to each other. S_5 stands on his chair and fidgets. As the bilingual teacher says, "OK" (line 1), S_1 slides back his chair and stands up; S_6 moves his chair back, stretches, and looks at the books in the bookcase along the wall behind him. As S_7 asks the bilingual teacher, "We'll play that cards tomorrow?" (line 2), S_4 slides her chair back from Table B, stands up and fidgets. S_5 stands and stretches as the bilingual teacher responds to the question (lines 5-6).

Coincident with line 7 of the transcript, S_1 and S_3 begin moving their chairs to the locations indicated in Figure 8.1. S_4 begins relocating after commenting, "Oh boy," (line 7) on the bilingual teacher's response to S_7's question. S_3 also comments on this response from halfway across the room (line 8). S_2 stands and begins moving his chair after notifying the class that "Time's up" (line 9). While the students continue relocating, the bilingual teacher leaves the room.

The dissolution of the organizational structure of the bilingual lesson by the teacher and the students partially accomplishes the *transition* between the bilingual lesson and the readiness exercise. The general structure of interaction during the bilingual lesson and the working through of the reading readiness exercise is organized around the accomplishment of instructional activities. The general structure of interactions during the transition accomplished in Segment 1 is organized around *getting ready* for an instructional activity.

The videotape behavior record shows the teacher and the students "getting ready" for the reading exercise by completing the following tasks:

1. The students relocate from their positions during the bilingual lesson to the positions indicated in Figure 8.1.
2. The workbooks are distributed to the students by the teacher.
3. The students find the page in the workbook containing the readiness exercise.

The ways the students and the teacher mutually go about completing these tasks also establishes the social organizational framework for working through the reading readiness exercise as a whole group activity.

As S_1, S_2, S_3, and S_4 are moving their chairs after the close of the bilingual lesson, the certified teacher clears her desk and gathers up the workbooks to be passed out. When the students begin to arrive at their destinations, the teacher stands, goes to Table D and starts to lay a workbook at S_3's position (see Figure

8.4). S_3 and S_4 are involved in a "traffic jam" at the lower end of Table D and are not yet in place. S_2 has reached his destination, but he is not yet sitting down. The teacher puts S_3's workbook back in the pile she is carrying, turns and goes to look out the window between the bookcase and the piles of materials shown at the top of figure 8.4. She remains looking out the window until S_2, S_3, and S_4 are seated in position.

As they settle in, she turns from the window, moves to Table D and hands S_2 and S_4 their workbooks. While this is happening, S_3 begins to dig in her desk. The teacher does not hand S_3 her workbook, but goes to Table A and hands S_1 his. She then moves back toward Table D, but pauses about halfway there. S_3 is still looking in her desk. The teacher turns, goes to Table B and gives S_5 and S_6 their workbooks.

S_7's workbook is missing from the stack being passed out by the teacher. It is not until this point in the segment that the teacher speaks:

(21)   T: (S_7's name), where's your book like this?
      S_7: (shrugs)
      T: Look in your desk.
(25) S_7: Do you remember Miss _____ took it.
(27)   T: That was (S_3's name)'s.

The teacher then turns, goes to Table D and hands S_3 her workbook. Moving from Table D to the piles of materials indicated in the upper left of Figure 8.3, she looks for S_7's workbook. On finding it, she exclaims, "Oh, here it is!" (line 29) and returns to Table B and hands S_7 her workbook.

S_5 asks, "Are we here, (teacher's name)?" (line 30). The teacher responds, "Yeah" (line 31). S_7, who by this time has opened her workbook, points to the proper page and asks, "Here (teacher's name)?" (line 33). The teacher, leaning over and pointing at the correct page in S_7's book, replies "Yeah on this side" (line 34). S_7, seemingly still not sure of herself, again points to the page and asks, "This one?" (line 34). The teacher responds "Yeah" (line 35).

Turning from Table B, the teacher moves to Table A. As she does so, S_1 turns around with a puzzled look on his face. The teacher, arriving at S_1's location, points to the correct page in the workbook lying open in front of S_1 and comments, "Right there" (line 40).

She then moves to the end of Table A and sits on top of it, facing the class. By the time the teacher is seated, all the students have their workbooks open to the proper page. All the students, with the exception of S_2, are also either looking up at the teacher or looking at their books, ready to begin the exercise as a whole group. The structural transition between the bilingual lesson and the readiness exercise has been completed.

The most evident aspect of the teacher's behavior during the accomplishment of the transition is her movement around the room (see Figure 8.4). One of the functions of this movement is the exercise of control over the behavior of the students (Erickson and Mohatt, 1977). This exercising of control through "pounding the classroom beat" is more the product of the teacher synchronizing her

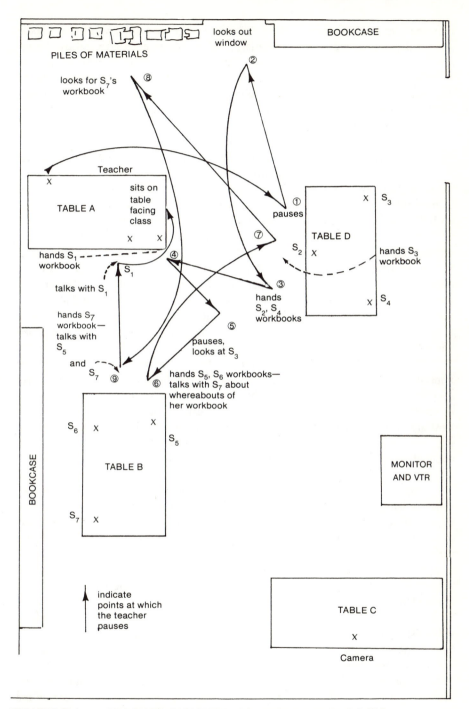

FIGURE 8.4   TEACHER MOVEMENTS AROUND THE ROOM DURING SEGMENT 1

movement around the room with the students' readiness to receive the workbooks and to begin focusing on the material, than it is deterrence effected by the immediate presence of the "fuzz." The teacher does not begin moving around the room when the students begin relocating; she also remains seated when the bilingual teacher leaves the room. She allows the students to proceed to their new locations without exercising "teacher stares" or other overt nonverbal control devices. The teacher also abstains from exerting control verbally.

It is not until the students have essentially arrived at their destinations that the teacher stands up and begins moving around the classroom. When she arrives at Table D, S_2 is not yet sitting down and S_3 and S_4 are still positioning their chairs and also are not seated. Rather than invoking verbal or nonverbal sanctions or prompts to "hurry them up," the teacher moves to the window and looks out until S_2, and S_3 and S_4 are ready to begin focusing on the material.

As she hands S_2 and S_4 their books, S_3 begins looking in her desk — she is not yet ready. Once again, the teacher does not invoke sanctions or overtly direct S_3's attention to the workbook. She proceeds to Table A and hands S_1 his workbook. Leaving Table A, the teacher pauses and checks on S_3. She is still not ready, so the teacher moves without comment to Table B. When she leaves Table B, on the way to look for S_7's workbook, the teacher again checks on S_3. S_3 is no longer looking for something in her desk and is now ready. The teacher then hands S_3 her workbook.

Examination of the teacher's verbal behavior during segment 1 furthers the impression that the teacher is *acting in concert* with the students, rather than *overtly controlling them*. Seven of the eight teacher utterances in the segment are directed to individuals and occur in private performance — the teacher and student are at an intimate distance from each other and the rest of the students do not serve as an audience to the interaction. The teacher's verbal behavior is thus coupled to her movement around the room; she talks with the students she is close to.

Just as she does in her movements around the room, the teacher seems to be synchronizing her verbal behavior with the "rhythms" of the class. The interactional device she employs is that of allowing students to be the primary initiators in successful verbal exchanges. She initiates only two of the seven successful verbal exchanges in which she is involved during segment 1. Both of these instances concern the whereabouts of S_7's workbook and are tangential to the accomplishment of the transition. The remaining five exchanges are initiated by the students.

This portrayal of the Koyukon teacher's exercise of her classroom authority is consistent with Erickson and Mohatt's description of the exercise of authority by the Indian teacher in a classroom on the Canadian reserve. The absence of the exercise of overt control by the teacher over the behavior of the students, and the distribution of social control as a "shared quantity" during the segment, directs attention to the accomplishment of the transition as a *mutual achievement* by the teacher and the students.

The establishment of the whole group structure which completes the transition is a *mutual assembly* by the teacher and the students as they engage in "interactional work" during Segment 1. "Interactional work" is used here to mean the ways the teacher and the students, in negotiating the definition of the situation, "inform" each other of "what is going on." This interactional work is "framed" by the classroom routines established over the course of the year. The students know that at the end of the bilingual lesson, S_1, S_2, S_3, and S_4 will move their chairs to the locations shown in Figure 8.1, as they have been doing for nearly the entire school year. The students also know that reading typically follows the Bilingual class in the daily schedule.

One aspect of the "interactional work" going on between the teacher and the students is the confirmation that students are to proceed according to "normal form." The teacher, by *not indicating* that the students are to do *otherwise*, "informs" the students that S_1, S_2, S_3, and S_4 are to move their chairs back to their seats as they do each day. The students, thus, proceed according to a "business as usual" pattern without requiring direction from the teacher on who is to move, where, or how.

For the students, there is some ambiguity inherent in the normal form of the social organizational structure to be used on any given day to accomplish reading — sometimes reading is done by students on an individual basis, sometimes it is done in small groups and sometimes it is done by the class as a whole group (teacher personal communication). There is ambiguity, too, for the students in the normal form of the instructional activity for reading on a particular day — it may be working in a workbook, playing games, listening to a story, or doing seatwork made up by the teacher.

A second aspect of the interactional work going on in the accomplishment of the transition is the reduction of ambiguity when the normal forms contain an array of options. The ambiguity inherent in the normal form of the instructional activity for reading is reduced when the teacher informs the students of the coming instructional activity by passing out the workbooks. Evidence of the workbooks also indicates that reading comes next, confirming that the daily schedule is proceeding as it typically does.

The students still do not know which page in the workbook they will be working on. Typically, when the students have worked in this particular workbook, they have taken each page in sequence. Occasionally, they work on pages out of sequence. All the students open their workbooks to page 40, the page following the last page worked on. S_1, S_5, and S_7 are still uncertain that page 40 is the correct page. S_5 and S_7, individually, in private performance, verbally elicit confirmation from the teacher. S_1 elicits confirmation from the teacher by turning and looking at her as she leaves Table B and begins heading in his direction. The teacher, without a word from S_1, continues to his seat and confirms he has the correct page.

There is yet ambiguity as to whether reading will be conducted as individual work, small group work, or work done by the class as a whole group. The first bit of information the students process to reduce this ambiguity is that, generally, pages in the particular workbook being handed out by the teacher are worked through as a whole group. Secondly, if the work is to be done on an individual basis, the teacher typically indicates this in private performance as she hands out material. If the instructional activity is to be completed as a small group, the teacher typically begins convening these groups as she moves around the room. That she neither establishes that the work be done on an individual basis, nor indicates the formation of small groups, informs the students that reading will be conducted as a whole group activity.

The accomplishment of the transition by the class without explicit directions or the exercise of overt control by the teacher suggests a high degree of congruence between the assumptions and knowledge about the appropriate conduct of everyday social life in classrooms held by the teacher and the students. For a group of students and a teacher to be able to leave many things unstated as they accomplish a classroom transition which includes a change in teacher, the relocation of more than half the class, the distribution of material and the orientation of the students to the material, requires that the teacher and students continually arrive at mutually consistent interpretations of what is going on and share mutually consistent understandings and expectations for how to proceed.

Not only are many things left unstated in accomplishing the transition, but the interactional work between the teacher and the students proceeds smoothly. Segment 1 takes some 131 seconds from juncture to juncture. Thirty-seven seconds of this time were taking up in locating S_7's workbook, leaving about 94 seconds for the completion of the transition. That a group of kindergarten students and a teacher complete the tasks they do and get ready for reading in such a short time is an impressive indicator in itself of the smoothness of the interactional work going on between the teacher and the students.

A second indicator of interactional smoothness in Segment 1 is the relative infrequency of "repair work," the channeling or correction of divergent student behavior by the teacher. Equally important is that the repair work is done smoothly by the teacher without issuing explicit directions or otherwise overtly exercising control over the students. The repair work done by the teacher during Segment 1 is accomplished by not replying to particular verbal initiations by students.

Two instances of repair work by the teacher involve the non-Indian student in the class, S_2. While the teacher is involved in verbal exchanges in private performance with S_7 (concerning the whereabouts of S_7's workbook; lines 21-27), S_2 turns in his seat, looks directly at the teacher and says, in a loud voice, "OK, ah, we're on page 40" (line 24).

The teacher does not respond or acknowledge S_2's contribution. S_2 fidgets a bit and again, looking directly as the teacher calls out, "We're on page 40." Again, the teacher does not acknowledge S_2. S_2 fidgets a bit more and continues looking at the teacher, seemingly waiting for acknowledgment. He then turns back in his seat and looks at his workbook. By not responding to S_2, the teacher channels his behavior away from calling out and interrupting an ongoing exchange in private performance, without overt direction or control.

The process of getting ready is accomplished without the exercise of overt control over the behavior of the students by the teacher with one exception. As the teacher begins to sit on the end of Table A facing the class, all the students, with the exception of S_2, are quiet and are either looking at page 40 or up at the teacher. S_2 continues to talk to S_4 (who is looking up at the teacher, not attending to S_2). The teacher marks the juncture between Segment 1 and Segment 2 by asking, "OK, what page are we on?" (line 42). The students with the exception of S_2 respond in chorus, "Forty" (line 44). S_2 continues talking, addressing his talk to S_4, who is attending to the teacher (lines 41 and 45). The teacher orients towards S_2 and in a noticeably louder voice says, "What page are we on?" (line 47). S_2 turns toward the teacher, stops talking toward S_4 and says, "Ah" (line 48). The rest of the class responds in chorus, "Forty" (line 49). S_2 then responds, "Forty" (line 50), having been brought into the fold.

The teacher, in orienting her posture and gaze to S_2, raising her voice and asking the question again, escalates to a more overt exercise of her control in informing S_2 of what is going on. It is worth noting that this escalation to a more overt form of control by the teacher is yet somewhat oblique. The teacher does not spotlight S_2 in verbal rebuke or sanction; rather she informs him by orienting to him, raising her voice and repeating to the class as a whole question that has already been answered.

The Koyukon teacher's exercise of her classroom authority is consistent with what might be expected for an Indian teacher, generalizing from Philips (1972). First, the students are allowed a great deal of self-determination in their actions as they "get ready" for reading. The teacher does not attempt to exercise continual and pervasive control over the student's behavior. Second, the teacher does not "single out" in public performance either divergent student behavior or student uncertainty about what is going on; rather, she uses a variety of channels for communication to inform the students of what is going on.

Conclusions

This example suggests that more comprehensive study of how Athabaskan teachers (who are few in number) and how non-Indian teachers exercise their classroom authority might provide illuminating insights into the workings of Alaskan cross-cultural classrooms. The consistency of the example with the findings and interpretations of Philips (1972) and Erickson and Mohatt (this volume) suggests that systematic inquiry into discontinuities between the ways social life is conducted in Alaskan native communities and in Alaskan classrooms may provide useful information for developing and effecting styles of teaching and classroom control more appropriate to Alaskan native students.

The analysis presented in this paper is a limited example of a Koyukon accomplishment of a classroom social organization. The analysis assumes the point of view that the ways the teacher and the Athabaskan students conduct themselves during the segment are *culturally* organized. Within the context of this paper, this assumption remains unexamined. Erickson and Mohatt, however, argue that such an assumption can be empirically examined and tested.

While this paper has displayed the smoothness in the conduct of the inter-actional work between the teacher and the students, it does not argue that this smoothness is the product of the "Athabaskanness" of the participants. To be able to do so requires that lack of smoothness in the non-Indian student's interactional work be demonstrated. This is indeed the case in S_2's behavior during the segment. At the end of the bilingual lesson, S_2 does not begin relocating until he announces "Time's up" (line 9), even though the other students are already moving their chairs. S_2 tries to interrupt an ongoing verbal exchange, in private performance, to let the teacher know, in public performance, that he knows the correct page. It can be argued that, while a student's seeking the classroom spotlight is inappropri-ate social behavior in an Indian classroom, it would be considered reasonable be-havior for a white student in a white classroom. However, interrupting an ongoing teacher-student exchange would probably be deemed inappropriate in a white classroom too. Finally, S_2 is not "ready" when the instructional activity begins. These demonstrations of interactional incompetence by the white student are too few and too varied to allow convincing demonstration, but they are suggestive. They may well be the product of differences in the cultural organization of behavior between the white student and the Indian members of the class.

Elaboration of the analysis to include the entire lesson would also provide an example to contrast with one of Philips's findings in classrooms with non-Indian teachers. The prevailing participant structure during Segment 2 of the lesson is the first participant structure described in Philips — the teacher interacts with all of the students. In Warm Springs classrooms, the Indian students partici-pated infrequently in classroom events organized in this way. In this lesson con-ducted by an Indian teacher, the Indian students participate freely and frequently. Microethnographic analysis of how this is accomplished by the teacher and the students could provide some illuminating insights into "the silent Indian student" syndrome.

9

*TEACHING READING TO HAWAIIAN CHILDREN: FINDING A CULTURALLY APPROPRIATE SOLUTION**

Kathryn Hu-Pei Au
Cathie Jordan

The problems faced by minority culture children when they enter the typical American public school are many. One of the most prevalent is that the school is often not successful in teaching them to read well. Because competence in reading becomes increasingly important as children progress through the grades, an early failure to learn to read is a sign that the child will experience increasing frustration and difficulty in school. While it is doubtful that there is any area of education that attracts more attention, generates more research, or engenders more debate than the subject of how best to teach reading, none of this interest has substantially changed the situation for minority culture children. Many still do not learn to read.

Children of Hawaiian ancestry are no exception to this rule. As a matter of fact, it is possible to argue that they are the most educationally deprived group in the United States. At the Kamehameha Early Education Program (KEEP), a research and development project located at Honolulu, a team of teachers, psychologists, anthropologists, and linguists has, as one of its primary goals, discovering better ways to teach Hawaiian children to read. As its primary research arena,

*This paper is based on one section of a symposium, "A Multidisciplinary Approach to Research in Education: The Kamehameha Early Education Program," presented to the American Anthropological Association, Houston, December 1977. The authors wish to acknowledge the intellectual contributions of the other panel members, Ronald Gallimore, Roland G. Tharp, and Thomas S. Weisner, and of the discussants, Frederick Erickson and Kekoa D. Kaapu. The work reported here was supported by the Kamehameha Early Education Program, Kamehameha Schools/Bernice P. Bishop Estate, Honolulu, Hawaii.

KEEP operates an experimental school, *Ka Na'i Pono*. This school is composed of one class of about thirty students each at the kindergarten, first, second, and third grade levels; three-quarters of these students are of Hawaiian ancestry; most of them are from families on welfare, reside in public housing projects, and are in other ways representative of those urban Hawaiian children who typically experience the greatest difficulties in school (Mays, et al., 1975; Weisner, Gallimore and Omari, 1978).

The story of KEEP is not one of overnight success; the first section of this paper is a review of the major explanations for the poor reading achievement of Hawaiian children which were explored before effective teaching methods were developed. The next section describes the current, successful KEEP reading program and examines closely the small group reading lessons which constitute one of its chief elements. It will be argued that these reading lessons succeed at least partly because, through their resemblance to a major speech event in Hawaiian culture, *talk story*, they capitalize on the pre-existing cognitive and linguistic abilities of the children. Finally, the implications which the KEEP experience may have for other educators and researchers working with minority culture children are considered.

Background

The term "Hawaiian" is used here to refer to persons who are descended, wholly or in part, from the original Polynesian inhabitants of the Hawaiian chain and who identify themselves as belonging to the Hawaiian ethnic group. Today there are approximately 150,000 Hawaiians living in the state of Hawaii, about 36,000 of them children of school age (Hawaii State Department of Education, 1978). In general, Hawaiian children, especially those from poor families, fare very badly in the public elementary schools: Schools with large Hawaiian populations typically score within the first or second stanine on standardized tests of reading achievement.

The problem is not that Hawaiian parents do not value education; almost unanimously they feel it is "most important" for their children to graduate from high school and "important" for them to go to college as well (Alu Like, Inc., 1976). Hawaiian parents do, however, have mixed feelings about the effectiveness and responsiveness of the public schools (Alu Like, Inc., 1976). This is not surprising, since their children do not often have successful school careers. In our opinion, nevertheless, the difficulties that the schools of Hawaii experience in attempting to address the educational needs of disadvantaged Hawaiian students have to do only secondarily with institutional intractability; generally, there is considerable concern with these problems among school personnel at all levels, from classroom teachers to members of the Board of Education. The more important problem, we think, has been with the types of options that have been generally available to school personnel. The typical range of solutions to poor reading scores have all been tried with Hawaiian students (tutoring, classroom aides, different types of commercial curricula), with little data-supported success. It became clear at KEEP that answers to the reading problems of Hawaiian children needed to be sought through an ongoing process of data-responsive classroom innovation (Tharp and Gallimore, 1979) which included a sensitivity to issues of cultural congruence in classroom practices (cf. Erickson and Mohatt, this volume; Jordan, 1974, 1975a, 1975b, 1976; Philips, 1972).

During its first three years of operation, the KEEP school was not successful in teaching its pupils to read, as can be seen from the standardized test scores presented in Table 9.1. The reading scores of our first three classes were not significantly different from those of control group children drawn from nearby public schools. Class IV, however, received a full year of instruction with a new reading program; the result was a dramatic increase in reading achievement, to a mean score above grade level. These results have now been replicated, and KEEP is beginning to export its reading program to the public schools. A full data analysis has been presented elsewhere (Tharp, 1979).

TABLE 9.1   **Percentile Equivalents of Mean Total Scores: Gates-MacGinitie Reading Test**

First Grade Classes	I	II	III	IV	V
Percentiles	8	15	38	67	52

The reading program was developed as part of a process which involved the successive elimination of a number of alternative hypotheses which had been advanced to account for the poor reading performance of Hawaiian children (Crowell, 1977). It would be misleading, however, to describe the development of the reading program as linear in nature; it was *not* a matter of the researchers first choosing a theoretical base which subsequently generated a reading curriculum (Erickson, 1978). Rather, the reading program emerged from a combination of social science theory, teachers' experience in the classroom, ongoing research, and professional knowledge of reading curricula, all operating simultaneously (along with a certain degree of serendipity). These converged to produce a large degree of consensus among members of the KEEP staff about the desired features of an effective reading program, although in many cases similar recommendations were made for quite different reasons.

Since its introduction, the new reading program has been undergoing continual modification, based on teachers' intuition and experience as well as on research data. Also, the program is being carefully examined in order to determine which of its features might be eliminated without damaging its effectiveness and which are, in practice, necessary and sufficient to its successful operation. This paper represents one such effort to identify critical elements within the program.

One of the major principles of KEEP's operation has been that of "least change" (Tharp and Gallimore, 1976). That is, it is assumed that in introducing educational innovations into public school systems one has the most chance for success with those innovations which require the "least change" from standard practice while still achieving the desired outcome. In the present case, KEEP wished to work toward a "least changed" school environment in which Hawaiian children could learn to read well. This principle dictated a certain order in addressing hypotheses concerning reading problems. The first addressed, because the most susceptible to remedy, was that Hawaiian children did not learn to read because they did not *work* at learning to read.

At the time of the inception of KEEP in 1971, one of the most popular explanations current among educators for the failure of Hawaiian children to learn to read was that they were "unmotivated"; that is, they (and their parents) were uninterested in education, and, consequently, they were inattentive in school and did not work hard at teacher-assigned tasks (Tharp and Gallimore, 1975). A well-developed theoretical base and a proven technology (social learning theory and behavior management techniques, respectively) for shaping social environments to encourage attentiveness and industriousness were already available, and introducing these techniques into the classroom required little alteration in classroom organization, curricula, or teaching methods. Thus, acting on the "least change" principle, the first innovation in the KEEP program was to train teachers in effective classroom management strategies. This innovation was successful in the sense that it produced high rates of attending and industriousness on the part of the children. KEEP students worked very hard and engaged wholeheartedly in their lessons. Yet under these conditions, with a conventional, middle-of-the-road, basal reader program, the children learned to read no better than control group children. It was concluded that effective classroom management was necessary, but not sufficient for the solution of the problem (Au, 1976; Tharp, 1978).

The second hypothesis, or more precisely, group of hypotheses, may be given the rubric of "cognitive/linguistic factors." KEEP children, after a year in kindergarten, have a mean I.Q. of almost exactly 100, as measured by the Wechsler Preschool and Primary Scale of Intelligence (WPPSI), even though this test was not designed to accommodate the differences in cultural background of Hawaiian children (For complete I.Q. results, see Gallimore, Tharp, and Sloat, 1979). The same result is true of the Cattell "Culture-fair" test of intelligence (Speidel and Tharp, 1978). The children's failure to learn to read, then, clearly cannot be attributed to any general intellectual deficit. However, it did seem possible that the children, who grow up as native speakers of a divergent dialect (Hawaiian Creole English), were handicapped in learning to read because of general or specific interference between their linguistic code and the Standard English of their teacher and textbooks. A series of studies was conducted to test several forms of this hypothesis (see Gallimore and Tharp, 1976, and Au and Spiedel, 1976, for reviews), but no evidence for dialect interference was found which could plausibly account for the low reading scores (Gallimore, 1978).

The children, then, were known to possess the basic cognitive and linguistic skills required for learning to read; this was clearly demonstrated by extensive testing and experimentation. What was not known was how to encourage consistent use of the appropriate cognitive/linguistic skills in school learning situations. A method was needed for calling up these skills in such a way that the children would apply them to learning to read.

A third hypothesis, which was not intensively investigated until the other two were explored, was cultural; perhaps there were differences between the ways the children learned at home or among their peers and the ways in which they were expected to learn in school (Jordan, 1974, 1975a, 1976). These differences might prevent or interfere with learning to read because the children would find themselves in instructional situations which would not be congruent with the learning strategies already familiar to them. If school learning contexts and teaching strategies could be changed in ways that would make them more similar to those that the children were accustomed to, learning might be improved (Jordan, 1977, 1978a, 1978b). The new KEEP reading program is successful, we believe, partly because it does just that.

The Reading Program that Worked

KEEP's new, successful reading program differs from its previous unsuccessful one in several important ways. One of these is its emphasis on *comprehension*, or the understanding of what is read. The previous program was *phonics*-oriented and emphasized the learning of sound-symbol relationships. Another difference is the organization of the classroom employed as the framework for teaching reading. Each classroom is organized into a system of learning centers. Each child has his own schedule, which takes him to five or six of the ten or more learning centers in the room each morning. During one of the time blocks he meets with the teacher for a small group reading lesson; during the rest of the time he works independently of the teacher at the centers, usually in the company of and often cooperatively with one to five other children. While at the learning centers he may complete pages of his reading workbook, read a book of his choice, practice words for a spelling test, write a story and draw a picture to accompany it, or participate in any of many other language arts activities. Each child, then, spends 20-25 minutes per day in direct interaction with the teacher, in a group with three to five other students. The rest of the time he works at learning centers where almost all of his interaction is with small groups of other children. We believe that the interaction within these peer groups may be one significant factor in the success of the reading program (Jordan, 1978b; Jordan and Tharp, 1979). However, it is the form and content of the interaction within the teacher-directed reading lesson that we wish to consider here.

In the reading lessons, groups of about five children meet with the teacher for approximately 20 minutes of daily instruction, almost always centered on a story from a basal reader. Lessons are composed largely of rapid interactions between the teacher and the children, the teacher asking questions and the children answering, and among the children, complementing and building on each other's responses. Some examples of these exchanges, taken from a lesson taught in a second grade class, follow. The story on which this lesson was based was entitled "Freddy Finds a Frog." This lesson, as is typical, started with the teacher showing the children that they had experiences which could be useful in interpreting the story.

T: What would you do with a frog, ⌈L.?
(Looks and points at her.)

A: │But if you put it in
a pan —
(T. raises open hand toward A.'s face, continues to look at L.)

L: ⌊If you eat it,
not going taste ucky, going taste like chicken an going taste good.
(T. continues eye-contact and affirmative nodding.)

T: Have you eaten it too?
(Nods at L.)
(A. and C. look at L.)
(L. nods 'yes.')
(A. and C. look at L.)

T: A-a-ah, (nods her head)
two people in our group ⌈have eaten it.
(S. looks up at T.)

S: ⌊I did.
(T. looks at him.)

T: If you have a frog, L., what would you do with it?
(Looks at her.)

L: I would — I would — I would — I would let um go, put um in the grass.

T: You would put him in the grass and let it go.

An important feature of this part of the lesson is that the teacher is giving the children the messages (1) that their everyday experiences have a place in the school and (2) that information from their own experience can be brought to bear on a text and used in combination with information from the text to make sense out of what they read.

After this opening, the teacher then had the children read a short section of the story, and followed with questions about the material read. Sometimes the children were able to answer quite easily, but at other times, as in the following example, they needed the teacher's careful guidance.

T: K a y.
C. (nominates C.)
What did Mr. Mays say he would do with the frog?

C:⌈He would take
│   (T. and C. exchange eye-contact.)
│   (All children put down their hands.)

L:⌊. . . water

C: um fishing.

T: He would take him fishing.
   Do frogs like to go fishing?

X$_1$:   N-o-o-o.
X$_2$:   N-o-o.

   (A. puts down her hand.)
   (L. puts elbows on table, but one of her hands is up.)
   (T. looks at C.)

T: C.___ do frogs
S: Y-e-e-s.

   (T. raises open hand to S.'s face.)

T: like to go fishing?
   (Pause)

L: N-o-o-o.
C: N-o-o-o.

T: Why don't they like to go fishing?
A: Cause they
   hate water.

   (T. raises open hand to A.'s face, gives her a "surprised" look, mouth open eyes wide.)
   (L. momentarily waves hand.)

L: They don't — they don't like fish, they like — they like flies.

   (As L. begins, T. points to her, but continues expression except for closed mouth. At end T. and L. exchange eye-contact.)

T: O k a y,
   what was he going — what was
A: They might —
   they might —

   (T. raises open palm to A., looks at her.)
   (L. raises hand, waves momentarily.)

T: E x c u s e m e.

L: They use for da bait.

   (T. gives her another "surprised" look, this time with her mouth open.)
   (S. raises his hand.)

T: Mr. Mays was gonna use the frog for bait, wasn't he?
   (Looks at L. and A., nodding affirmatively.)

It is crucial in the teaching situation that the children remain actively involved in the lesson, that they do not tune out and stop answering even when they are uncertain of the answers. Their willingness to participate, which in the example just cited included the risk of being wrong, suggests that the children do not see the reading lesson as an ordinary classroom recitation situation, but as something quite different. It will be argued that the children's responsiveness may result partly from similarities between the reading lesson and linguistic events of importance in Hawaiian culture, namely *talk story* and *storytelling*. In responding to these similarities the children apply to the reading task the cognitive and linguistic capabilities which they have been shown to have in other situations.

There are a number of similarities between the reading lesson and talk story and storytelling, one or all of which may be significant to the children. First, the teacher in each KEEP classroom has established herself as a socially relevant figure, an adult whose approval is highly valued (Tharp, 1978; Jordan and Tharp, 1979). The status is not automatically accorded to all adults by Hawaiian children; it must be earned (Gallimore, Boggs, and Jordan, 1974). The teacher accomplishes this by demonstrating both warmth and control. Children are warmly praised for their efforts, individually and in groups. They are encouraged to work hard, to try their best, and are given credit for the smallest bit of progress made. The teacher expresses her expectations for classroom conduct and academic work. She holds high standards for the childrens' industriousness and is likely to express disapproval when "slacking off" occurs or carelessly completed work is submitted, but individuals are not criticized or shamed for mistakes made in the process of trying. Her clear expressions of both approval and disapproval and her consistent and contingent dispensing of the "good things" in her control, such as privileges, establish her in the role of a firm but friendly adult, one whose positive regard is actively sought. Hawaiian children will talk story with such an adult, when she gives cues that she is receptive to what they have to say (cf. Boggs, 1972). The social context of the lesson is highly important to the children. A teacher who has not already established the proper interpersonal relationships between herself and the children would not be able to teach reading lessons in the talk story style; the children simply would not be responsive.

The second similarity between the reading lesson and talk story is that both interactions are characterized by *mutual participation*. Mutual participation is a major characteristic of the children's peer teaching/learning interactions identified by Jordan (1978a); the term is used to indicate that both the teacher and the learner(s) are participating in the task at hand together. In the reading lesson, although the teacher structured the discussion with her questioning, she clearly did not want to provide a full interpretation of the story herself. Neither did she simply quiz the children about the story while remaining aloof from the process of narrating and interpreting it. Rather, she constantly tried to elicit ideas and information from the children, and at the same time participated actively in the conversation and the *co-narration* of the story.

T: O k a y,
the frog —
(Makes hand gestures towards L., exchanges eye-contact with S.)
(S. sits back in chair smiling.)
S: O-o-h-h-h.

T: gave a jump in Freddy's pocket.
Does it mean it jumped *out* of Freddy's
(makes hand gesture of something jumping out of make-believe pocket, looks at C. and S.)
pocket?

X_1: N-o o-o.
(L. and C. shake heads 'no.')
(A. looks down at her book.)

X_2: N-o-o o-o.

X_3: N-o-o-o.

T: No, it's inside — I don't have a pocket but it's inside the pocket and it jumps, it goes like this.
(Demonstrates frog movement inside a pocket, looking at S.)
It wasn't in his hand, and it didn't jump out and run down the street.
Who ran down the street?
(Looks at S.)
(L. and C. are attending to her.)
(A. appears to be reading. T. glances at her.)

L(?): Fre dd-y-y-y.
(Sits back in chair, almost collapsing.)

G: Fredd-y-y-y.
(T. repeats response with group, giving a large nod of affirmation.)

T: Freddy ran down the street.
(Nods, looking down at her book.)

S: Because —
because

T: O k a y.

S: he didn't want
Mr. Mays to make him a bait.

T: Exactly right S., good reading.
(Sits back in chair while exclaiming, points to S.)

In this example, it can be seen that the teacher clarified points of confusion and tried to contribute information which might not have been available to the children. She attempted to give them a more precise understanding of the story than they might otherwise have gained. She further communicated to the children the idea that their contributions to the discussion were no less important than hers. Thus, in the example, S. spontaneously elaborated on the teacher's last statement and was praised for providing this additional piece of information.

In the context of pure talk story and of the KEEP reading lesson, the major manifestation of mutual participation is the feature of *co-narration*. Co-narration, or the joint narration of a story by two or more people, is a feature of Hawaiian storytelling which has been observed in children of the same age as the KEEP students (Watson-Gegeo and Boggs, 1977). The reading lesson can be conceptualized as a speech event in which teacher and children co-narrate a story. Furthermore, according to Watson-Gegeo and Boggs, if the narrators are close friends, co-narration may serve to reconfirm their relationship. Similarly, the children's willingness to participate in the lesson, their acceptance of the role of co-narrator with the teacher, as well as with each other, may be a reflection of the importance they attach to their relationship with her.

The following excerpt shows the types of close cooperation and careful synchronization of speech between children and teacher necessary in co-narration.

T: Mr. Mays was gonna use the frog for bait, wasn't he?
(Looks at L. and A., nodding affirmatively.)
If you use it for bait, what do you have to do
to the frog, A.
  (T. glances across the rest of the group, then back to front, notices that A. has her head face down on desk, head resting on her hands. T. then centers attention on A.)
S: Put it —
(Had lowered his hand.)
(Pause)
(A.'s head still down.)
T: If you're gonna use it for bait, what do you have to do with that frog?
(Orients body and face towards A., gazes at her, glances momentarily to the side, looking at a distraction.)
You just throw it in the
(A. finally raises her head.)
w a t e r ?
X: Uh-uh. (negative)
A: Put it on a hook.
(Still leaning forward over desk.)
T: Oh no-o-o ! (grimaces)
He's gonna have to stick it on a hook.
(Gestures hooking something with hands, glances at S., then back to A.)
L: And den go like dat, an den dat.
(Gestures casting a line.)
(S. and C. glance at her.)
T: And throw it in the water,
and, (also makes gesture of casting)
(Glances at S. on word final.)
(A. puts her head down again.)
L: En den, en mi ight
S: The
fish
might come and eat it.

A: Da fish might come and eat it.

(Raises her head.)

(All look at her.)

So far we have suggested that the KEEP reading lesson is successful partly because it shares with talk story and story telling the features of a socially relevant, receptive adult, mutual participation and co-narration. The reading lesson and talk story and storytelling are also alike in that all may be settings for learning, although a reading lesson is always directed at this goal while talk story and storytelling are only occasionally so directed. Still, talk story and storytelling may be viewed as instances of informal learning.

Another way of understanding the adaptive nature of the KEEP reading lesson is by considering the general distinction between *school learning* vs. *informal learning*, as defined by Scribner and Cole (1973). We argue that all features of both types of learning are present in the lesson, if the perspectives of both teacher and child are combined. Figure 9.1 is a summary of the major features of each type of learning.

School Learning	Informal Learning
1 What is being taught is most important	Who is doing the teaching is most important
2 Unfamiliar content	Familiar content
3 Language as main vehicle for learning	Watching, doing as vehicles for learning
4 Rule-orientation	Task-orientation

FIGURE 9.1   FEATURES OF SCHOOL VS. INFORMAL LEARNING

1. *What is being taught is important in school learning, while who is doing the teaching is likely to be more important in informal learning.* Certainly the point of the lesson for the teacher is to teach the process of reading comprehension. Yet, because the teacher must first have established herself as a socially relevant figure to the children, *who* is doing the teaching is important as well.

2. *The content of school learning is often different from that of informal learning and often unrelated to the child's culture.* Although many stories in a basal reader are likely initially to be somewhat foreign to the KEEP student, the teacher tries to show the children that their own experiences and the information in the text can be linked together in meaningful ways and that text information can be used (as can their own experiences) in making sense of the world.

3. *In school, language is often the only means of communication, while in their own world children may be able to learn by watching and doing.* But, as Scribner and Cole (1973) also point out, there are certain situations in everyday life in which children gain knowledge through language when the referents of the words are not physically present. While language is the chief means of communication in the reading lesson, the lesson resembles events in Hawaiian culture (talk story and storytelling) where the child is accustomed to relying heavily on language.

4. *School learning is often rule-oriented, with the teacher explicitly stating the principles involved; informal learning is generally task-oriented and unaccom-*

panied by rule statement. In the Hawaiian case, Jordan (1978a) has found task-orientation to be characteristic of peer teaching-learning interactions. KEEP children working with other children rely very little on rule statement as a teaching device; rather, their teaching-learning interactions revolve around the successful completion of the task at hand. Adult school teachers, in contrast, are likely to use much more rule statement. They are inclined to tell children general principles, then leave them to work out particular applications of the principles to particular tasks. With both the peer and "school teacher" styles, rules are eventually learned; the difference between the two styles is that the former depends on inductive reasoning through experience with repeated examples while the latter depends on deductive reasoning.

The KEEP reading lesson, unlike many other classroom instructional situations, is notably free of teacher rule statement. Obviously, the teacher wants the children to learn the principles of reading, but she teaches these principles by leading the children through the reading process over and over again. In her questioning she guides the children step-by-step through the process which a mature reader might follow in reading and interpreting the story. At the same time, the task-oriented nature of the reading lesson makes it possible for the children to relate the reading lesson to talk story and storytelling. The children see themselves as working with the teacher on a common task (the successful narration and interpretation of a story), although the long term effects of the lessons may be that the children learn a set of rules. Thus, the reading lesson can be seen as either rule- or task-oriented, depending on whether one takes the view of the teacher or the child.

Because the KEEP reading lesson is a blend of school and informal learning, it is possible, in Wallace's (1970) terminology, for the teacher and the children to have different cognitive maps, which nevertheless imply the same equivalence structure. Thus, another reason the KEEP reading program succeeds may be because it allows the participants to have views which are different, yet compatible, as depicted in Figure 9.2. The teacher is rule-oriented, and her perception of the lesson is that she is teaching the rules of reading comprehension. The child, however, is task-oriented and perceives the reading lesson as an event resembling talk story or storytelling in which he or she participates with peers and a socially relevant adult. Yet the participants' different perceptions do not conflict, because by acting according to his or her own perceptions of the situation, each is simultaneously fulfilling the other's expectations.

	Teacher	Child
Orientation	Rule	Task
Perception of the Self	Teaching rules of story comprehension	Telling story with teacher and other children
Perception of the Other	Learning rules of story comprehension	Telling story with children

FIGURE 9.2　　TEACHER AND CHILD PERCEPTIONS OF THE READING LESSON

Now, if this comprehension-oriented program is compared to the old, phonics-oriented program, it can be seen why the phonics program was not effective. The use of a phonics approach destroys the compatibility of the perceptions of the teacher and the child. If the content of the lesson is not a story but a relatively meaningless collection of words, sounds, and letters, the Hawaiian child will find it difficult if not impossible, to relate the reading lesson to anything he knows or finds important. In addition, the teaching of phonics does not lend itself to a mutual participation, co-narration style of interaction.

Conclusion

In summary, a major problem in teaching Hawaiian children to read appears to be that they do not recognize ordinary reading lessons as situations which call for the application of their full range of cognitive and linguistic abilities. The KEEP program seems to be effective at least partly because it employs a special type of reading lesson, one which resembles talk story and storytelling, major speech events in Hawaiian culture. It must be emphasized that the reading lesson is *not* isomorphic with these cultural forms (for discussions of cultural isomorphism as an educational issue, see Weisner, 1978; Jordan and Tharp, 1979). It does, however, exhibit several similarities to them, and in responding to these similarities, the children are able to apply their abilities to the task of learning to read to a greater degree than they can in conventional reading lessons.

The implications which may be drawn for the education of other groups of minority culture children from the KEEP experience are to be found less in the details of the talk story hypothesis than in the process involved in the development of the analysis. Hawaiian culture is of course quite different from the cultures of other Native American groups, Black culture, or Chicano culture. Yet it may share with these other cultures the incorporation of methods of teaching and learning which differ significantly from those of the conventional American public school. Hawaiian children, like other minority culture children, are greatly handicapped in learning academic content, we suggest, because the school is ordinarily not adjusted to their ways of learning. As a result, the children appear to be much less competent in school than they appear in other settings. We think that one avenue of improvement is for the school to develop learning situations which are more congruent with those the child has experienced in his own culture.

Yet we realize that this recommendation is much more easily stated than carried out. As our experience at KEEP has taught us, it is not simple to deduce exactly what a culturally appropriate solution will be. One of the main reasons for the complexity of this undertaking is that effective classroom learning contexts need not always be similar to any of the learning contexts present in the child's nonschool environment (Jordan and Tharp, 1979). Roughly parallel situations such as talk story may be identified, but the exact ways in which elements of such a speech event should be translated into a reading lesson are not automatically given.

Perhaps a more immediately productive approach to the problem might be to study classrooms with minority culture students in which an exceptional level of achievement is already present. The behaviors of the teachers, the social organization of the class, the types of participation structures, and the physical arrangement of the classroom could all be analyzed. If the observer is sufficiently knowledgeable about the children's culture, he or she may be able to identify specific features of the total learning environment which are culturally congruent. Once this identification is made, hypotheses about effective elements can be tested by encouraging other teachers to try similar methods, or by enhancing the potential effectiveness of the culturally appropriate feature. In the Hawaiian case an example of the latter might be to increase the opportunities for informal peer teaching/learning interactions among the children. If the academic performance of the children is improved, we may be more certain that we have identified a critical variable.

To a large extent we may find that we must place considerable reliance on the intuition of particularly skilled teachers, such as the one whose lesson was discussed here. These teachers are valuable resources for the ethnographer who wishes to understand how culturally appropriate programs can be developed. Cooperating with such teachers in analyzing instructional contexts which are especially successful with different groups of minority culture children may be the most productive method currently available to us. Through such cooperative endeavors we may eventually gain more insight into the general principles underlying the development of culturally appropriate school programs and be able to move from the level of description to that of prescription.

10

EXPANDED AWARENESS OF STUDENT PERFORMANCE: A CASE STUDY IN APPLIED ETHNOGRAPHIC MONITORING IN A BILINGUAL CLASSROOM*

Robert L. Carrasco

Introduction. In every classroom there always seems to be at least one student that "just isn't making it" who is assessed by the teacher as incompetent in various school tasks and who, therefore, is expected to achieve less than others in the classroom. This was the case with a bilingual student and her teacher in a bilingual kindergarten classroom I recently observed in Santa Barbara, California (April-May, 1978). The teacher told me:

> "I had written her off. Her and three others. In other words, they had met my expectations and I just wasn't looking for anything else." (Teacher, Interview Transcription, May, 1978).

This case study will document how the "ethnographic monitoring" process (Hymes, 1976) was applied in a bilingual classroom setting. Using video equipment and ethnographic procedures, I systematically captured on videotape this bilingual student as she was performing a task out of the teacher's awareness. I immediately shared the tape with the teacher and her aides in the field. After viewing the tape, the teacher looked at me and in a very reflective manner stated, "I'm going to have to suspend my full assessment of Lupita[1] until I get a closer look at her." The videotape has an impact on the work of the teacher and her aides as well as on the life of the bilingual kindergarten child.

---

*An earlier version of this paper appears as Sociolingustic Working Paper, Number 60, by Southwest Educational Development Laboratory, 211 East Seventh Street, Austin, Texas.

In general, this study will speak to the issue of what can be done to bring research more in line with the reality of the classroom and the needs and concerns of teachers. It will show how a teacher's "early-in-the-school-year" classroom observation of a child in her classroom and her knowledge of the child's home background and of the child's pretest scores all played a role in determining not only the teacher's perception of the child's competence, but also the nature of the interaction between the teacher and student for most of the remaining year. More importantly, this study will show how a teacher's "expanded awareness" of a child's communicative competence and other positive social qualities resulted in positive changes not only in the interaction between teacher and student, but also in instructional strategies and teacher expectations for that child, and therefore, in the child's performance in the classroom.

I have tried to present this case study in simple narrative form, free of most of the jargon used by social scientists and of the shared assumptions within this area of research because I believe that studies such as this one are of value not only to social scientists, but to practitioners in the field — teachers, administrators, aides, and college education majors.

The basic reasons for presenting this case study are:

1. To show the efficacy and validity of classroom ethnography
2. To show the value of teachers (and aides) as collaborating researchers (for it is the teacher and aides who know the classroom and the students better than any outside observer, including the school principal)
3. To demonstrate how information gathered in natural classroom settings is useful to teachers as immediate feedback and how this information is incorporated into ongoing planning (That is, how functionally relevant research in the field is useful to the educational process)

Ethnography and Ethnographic Monitoring. Social and intellectual assessment of children depends not only on formal measures (e.g., tests) but also on interactions between teachers and students. Although other factors, i.e., textbooks, materials, etc., play a major role in the type of education a child receives, the effectiveness of such factors is bound by the day-to-day communication the student has with his/her teacher. When students are performing various school tasks and activities with the teacher, teachers use what they see and hear as ways of assessing their social and intellectual competence. What students are called upon to perform in the classroom is an important factor which shapes their educational careers (Cicourel et al., 1975; Florio, 1977; Mehan, 1974; McDermott, 1974; Erickson et al., 1975). An important fact to keep in mind is that teachers see and hear only a limited sample of a student's total "communicative repertoire."

> Because of individual and cultural differences, children are differentially sensitive to various dimensions of these contexts, so some children employ a wide range of speech styles in performing ordinary school tasks in the teacher's presence, while other children employ a narrow range of styles in those contexts. In observing children of the latter type, the busy teacher is likely to commit the logical fallacy of inferring lack of competence from their lack of performance. (Erickson et al., 1975: 4)

Thus, basic to the educational process in classroom settings is the communicative competence of children. In general, the notion of communicative competence, as defined by Goodenough (1971), is based on what a speaker needs to know to communicate effectively in culturally significant settings. I would like to refine that definition here: "Communicative competence is based on what a person needs to know and do to communicate and perform effectively in culturally significant settings." If one views the classroom as a small society or community, it is therefore a socially and culturally organized system. Classroom researchers should then ask, "What do students need to know and do to be competent members of the classroom community? What skills and knowledge must students employ to be judged successful in the eyes of other members of the classroom, notably the teacher?"

To tackle such questions one must begin by attempting to understand the qualitative nature of the interaction a student has with his/her teacher. The importance of this assumption is expressed by the U.S. Commission on Civil Rights (1973):

> The heart of the educational process is in the interaction between teacher and student. It is through this interaction that a school system makes its major impact upon the child. The way the teacher interacts with the student is a major determinant of the quality of education that the child receives. (Ibid: 7)

Another important step is to understand the qualitative nature of classroom peer interaction. This insight can reveal the range of communicative competence and other social qualities children may possess (such as leadership, teaching abilities and mediating skills) outside-of-teacher awareness. The teacher can then use this knowledge to better educate the children. Research then, should focus on all the communicative arteries of the classroom, for therein lies the heart of the educational process.

If the subtle process of education is to be understood, methods which simply codify and quantify the behaviors of classroom interactants (e.g., Flanders Interaction Analysis System) are inadequate. While such methods have yielded important summary findings (such as those reported by the U.S. Civil Rights Report #5, 1973), are of limited usefulness to any individual classroom. "It is when one tries to move from such important summary findings to search for the classroom dynamics which produce them that different methodologies are needed," Cazden (1974) states in reference to the Civil Rights Report. (For reviews of such quantative systems, see Dunkin and Biddle, 1974, and Good and Brophy, 1973.) A different methodological approach is also required to provide ways of studying everyday life in classrooms that make more sense to teachers than previous approaches have done.

The approach used is specifically, that of "ethnographic monitoring" (Hymes, 1976). "Ethnographic monitoring" involves a microfocus on particular aspects of variation in data — or variation that is salient theoretically, and also relevantly salient to practitioners (Erickson, 1977). Relevant classroom phenomena can be identified on the basis of prior quantitative and qualitative research in the same or similar settings, the needs and concerns of the participants in the setting, or a combination of these (Hymes, 1977; and see Shultz and Harkness, 1972, for an example of this). Such a focus on salient issues of value to those affected by and involved in the research make possible "intimate familiarity" and genuine collaborative relationships between the researcher and the teacher (Lofland, 1976; Florio and Walsh (this volume), for an account of this type of relationship).

Basic to all research is the issue of validity. For ethnographic inquiry, validity is commonly dependent upon accurate knowledge of the meanings of behavior and institutions to those who participate in them. "Accurate knowledge is *sine qua non*," (Hymes, 1977: 9) — knowledge that comes from participation and observation — "if what one thinks one knows" is to be valid. Moreover, giving meaning to behaviors cannot also be assumed in advance of inquiry; this can be discovered only through participation and observation over time by the researcher.

> Before classroom research can proceed further we need languages of description at the level of primary data collection which make contact with the theories of action that are being used in moment to moment decision-making by participation in the events we observe and describe. (Erickson, 1978: 3)

Thus, the issue of descriptive validity is essentially one of the functional relevance from the participants' points of view (see Hymes, 1977; Erickson, 1977, 1978, for elaboration on standards and issues of validity in qualitative research, and more specifically, ethnographic monitoring). Ethnographic monitoring involves working with definitions of what is relevant taken from the "conscious" awareness of school practitioners and from existing literature in educational research.

Ethnographic monitoring may involve "discovering" new phenomena of functional relevance — new relationships among variables — that may not be accounted for in the conscious awareness of school practitioners, but may be suggested by recent research and theory development in social sciences (Erickson, 1977). In this case study, the teacher was unaware of a child's communicative competence in peer relationships in the classroom setting. I was able to discover this phenomenon because I had been involved in a prior study (Carrasco, Vera and Cazden, in press) in a similar setting.

Ethnographic Background

Entry Negotiations. The type of inquiry I was proposing to do required establishing "trust" not only with the teacher but also with the school system as a whole. Knowing that the shortness of my planned time frame for research would not allow me to independently develop this trust relationship with the teacher and the school, I tapped into an already established relationship between a professor at the local university and the school system nearby and was introduced through this established social network.

It was made clear to all personnel at Riverdale School[2] that my role was not to evaluate the program nor the quality of teaching/learning but rather to explore the daily natural interactions between the teacher and her students, and to collaborate with the teacher as a researcher-practitioner. I further explained that I would not interfere with normal daily classroom schedule of events, as I wanted to observe and capture routine events and behaviors of participants in a natural classroom setting.

School and Community Background. Riverdale School, located in a small town just outside Santa Barbara, California, is set in the center of a multicultural, middle-class residential area surrounded mostly by alfalfa, fruit trees and animal farms. Beyond these farms is the older, predominantly Chicano and Spanish speaking community which was once the center of this expanding town.

The new residential area (in which Riverdale School is located) is much like any suburban community whose residents mostly work in the nearest city (in this case, Santa Barbara). The majority speak English, while some are Spanish speakers, usually bilingual.

The residents of the "old" part of town generally either work there or are farm laborers. Some families live on ranches in migrant homes provided by the farm owners. There is a large portion of first, second, third and fourth generation Chicano residents and ever-increasingly newly arrived Mexican "green card holders" (legal residents), both using Spanish as their primary language in stores, theatres, and homes.

The bilingual classroom is an "enrichment" program because of the emphasis on multicultural education and because all children receive instruction in a second language. Moreover, it is a "volunteer" program — the parents have the choice of sending their children to either a bilingual or a regular English only classroom (both are available to the community). The goal of the bilingual program is to have the children emerge as equally competent in Spanish and English.

Because there are only two elementary schools in the town, in Ms. Padilla's kindergarten classroom approximately half the children come from the local neighborhood, making this class a multilingual, multicultural classroom. The students were either newly arrived Mexicans, Chicanos or Anglos, Spanish or English speaking (or both), or a combination of these.

Classroom Environment. The large classroom (approximately 32′ x 46′) is very well-lighted and airconditioned. In general, the walls of the classroom are rich in very colorful decor and busy looking, with lots of individual children's art and academic work displayed on bilingual bulletin boards and other areas along the walls (including the windows).

There are four or five independent learning centers (areas) — an audio-assisted reading center (with headphones), a manipulable (hands-on) game center, an art culture center, a science area and a puppet theatre area. These centers change from time to time, week to week, depending on the teacher's lesson plans, and serve as enrichment areas. The classroom library is well-stocked with a variety of bilingual preschool, kindergarten and first grade books, including a unique collection of teacher-made bilingual materials.

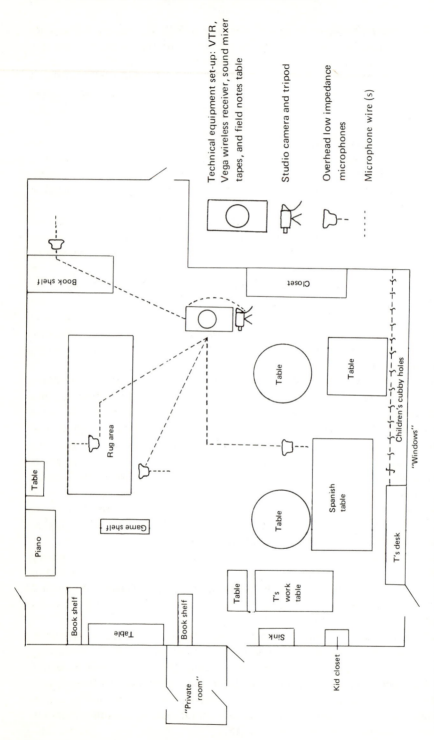

Technical equipment set-up: VTR, Vega wireless receiver, sound mixer tapes, and field notes table

Studio camera and tripod

Overhead low impedance microphones

Microphone wire (s)

FIGURE 10.1   CLASSROOM FLOOR PLAN AND TECHNICAL EQUIPMENT SET-UP

Along with the normal bookshelves and general storage areas, there is a piano, four large working tables and chairs (both kindergarten size) and a large rug that is normally used for teacher-led whole group events (Please refer to Figure 10.1, Floor Plan and Technical Equipment Set-up for top view of class-room environment). No child has claims to any seat or particular table space since the children are always assigned to different work areas during the day. But each child does have a personal storage space, a "cubby," a box drawer (1' x 1' x 2') against the wall under the windows.

Other than the working tables, there are two other small working areas, private and semi-private, where the children can work with the teacher and/or aides. The private space is a small room adjacent to the left side of the room (See Floor Plan) and the semi-private space is within the classroom walls, an alcove-like space on the upper right of the Floor Plan.

Through the windows there is a view of a vast, neatly manicured playground lawn with many swings, bars, sand boxes, and benches near baseball-kickball fields.

Normal Classroom Events. Table 10.1 illustrates the weekly/daily schedule of instructional events noted in my first week of observation. *Opening, activities, music story,* and *end prep* are events in which the entire class (whole group) participates with the teacher (with aides helping or preparing for the next event or on "coffee break"). For the other events, small groups are formed according to ability groups (e.g., high, low, medium groups for math; Spanish-dominant, English-dominant, bilingual for *Spanish Reading*, etc.). *Spanish as a Second Language* (SSL) is made up of groups who are dominant English speakers, while *English as a Second Language* (ESL) is taught to dominant Spanish speakers. Bilinguals receive both ESL and SSL on alternating days or receive special instruction as a third group.

During the second week in which I videotaped, "Cinco de Mayo" was cele-brated. This is one of two Mexican Independence days celebrated in Mexico and in the United States by Mexican-American communities throughout the South-west and other areas where Chicanos are in large numbers. Therefore, the activities during the week were mostly culturally aimed to accommodate the coming school/community celebration.

The teacher keeps a very strict and efficient time schedule always beginning and ending each lesson on time (as scheduled in her daily lesson plans). She always gives the children explicit cues marking the beginning and end of each instructional event (e.g., a few notes on the piano means two minutes to get ready for the next event or two minutes to end the present event).

All whole group events are conducted in Spanish and English, alternating from one language to another and repeating each sentence in the other language. Children are allowed to speak in either language when they initiate or contribute to a discussion. During certain events, especially during *opening*, the teacher makes it a point to ask Spanish-dominant children questions in English, expect-ing/requiring answers in English and *vice versa* for English-dominant children.

In small group lessons, if the group is made up of Spanish speakers only, then the lesson is conducted in Spanish (e.g., *Spanish Tables*). But if the Spanish

TABLE 10.1 Normal Weekly Classroom Events

	MONDAY	TUESDAY	WEDNESDAY	THURSDAY	FRIDAY
12:00 12:30	MATH	SPANISH READING	SPANISH READING	SPANISH READING	MATH
12:30 12:45	OPENING	OPENING	OPENING	OPENING	OPENING
12:45 1:00	SPANISH SECOND LANGUAGE/ENGLISH SECOND LANGUAGE	SPANISH SECOND LANGUAGE/ENGLISH SECOND LANGUAGE	SPANISH SECOND LANGUAGE/ENGLISH SECOND LANGUAGE	SPANISH SECOND LANGUAGE/ENGLISH SECOND LANGUAGE	SPANISH SECOND LANGUAGE/ENGLISH SECOND LANGUAGE
1:00 1:15	SNACK	SNACK	SNACK	SNACK	SNACK
1:15 1:30	RECESS	RECESS	RECESS	RECESS	RECESS
1:30 2:00	SOCIAL STUDIES	SPANISH TABLES	ENGLISH READING	SPANISH READING	SOCIAL STUDIES
2:00 2:30	ACTIVITIES	ENGLISH READING	ACTIVITIES	ENGLISH READING	ACTIVITIES
2:30 2:45	MUSIC STORY	MUSIC STORY	MUSIC STORY	MUSIC STORY	MUSIC STORY
2:45 3:00	END PREP	END PREP	END PREP	END PREP	END PREP

speakers are in an event such as *English as a Second Language* or *English Reading*, then Spanish and English are both used.

In this taped event under study, *Spanish Tables*, the lesson is conducted in Spanish since it is for Spanish speakers. The task at the *Spanish Tables* requires the children to read a teacher-made book, about Mexican culture titled *Mi Libro de Cultura* (My Cultural Book). The child must read what is written under the picture and then color the picture with crayons using the appropriate color indicated by the underlined word in the sentence (e.g., "Es un huarache *cafe*," translated, "it's a *brown* sandal"). Thus, the objective of the lesson is to understand the meaning of the color words and to demonstrate that understanding by appropriately coloring the pictures.

Teacher, Aides, and Children's Background. Ms. Padilla is a bilingual (Spanish-English) Chicana in her late twenties (age), who is very knowledgeable in early childhood and bilingual education (B.A. and M.A. in Elementary Education with special emphasis on Early Childhood Education). Her previous experience includes kindergarten bilingual teacher, preschool director of Bilingual Education, migrant school director, and a research assistant at an institute for retarded children. She is actively involved in school/community relations, and is often asked to present teacher/parent workshops in bilingual education and community involvement in the schools.

Her teaching style can be described as enthusiastic and fast-paced. She consciously praises children in a variety of ways (privately, publicly, and most often nonverbally at the one-to-one level). Her lessons seem to be well-planned in time, content, and strategy. She also seems to be aware of what is going on in her classroom at all times.

When I asked her how she knew so much about a child's background, she informed me that at the beginning of the school year she had visited all of her students' homes and kept notes on their environment.

Ms. Padilla has three bilingual community aides whom she selected, two at the beginning and the third in the middle of the school year. The teacher informed me that she chose the aides to complement her teaching style, which she admits is very quick and energetic. The aides are provided by the Migrant program (two aides) and Title VII/ECE funds (one aide). Ms. Padilla knows the capabilities of each aide and manages them in a highly planned manner so that they are clear about their roles each day.

There are 28 children in the classroom. Eighteen are registered "migrant" children, all bilingual, accounting for the presence of two migrant aides (Ms. L and Mrs. H). Approximately half of the class is bussed to the school from the other (predominantly Chicano) community. The rest of the class lives in the immediate community surrounding the school.

Lupita's Background. The focal child, Lupita, was born and raised in Mexico before attending kindergarten at the school site. According to the teacher, in Mexico Lupita lived with her grandmother while her parents were working in the United States as migrant workers. In Mexico she did not have access to radios, television, toys, puzzles, crayons, paper, paste, and scissors. She rarely (if ever) interacted with other children, mostly interacting with her grandmother.

Lupita's parents brought her over from Mexico and enrolled her in school several days after school had officially begun. Once in school (kindergarten) Lupita was given a pretest. The teacher explained that this was actually a "placement test," consisting of "those skills we hope our kids will have at the end of the year." While the norm for that test for entering children was 12/32, Lupita scored only 3/32. She was only able to give her name (3 points). She wasn't able to name colors or numbers, say how old she was or give her address. The test was administered in Spanish by the teacher, since Lupita did not speak English.

Lupita was six years old at the time, while normal age for kindergarten was five years. She has one younger brother or sister, and now lives with her parents whom the teacher described as "real young." The parents' major concern with Lupita in school is that she *behave*, a concern not shared by the teacher since Lupita is considered a model student.

When observed in class, Lupita was always very attentive, quiet, well-mannered, and seemed to always behave appropriately.

> One thing I have to say about Lupita is she's always been a good little girl ... to the point that I lose her! I forget about her. She becomes part of the other kids. So I have to keep reminding myself that Lupita is there. (Teacher Interview Transcriptions)

In the beginning of the academic year, Lupita was given the opportunity to perform in various group tasks until she "weeded" herself out into what the teacher called "my preschool group." The teacher defined that group as children who needed school environment experiences that other children possessed before entering school. She intended to give this group a strong preschool year.

In the middle of each school year, the school teachers must decide which children in their classes are below grade level and who is most likely to be retained, in order for the school administration to plan for the following year. Upon reflection, the teacher admitted that it was then that she "wrote Lupita off." Since Lupita had fallen so far behind, the teacher decided to make this year a preschool year for her (with the permission of the parents), and retain her in kindergarten. While the teacher did realize that Lupita was probably competent in other areas (such as oral language skills), she was not competent in the skills required to pass first grade. Ms. Padilla estimated that she (Lupita) would not catch up with the rest of the students at the end of the year.

Steps of Inquiry at the Field Site

Some pertinent details of the actual steps of inquiry are presented in this report for the following important reasons:

> In writing up research, while most researchers concentrate on the analysis of data and results sections, in this study I have focused on the procedures because it was the actual steps of inquiry that led to the discovery of a salient phenomenon of functional relevance to the teacher and should therefore merit special attention. Important details such as "how contact with informants were made, how trust between teacher and researcher was established and maintained, how initial inquiry questions and methods

changed as the conditions in the field changed, and how videotape equipment was in-troduced to a natural classroom environment," are among the many aspects of field inquiry of this type that are essential to report here if the results are to make full sense to the reader.

The second reason for highlighting this section is to present an actual account of how initial questions of ethnographic inquiry can change in the field as new salient pheno-mena become more important and relevant to the participants involved.

Finally, this section is important because it tests the idea that not all classroom ethno-graphic research need be so time consuming. My goal was to try to quickly feed back to the teacher what knowledge was found in hopes of making research data relevant to action (on the part of the teacher).

It seems like standard procedure in social science to take an inordinate amount of time between initiation of a research project and the writing up of the research data. The applied researcher has no such luxury. If the key decision must be made in a week, then research procedures and analysis must accommodate that time frame or the entire procedure may be rendered useless. (Schensul, 1974: 207)

These steps of inquiry will show that in a relatively short time frame (less than three weeks — See Table 10.2, Calendar of Field Site Events), it is methodologi-cally possible for classroom ethnographic research to have immediate and relevant effects on those participants involved — the teacher and the students.

Purpose. Before I entered the classroom to observe, it was clear to the teacher and her aides that my intent was not to evaluate, but rather to investigate the nature of classroom interaction with a special focus on the interaction between the teacher and individual students. However, so as not to affect the nature of her interaction with students, I did not tell her what specific questions I was addressing.

I initially came into this study with these questions, "How do Chicano teachers praise Chicano children? Does this praise differ from the praise given Anglo or other ethnic children in the classroom? And what are the ways, means, and forms of praising?" These questions changed during inquiry in the field as "new" questions became relevant to the teacher and her aides.

Classroom Observations. A few hours into my first day of classroom observation, I quickly became friends with one of the teacher's aides, Mrs. H, mainly because we were the same age, spoke in the same Chicano jargon, and because I had become friends with her husband. Near the end of the first day of observations, Mrs. H privately pulled me aside and told me that it was unfortunate that I couldn't capture on vidoetape how Chicano children "really" speak. She explained that Chicano children are basically very shy in front of the teacher, in small or large group sessions, and in those contexts speak very little, expecially the dominant Spanish speaking children whom she felt were very strong in Spanish oral language skills. She said that these skills were rarely displayed in the classroom except at the peer and one-to-one levels with an adult — mainly the aides from their community. This participant-informant suggested that I might investigate the speaking abilities of those children.

The next day of observation, I asked Mrs. H if she could identify some dominant Spanish speaking children so that I might talk to them individually just

TABLE 10.2   Calendar of Field Site Research Events

	MONDAY	TUESDAY	WEDNESDAY	THURSDAY	FRIDAY
WEEK 1 April 24-28	– No School – Meet with teacher in her home	– Observation field notes (P.M. 12-3:00) – Meet principal (A.M.) – Meet Early Childhood Education Coordinator (A.M.) – Tour School - meet teaching staff/aides – Aide informant	– Observation field notes – Verify/test aide's opinion	– UCSB Campus (A.M.) – Test technical equipment – Photos of children (P.M.) – Make floor plan set up (P.M.) with okay by teacher	– UCSB Campus – Final testing of equipment (UCSB - ALL DAY)
WEEK 2 May 1- May 5	– UCSB-Repair some equipment (A.M.)-transport to field site – Set up equipment at site (after school w/teacher) – Test VEGA wireless	– Trial testing audio/visual – Introduction of equipment to class (demo) – Taping Day No. 1	– Taping Day No. 2 – Large/small group lessons – Repeated viewings of videotapes (after school by researcher)	– Taping Day No. 3 – Large/small group (1 hour) – Maria-2 hrs. w/ teacher's permission, – Field site viewing of Maria tape (after school w/ teacher and aides) – End taping session	– CINCO DE MAYO CELEBRATION – No taping
WEEK 3 May 8- May 12	– View tapes by researcher (alone) – Time-date *corpus* of videotapes – Make duplicates of data tapes – Generate questions for teacher interview session	– Interview teacher at her home (P.M.)	– Field site to thank teacher, aides, coordinator and principal – Special thanks to children	– Return to Harvard	– Harvard write-up begins

to satisfy my curiosity. I talked to two children one of which was Lupita, the other, her friend Graciela. I sat next to where Lupita was sitting doing individual group work (art). She initiated our discussion by asking me if I had children, a wife, and where I lived. Having satisfied her curiosity, she then began to tell me (without elicitation) what had happened most recently at home — in rich, descriptive detail and in excellent oral Spanish. She painted a vivid picture of the story in my mind. After speaking to both children, I went to the aide and thanked her for her interesting insight and told her that I thought it deserved further investigation. And I momentarily dropped the subject since my initial intention then was not to investigate how individual children speak and perform.

On the third day of observation, I decided to take naturalistic still-photographs (using fast indoor film that does not require flash lighting) of each child. I knew that in my planned limited observation and taping schedule I would not be able to remember each of their names, and photographs of each child would be valuable for future use of the *corpus* of videotapes. I gave the pictures to the teacher, asking her to write on the back of each the child's name, age, language dominance, ethnicity, estimated SES, and a brief assessment of their academic and social competence in school.

Immediately after the third day of observation, with my field notes I began to identify key instructional events which I felt were rich in teacher praising instances. I decided that whole group events such as *opening* and *activities* would be taped because the teacher seemed to ask each child something instructional requiring reinforcement by the teacher when the children answered. This would allow me to see how the teacher praises each individual child "publicly." I also decided to videotape small group table events because I had observed the teacher and aides "making the rounds," monitoring each child's individual work and stopping to help and/or to praise the children "privately."

Setting Up the Technical Equipment. In my field notes I sketched a physical layout of the classroom (See Figure 10.1), taking note of which areas were not frequented by children or teacher and aides, looking for a vantage place to set up the technical equipment which would allow me to capture those events of interest to me. The teacher and I decided that the puppet theatre area would be appropriate since it is rarely used and because from that area I could capture all the areas where instructional events normally take place.

Relying on my field notes and observation of that classroom, I was able to decide where I should place the overhead microphones (knowing what classroom areas were normally used for certain instructional events I wanted to videotape). Using my classroom layout sketch, I showed the teacher where I thought the microphones should be placed, asking her if they might interfere with her normal routines. The first day of the following week (after school), I set up all the equipment using four overhead microphones strategically placed, a sound mixer, a wireless microphone system, and a video-camera set-up (studio camera and tripod with a videotape recorder [VTR]. The wireless microphone was to be worn by the teacher throughout the scheduled two-day taping sessions.

Overcoming Obtrusiveness: Taping Days 1 and 2. The following day the children arrived and all were curious about the equipment. I was allowed by the teacher to show them how the equipment worked, and the teacher briefly explained to them that I was going to videotape the class for the next few days. For the first hour or so, the children were conscious of the camera's presence, sometimes coming over to that area to glance at what was being taped. I was taking this opportunity to field test the equipment with live subjects and natural classroom noise to adjust for quality pictures and sound before actual videotaping of selected instructional events I had decided to record.

After that first hour, the children seemed to accept the equipment as part of their normal environment. The camera quickly became unobtrusive, and since the teacher and I both decided that it was not bothering them, we went ahead and began taping that afternoon. One of the key behaviors I discovered to help speed up "unobtrusiveness" was for me to keep away from the camera area once I had set up the camera with a wide angle lens and checked the audio levels, leaving the camera to do all the work in a static position, yet capturing the entire scene. Knowing the instructional event routines in time and space from prior observations allowed me to do this. Whenever the event space changed, I walked up to the set-up, changed the camera, focused on the event, switched microphone inputs, checked the audio quality, and left the area. This strategy was no longer necessary the second day of taping since the equipment (and I) had become part of the children's normal environment.

A General Review of Collected Tapes and The Birth of New Questions. After taping two days of selected instructional events (as scheduled), I reviewed the *corpus* of tapes alone that evening to begin to catalog and edit analogous events rich in praising instances for comparative analysis. To do this I had to repeatedly look at all the events, focusing on how the teacher praised, how many times she praised, and to whom the praises were directed. This became the turning point of this study for it was during this process that I came across a pattern of teacher behavior which didn't make sense to me. Having become very familiar with Lupita, I was always aware of her while viewing the taped events. I became aware of Lupita mainly from our earlier conversation during my observation period and because we usually had short conversations before and after school. I found that in each taped event that Lupita participated in, whether in large or small group discussion, the teacher rarely called on her to participate, although a few times she was recognized for her appropriate behavior. I began to wonder why it was that Lupita was not called upon by the teacher in those events, and why it was that in some events (particularly those on the rug where children must sit on the floor) Lupita sat away from the teacher and on the edge of the group. These became such nagging questions in my mind that I decided that evening to extend my taping schedule one more day to further investigate this feature. (As a safeguard, I intentionally had not taken down the technical equipment that afternoon in case the quality of some of the tapes were poor and I needed to tape additional segments.)

Taping Day 3 — The Lupita Tape. The next day, I asked the teacher if I could tape Lupita's actions during that day's events with an explanation that I wanted to see her operate in various contexts with and without the teacher. The teacher, somewhat surprised, informed me that she would be very interested to learn more about Lupita because she (teacher) had decided to retain her in kindergarten for one more year "because she was incompetent in those skills, prerequisite skills required to succeed in first grade — skills that should be learned in kindergarten." Not asking any questions about Lupita's performance in class, I asked the teacher to save her explanation of why she felt Lupita should be retained until after the taping session was over that afternoon. Then the questions became, "What is Lupita doing to be judged incompetent in the eyes of the teacher? Is she competent in other contexts?"

Before all videotaping had begun, I anticipated using a wireless microphone not only with the teacher but also with some children. Mrs. M made five children's vests of various colors and sizes especially designed (by me) to carry the wireless pocket-size transmitter and the mini-microphone. The teacher made her own.

Lupita was asked to wear the vest (which had a special pocket on the back to insert the wireless transmitter), allowing her to get used to it. The mini-microphone was clipped and taped to her left shoulder close to her throat area, the microphone pointing away from her so as to capture not only Lupita's voice but also the utterances of those persons interacting with her. (The same wireless set-up was used by the teacher the previous days of taping using an adult version of the vest.)

When I saw that Lupita was no longer concerned with the vest and that the other children were no longer interested in what she was wearing, I began to videotape her after recess that same day.

Not concerned with the content of what I was taping, but rather concerned with obtaining quality audio and video pictures, I was not aware of a scene I was capturing. Working alone with technical equipment in such an active environment makes it almost impossible to concentrate on things other than making sure the equipment is working.

Immediate Feedback in the Field. At three o'clock, when the children were dismissed, I was rewinding and reviewing the tapes taken that afternoon, checking the quality of each. During this process, I came across a scene with Lupita and two other children working on puzzles during "free time." It was while watching this scene that I was caught by the teacher saying to myself aloud, "Wow. This is interesting!" The teacher came over to me and asked "What's interesting?" I then asked her if she wouldn't mind seeing what Lupita did in her free time during the Spanish Tables instructional event. She agreed and also asked the three aides and another kindergarten teacher who had come in to visit and view the tape. I was not reluctant to show the tape to this audience because they all understood that my interest was on the teacher's interaction with children and I knew that the teacher and aides (who up to this point in time had not seen any of the tapes) wanted to know more about Lupita. Preparing the tape for them, I said nothing evaluative about the taped scene. I sat away from the viewing session allowing the viewers to interact among themselves as they watched the tape.

The Taped Scene. Briefly, what they saw was Lupita performing and interacting outside of teacher awareness during free time. After having finished the Spanish Tables instructional event task (she was the first to finish the task), Lupita decided to work on a puzzle in the rug area. She was soon joined by two other bilingual girls, each independently working on their own puzzles. Lupita was immediately successful in placing a few pieces back on the puzzle template. Then Marta, a bilingual child assessed by the teacher as a very competent student, asked Lupita for help in placing her first piece on the template. Lupita not only helped but also taught her how to work with it by taking Marta's hand and showing her where and how it should be placed. Lupita continued to help her for a short while and then returned to her own puzzle. A few moments later, Lupita disengaged herself from her puzzle work and became interested in what a boy, who had just entered the scene, was doing with a box of toys. Lupita asked him if she could play with him, when suddenly the boy was interrupted by the classroom aide who asked him if he had finished his work at the Spanish Tables (trying to convey to him that he shouldn't be there). The boy did not quite understand, perhaps, what was being asked of him. Lupita turned around and told him that he should go back to finish his work. He left and Lupita continued working on her puzzle which was almost completed. Marta again asked for help after not having accomplished very much since the last "help." Lupita helped Marta for a short time, then returned to her own task. The teacher then entered the scene, moved past them toward the piano, and played a few notes to cue the children that the event would be over in two minutes and to begin to prepare for the next event. Lupita speeded up her effort while Marta continued to have trouble. Lupita finished her puzzle, then helped Marta with hers, while the third child in the scene (who was sitting next to Marta) approached Lupita's side with her puzzle and nonverbally indicated that she also needed help. Lupita told Marta to continue to work on hers alone while she helped the third child and asked if she could help them finish the puzzle. Lupita, working quickly with the third child's puzzle, directed Graciela to go help Marta since she needed the help. After Lupita and the third child put away their finished puzzles, Lupita looked around and noticed that Graciela and Marta were still at theirs. She quickly approached them, knelt down in front of them, took command and helped them finish in time for the next lesson. This tape scene clearly showed Lupita's competence as a leader and teacher, as well as her ability to work puzzles. Moreover, it seemed to reveal how Lupita's peers perceive her as compared to how the teacher perceived her.

Viewers' Reactions. Immediately after the viewing session, the teachers and aides were milling around, reflecting, talking about it, and appearing somewhat amazed about what they had seen. While I was rewinding the tape once more, the teacher approached me and said, "I'm going to have to suspend my assessment of Lupita until I get a closer look at her . . . and a couple of other children, too. That was *very* insightful. Thank you!"

The teacher remained very reflective that afternoon while she was preparing the classroom for the next day. Mrs. H seemed very glad (as she smiled at me) that I had in fact captured something she suspected about Lupita . . . and other children like her in class.

I did not pursue questioning the teacher about Lupita since I felt she was still thinking about this new awareness and because she was busy preparing for the next day's Cinco de Mayo celebration at the school. I left for the weekend to continue cataloging, editing, and analyzing the tapes, returning to her home on Tuesday. That evening I interviewed the teacher in her home while viewing the selected pieces of videotape rich in praising instances.

Teacher Interview Session. In the teacher interview session I was trying to get the teacher to help me identify and point out praises. It soon became obvious to me that neither she nor I were fully interested in "praising"; during a rest period, we began talking at great length about Lupita's tape. I audiotaped the conversation-interview and transcribed it. I asked very few questions and received long, informative answers, thoughts, and philosophical ideas without much probing. Ms. Padilla wanted to share everything with me about Lupita and a few other children as well.

I was extremely interested in what the teacher was saying because before the interview I had no knowledge of Lupita's background except that she was a dominant-Spanish speaker, that she was competent in the Spanish language, and that she was going to be retained in kindergarten. Moreover, while I had some idea, I didn't fully understand why the teacher and aides reacted as they did after viewing Lupita's tape. I wanted to hear about Lupita's background, for she then became central to my study.

Before I began audiotaping the teacher interview session regarding Lupita, I informed the teacher how I decided to isolate Lupita "for a closer look" at her behavior in class. I explained how, on the basis of having noticed that she had not called on Lupita to participate in either large or small group instructional event discussions on my tapes, I became curious as to why this was happening at least during those events I had captured on tape. I asked Ms. Padilla this question, knowing that prior to observation and taping she had earlier expressed to me that she made it a conscious point to try to interact with each child each day in each session. I found that the teacher was consciously aware of the nature of this interaction. She explained that because of Lupita's history and home background and her lack of the skills required to participate effectively in these sessions, she decided not to humiliate or embarrass Lupita in front of her peers for not being able to answer or perform adequately. The teacher was very concerned that Lupita not develop a negative attitude toward school and toward herself.

Here is a case in which the teacher was clearly aware of what she was doing and where the researcher was lacking in knowledge as to "why." Had I not talked to the teacher I might have misjudged her actions. This is a prime example of the value of teacher collaboration in classroom research: the teacher gave meaning to an action that may have been easily misinterpreted by an "outside" researcher working without the teacher.

Although Lupita was not called upon to participate by the teacher in whole or small group discussions, she was not excluded at the one-to-one level of inter-action in other instructional events. In Spanish Tables, for example, where the students individually work on certain tasks (e.g., pencil-paper tasks, art, cutting), the teacher and aides "make the rounds" going from one child to another, moni-toring their work and helping each student individually.

The nature of this teacher-student participation structure in small and large group discussions may have been further enhanced by Lupita's "invisibleness" due to her appropriate social behavior in class. That is, Lupita's model behavior may have added to her "invisibleness" because she was never doing anything wrong in front of the teacher. "Visible" children are usually those who misbehave or initiate discussion in the teacher's presence.

> One thing I have to say about Lupita is (that) she (has) always been a good little girl — to the point that I *lose* her. I forget about her. She becomes part of the other kids. So I have to keep reminding myself that Lupita is there.

> She plays the game; she plays it well. She plays my game *very* well. Behaviorally, she's not a problem. (Teacher, Interview Transcriptions)

The teacher expressed to me that she was very aware of Lupita's strong oral language skills (in Spanish), skills that she was not aware of early in the year since Lupita was very quiet. For example, she was able to tell a three sentence story with a "before, a middle and an end."

The teacher was also aware of Lupita's language competence in other con-texts — at the peer level, and was concerned with the child's psychological and social well-being in the classroom as expressed in her strategies in helping this child cope in and adjust to this new cultural environment — the school, the class-room and the people in the classroom, as well as the American culture in general.

The teacher began the audio-recorded interview by expressing that she had "pygmalion effected"[3] Lupita.

> "I've pygmalion effected her. In the last three months I haven't been testing her for anything. I wrote her off — her and three others." (Teacher, Interview Transcriptions)

She was reflecting on how she arrived at this state by explaining Lupita's history and home background and her lack of performance in skills prerequisite for entering kindergarten.

Because of this "behindness" and her genuine concern for Lupita's later success in school, the teacher had decided to retain Lupita (with the parents' permission) in kindergarten for the following year.

> I know what's expected of her over there (meaning the first grade). And she'd have problems. And I'd rather that she stay with me and get a really strong kindergarten. "Now boy, she's ready. Let's give it our go." And send her on. (Teacher, Interview Transcriptions)

Before I explicitly asked what effect the videotape might have had on her, the teacher mentioned that that very morning before the interview she had talked with Mrs. M, the teacher aide who worked closely with Lupita throughout the school year, about Lupita's present academic status.

> So I can truthfully say that talking with Mrs. M this morning, she (Lupita) is about where my kids were, my average kid was in December. She's there now. So we . . . no . . . we have not gotten past recognizing of letters . . . none of those prerequisites that are needed to get to first grade. And one prerequisite for all the kids to do well in first grade is to know the five 'vocales' (Spanish for 'vowels'). All five vowels must be in the child's repertoire. There's no way she could get them in the next four weeks (number of weeks left in the school year). So on that basis alone I have to come to grips, "Do I keep her or don't I keep her?" (Teacher, Interview Transcriptions)

The fact that she inquired about Lupita's academic standing and her newly stated indecisiveness to retain Lupita, as evidenced in her last sentence above, were some of the initial clues that the videotape had had an effect on the teacher's assessment of Lupita's abilities. The first clue was her immediate reaction to the tape just after viewing it in the classroom:

> "I'm going to have to suspend my assessment of Lupita 'til I get a closer look at her."

When I asked her why she had asked Mrs. M about Lupita's status, she stated:

> The videotape. And her aggressiveness on Friday (the day after the final taping). I couldn't get her down. I mean, she was just downright aggressive. She just wanted my attention — was demanding it! You know . . . which I have honestly not seen that in her, *never*!

To this researcher, it seems that this "expanded awareness" of Lupita's abilities as documented in this videotape segment helped make Lupita "visible" once more to the teacher. And while I wasn't there to witness this new interaction behavior the teacher described to me, it seems possible that Lupita's change in interaction style might have been due to changes in teacher's interaction style with Lupita — due perhaps to the teacher's renewed recognition or awareness of Lupita. Thus, Lupita — like any normal human being adapted her behavior to the teacher's new behavior. And while the teacher at first may not have been aware of changes in herself while interacting with Lupita, she was first aware of changes in Lupita, which in turn, allowed her to reflect on the interactional strategies she herself used to result in such changes.

Reflecting on this new interactive experience, the teacher wondered what might have happened if she had seen the videotape earlier in the year.

> I'm not sure that even if I had done it in December it would have helped. I don't think she was ready for that yet. But I'm not sure she wasn't ready for it last month! And I have had two months (instead of one) to have capitalized on what I see I could've done now. (Teacher, Interview Transcriptions).

When asked what further thoughts emerged from viewing the videotape, she raised many self-evaluative questions.

> Did you do that to her? Did you cause her to stop growing? Did you stop adapting for her? And yeah . . . you know, it's an easy way to say, "Now you belong to a preschool group and you will get the following things done." And that's why I say, perhaps with

guilt, two months ago, *three* months ago, that's what I thought, I could have observed her and maybe found the same things out. But I didn't. So, *one more learning process and one more learning thing for me to remember.* (Teacher, Interview Transcriptions)

The teacher's last sentence above corroborates what the principal and the Early Childhood Education Coordinator independently told me at the very beginning of this project:

She's one of the best bilingual bicultural teachers in the school, if not the entire state. (Field Notes, 1978)

There is no denying her sincere and genuine concern for personal growth as a professional teacher of young children. Her positive attitude can best be expressed in her own terms:

I really don't get upset even looking at myself. I don't say, "Gosh, I did it to that kid." No! Just like Lupita, I have a month left. You know, I could still give Lupita a whole . . . much more time. We still can give it a go. Try it . . . who knows? (Teacher, Interview Transcriptions)

Near the end of our interview, the teacher was considering new teaching strategies as a result of having viewed Lupita in another context.

Well, if nothing else, I've become more aware of trying to, quote, "Meet her needs" as a leader so that I will put her in positions where she *can* be leader. And . . . 'cause that's the important thing. It's an important quality. We have enough children there that I could set up activity time so that she *will* be the leader. She would direct kids. (Teacher, Interview Transcriptions)

This awareness not only had direct implications for the teaching of Lupita, but also opened up an awareness of other children like her in the classroom. The teacher was also taking a closer look at three other children. For example, in another taped event (while I was working on praising forms) she noticed an out-of-teacher-view behavior of a young boy, Miguel, and took note that "tomorrow I'll take more notice (of him as a result)."

She continued then with the validity of videotaping in the classroom:

. . . it's very quick feedback. To me it would be more nifty to have seen it yesterday (Miguel's behavior), the day it occurred and then I would come back and do it again (meaning changing strategies to correct Miguel's behavior). And manipulate some things so that I don't see that behavior occurring. What if I change it? What happens then? You know, I'm not sure that I can be on top of it to observe either. So . . . like videotape should be on me again. Doing a pre-post (referring to pretesting and posttesting using videotapes). You know, "Okay, so you caught me doing that." Now I'm sure you can come back and see what you think I'm doing. (Teacher, Interview Transcriptions)

At the end of the interview she began to explore other possibilities for using this "immediate feedback approach." She spoke about how videotaping might be used at the beginning of the school year to speed up "getting down to the business of teaching."

You know, you've got 28 kids and you're having to think, "Now, was he the one that was biting his thumb? Or, was he the one . . ." You know, just getting names and faces and behaviors together. It's nifty if you could get it all down over the weekend. You check it out, and 'Okay, now I know what you like. And what he doesn't like.' And those kinds of things. And at the end of the year . . . just to see the growth! Reinforcement alone! Just to see what reinforcement for each kid. How far along did they go along the scale?" (Teacher, Interview Transcriptions)

A Brief Discussion. Here is a classic case where the teacher's knowledge complemented the researcher's knowledge of the situation, for without this collaboration, this "special" taped scene in the life of a bilingual child in the classroom might not have made sense to me nor had an impact on both of us, and ultimately, a special impact on Lupita.

This case study might also be exemplary case of the essence of ethnographic inquiry that separates this approach from experimental models.

"It is the essence of the method (ethnography) that initial questions may change during the course of inquiry." (Hymes, 1977:7)

"The field worker brings a point of view and implicit questions with him to the field. His perspectives and questions may change in the field, but he has an idea base from which to start." (Erickson, Personal Communication, 1978)

I began this study with a point of view, a good theoretical and research background, and a purpose: "How Chicano teachers praise Chicano children." With this background and purpose, I was able to "shift" by direction in the field to discover a salient phenomenon of functional relevance to the teacher as well as her aides, one of whom directed me in developing in the field a new path of inquiry.

Post-Research Teacher Interview. In early July (1978) after the end of the school year, I telephoned the teacher for a post-research interview. I wanted an up-to-date report on Lupita and needed some more information on the backgrounds of her aides.

The teacher told me that since my departure she and her aides had been closely working with Lupita using such strategies as allowing her to become a leader in certain group activities. Lupita also became more involved in group participation. The teacher was very proud and surprised that in the kindergarten skills post-test, Lupita had scored very high, 22/32, with exceptional scores in language skills and mathematics. (Recall that upon entering kindergarten, Lupita had scored 3/32 — while the average score upon entering was 12/32). The high math scores should be compared with what she knew a month earlier. In the May teacher interview, in her desire to get a closer look at Lupita's academic standing and abilities, the teacher spoke with Lupita's aide about her mathematics ability. At that time, Lupita was only able to recognize three numbers: one, two and three.

As a result of her age and because she did so well in her post-test scores, Lupita was passed to the first grade but was to go to the kindergarten class for work on bilingual reading skills.

(Teacher, Phone Interview)

Near the end of the school year, the teacher talked with Lupita's parents and suggested to them that Lupita attend the Migrant Summer School Program. Having just visited that summer school the day I called, the teacher told me that the summer school teacher reported that Lupita was doing very well, is a leader, and is very competent in a variety of academic skills. Both teachers agreed that Lupita had "spurted" in academic growth — in the last two months. (That is, since my departure.)

Ms. Padilla now believes that Lupita will have no problem in the first grade.

Perhaps it should be mentioned that Lupita's summer school teacher was the "second" teacher who happened to be visiting Lupita's classroom that afternoon when the videotape was shown in the field. What effect this may have had on her is unknown.

Comparative Analysis

The only other classroom research effort similar to this (to my knowledge) is the work I was involved in most recently (Carrasco and Vera, 1977; Carrasco, Vera and Cazden, in press). We analyzed a taped "instructional chain" event (the process by which a teacher teaches a task to one child who then teaches it to one more of his/her peers) in which a Spanish-dominant bilingual first grade Chicano child, Veronica, was the tutor. Like Lupita, Veronica was a quiet, well-behaved girl who spoke very little English. At the time of taping, Veronica had been retained in the first grade due to her "weak" English skills (the classroom was not in a bilingual program, the teacher was not bilingual/bicultural, and the language instruction was predominantly English).

The camera captured the teacher teaching Veronica an English language arts task in the English language. After teacher instruction, the teacher asked Veronica to recapitulate what the task was about. Veronica was only able to feed back minimal information in broken English. After a few moments of "free time," Veronica then began to teach her tutee, a Spanish-dominant bilingual boy. Once accomplished, Veronica returned to the teacher who was privy to the peer tutoring process and who asked "how it went." Veronica was only able to give minimal information, again in broken English.

With this minimal information a teacher might make the logical argument that Veronica did not understand the task and by logical extension, was also probably not a competent tutor. We focused on the tutoring process since the teacher was not involved in the scene. We found that Veronica not only understood what was taught to her in the English language, but also that she possessed teaching skills much like an adult teacher. While she was not taught *how* to teach, Veronica was able to process the task information received in English to formulate a clear set of instructions for her tutee. And what was most interesting was that we were able to see and hear Veronica's remarkable job of effectively formulating those instructions and teaching the English language arts task in her native language — Spanish.

During her "free time," Veronica was also seen independently studying a set of English sight-words, pronouncing each of them to herself aloud, and in perfect, crisp and exaggerated English. Indeed, a self-learner.

In this study, Veronica, like Lupita, displayed hidden talents and abilities in class with her peers, out of view of the teacher. The major difference between these two case studies is that the Veronica tape was analyzed two years after it was taken — too late for the researcher and teacher to put this knowledge to use in that classroom.

A Closer Look at the Tape. While in this case study it has been shown that it is not always necessary for classroom ethnographers to analyze the videotape to have an effect on teachers, I went ahead and broke down the tape into constituent parts and analyzed them in descriptive detail, noting accurate verbal and nonverbal descriptions of the scene in real time.

A more focused look at this tape allowed me to further investigate similar behaviors that both Veronica and Lupita seemed to display. There are some hints about Lupita's continual "invisibleness" in other contexts in class. By taking a closer, more detailed look at the taped scene under study, for example, before Lupita had decided to play with the puzzle, she was standing behind Marta and monitoring the interaction between her and the teacher — the teacher was head-down focusing on Marta's coloring book, evaluating her Spanish Tables task. Having finished, the teacher looked up to say something to Marta face-to-face, and Lupita, caught in the teacher's line of vision, immediately began to look busy by bending down to get a coloring paper, a free time task assigned by the teacher which Lupita seemed reluctant to perform. Another instance on this tape was when the aide called the boy at the box of toys to go back to the Spanish Tables to finish his work. Lupita, again caught in the "authority's" line of vision, re-focused on her puzzle, to see "when it was appropriate" (when the aide was no longer looking) to turn around to tell the boy to go back to finish his work.

In the Veronica tape we found that she also seemed to display "invisible" behaviors in the "authority's" line of vision. During one episode, for example, Veronica was joined in her tutoring job by another bilingual student — a third party. Having noticed the third party at the scene, the "student teacher" (adult) in the classroom approached the group and pulled out the third student from the scene. But just before this occurred (and just like Lupita), Veronica and her tutee, Alberto, looked in the direction of the approaching teacher and immediately began to "look busy" — focusing on their job and acting as if the third party wasn't there. A detailed analysis of the Lupita tape allowed me to see this similar behavior Veronica and her tutee displayed. I feel this is important information for teachers to know because they usually spend an inordinate amount of time trying to keep discipline in their classrooms. "Behavior problem" children are always "visible" in the classroom. And "invisible" children who seem to behave well in the eyes of teachers may be getting less attention, less teacher-student interaction, and therefore, less instruction; or, as in this case study, children are "forgotten" because they are "invisible" to the teacher.

Most previous classroom ethnographic studies have focused on children's inappropriate behavior with the underlying assumption that teachers use these "bad" behaviors as a basis for assessing the social and intellectual competence of children (e.g., Bremme, 1976; Erickson, 1976; Erickson, Florio and Bremme, 1975; McDermott, 1974, 1976, and McDermott and Gospodinoff, 1976; Mehan, 1975; Rist, 1970). They found that educators do seem to make informal judgements about students on the basis of their interactional performances and these judgements do seem to influence educator's decision-making about students.

> As we study classroom interaction from the student's perspective, we are finding that the alignment of behavior and situation is a significant skill in the repertoire of the "competent student." It appears that the raw number of appropriate and inappropriate behavior does not vary across students in the classroom. But those students whom the teacher independently rates as "good students" are those who are able to keep their appropriate behavior in the eyes of the teacher, and their inappropriate behavior out of sight. The students who are not rated as "good students" have not made that distinction. They indiscriminately perform inappropriate action both in the teacher's gaze and out of it. (Mehan, 1976: 9)

Here are two cases in which both students are socially competent in the classroom and whose expanded view of their performance by their teachers in outside-of-teacher-awareness contexts revealed what *more* these kinds of children are capable of doing. In other words, teachers as well as researchers should not only focus their attention on inappropriate behaviors by children, but should also investigate what "appropriately behaved" children do outside of the teacher's gaze.

Finally, expanded awareness of student competence such as found here may not always have such impact on teachers. For example, in a semester-long observation study of a bilingual program in Boston, Rodriquez (1978) described how dominant-Spanish speaking bilingual junior high school students taught Spanish to monolingual English-speaking elementary school children, and he noted that the junior high school teacher expected very little from her bilingual student tutors. He described how an Anglo child had trouble pronouncing the Spanish word, "juego" (game). Out of teacher view, the tutor went to the blackboard and wrote the word phonetically, "Who-egg-o," and the tutee was able to correctly pronounce the word. After the tutoring session, the researcher observed the junior high tutee informing the teacher how he had accomplished this lesson. The teacher kindly but briefly acknowledged the student and went on with her business. Later observations by Rodriquez suggested that this new knowledge about this student's competence did not have an impact on the teacher's attitude toward the student. This may be partially due to the teacher's stated negative attitude toward the program. Nevertheless, in the face of such evidence of competence as tutor, the teacher was not affected by it; she did not incorporate such knowledge in her teaching strategies, and the student remained in the teacher's low expectation frame. Thus, when evidence of student competence unfolds, teachers have to be able to recognize and to accommodate such evidence to their conception of individual children if responsive education is to take place in the classroom.

Conclusion

Like most educators, I believe that teachers should know what skills, abilities, and talents children bring to school — what children already know and do. Teachers understandably have a limited knowledge of those skills and talents children bring to their classrooms. What they do know is what they have seen and/or heard about them from other teachers and what they learn at first hand mainly through interaction with the children in the classroom. The purpose of this study was to expand this knowledge, to broaden teachers' awareness of the various communicative abilities and talents children have in other school contexts so that ultimately these "other views" will help teachers (1) be more accurate in their assessment of children, (2) adapt their teaching procedures and learning environments to accommodate individual children's needs, and (3) raise their expectations of children.

In this case study it was shown that even the most conscientious teachers may have a limited view of their children's talents and abilities in the classroom. This is understandably so because the teacher must usually distribute his/her attention among many children, limiting the amount of time spent with any one child, and as a consequence, limiting his/her knowledge of each child's talents and abilities. In these short interactions, if the busy teacher sees and hears a child performing inadequately, especially at the beginning of the school year, the teacher is likely to infer that the child lacks competence. This could lead to lowered expectations for that child.

This study has shown, I believe, that ethnographic monitoring in classrooms can serve to at least expand teachers' information about children so that teachers can better assess children's performance and raise their expectations of them. Using videotape cameras in classrooms, while useful, may not be necessary to expand teachers' awareness of children's abilities. The videotape in this study merely served to validate what most educators already know — that children have a variety of "other abilities and talents that are not displayed in teacher-student contexts." Instead, what teachers *can* do is simply to periodically "look and listen in" — that is, focus on what an individual child of interest to the teacher *does* and *says* in various classroom peer contexts. This process may be useful especially when teachers are beginning to form assessments of children, but before those assessments become fixed in their minds. In short, in order for teachers to expand their own knowledge about children, I urge teachers to become "in-the-field researchers" in their own classrooms.

Notes

[1] Pseudonyms will be used to maintain agreed-upon confidentiality.

[2] Pseudonym

[3] The "pygmalion effect" is how a teacher's expectations for his/her pupils' intellectual competence can come to serve as an educational self-fulfilling prophecy. Thus, low teacher expectations, low student achievement. (See *Pygmalion in the Classroom*, Rosenthal and Jacobson, 1968).

11

THE PROCRUSTEAN BED: PUBLIC SCHOOLS, MANAGEMENT SYSTEMS, AND MINORITY STUDENTS

Margaret D. LeCompte

Public schools have been under fire for some time for their presumed lack of articulation with the needs and cultures of children from ethnic minorities. One set of critics decries the institutionalized racism in schools; others have attacked fundamental characteristics of school organization itself. They allege that the reward system and patterns of competition and achievement in public schools are incompatible with the backgrounds of many minority children. Schools also have been castigated for their stress on individual effort, their culturally biased tests, their bureaucratic orientation and impersonality, and even for their emphasis on science and mathematics (Illich, 1972; Ramirez and Casteneda, 1974).

In the study reported here, several types of elementary school classrooms were examined intensively to determine what, if any, major normative themes exist in classroom environment and teacher behavior, to indicate how such themes are manifested in the classroom, and to evaluate, in the light of the preceding critique of schooling, their potential impact on students of different ethnic groups.

Preliminary Investigations

Stage one of the research began with preliminary observations in six urban elementary classrooms not from the actual study site. Observational research in the style of Barker (1963) and Smith and Geoffrey (1968) was used as the most appropriate means for determining what teachers actually did in the classroom. Chronicles of teacher verbal and quasi-verbal behavior[1] were recorded in writing by the researcher, then used to determine the specific norms which teachers seemed to stress in their classrooms. These observations suggested that the most salient feature of classrooms was their task orientation; the school was different from other settings children participated in because it was a place of work. There were jobs to be done, whether or not the students wanted to do them. This task orientation shaped the demands teachers placed upon children, demands for behavior which was oriented around five work norms. Classrooms appeared to be places where children were expected to do the following:

1. Conform to authority
2. Conform to a schedule and avoid wasting time
3. Equate academic achievement with personal worth
4. Keep busy
5. Maintain order

Doing the job, then, seemed to include doing it in a specific way; students had to do what the teacher said to do when it was wanted, with minimal noise and movement. They also were expected to learn the distinction between work and play.

One school norm was a work ethic. It had two aspects: the virtue of keeping busy and work as a value in itself. Work in our society is often viewed as the road to salvation, and early gratification of desires is seen as an unnecessary detour. Schools emphasized both work and denial of present gratification (Jackson, 1968); teachers in this study, for example, told children that hard work on long division now would help them in high school algebra. Schools also stressed the concept of time as a commodity. Much classroom activity was devoted to emphasizing and clarifying class time-tables as well as stressing deadlines and proper usage of time. Working alone was also valued in school. Children spent a great deal of time engaged in activities which did not allow them to move physically or respond verbally to other people or situations, except when spoken to by the teacher. This seemed to be a reflection of a rugged individualism still alive in American social ideology (Riesman, 1955). In the classroom, maintenance of order and the flow of activities seemed to be predicated upon internalization of rule structure and a set of expectations usually enunciated and enforced by a woman to whom all had to acknowledge subservience.

As had been confirmed by others, schools also emphasized public recognition of academic achievement (Jackson, 1968; Dreeben, 1968) and the ranking of children into categories according to the evaluation of their schoolwork. Although this is a rather narrow set of criteria for determining an individual's worth, academic achievement categories tended to be used as proxies for other indicators. Just as knowing someone's occupation in this society tells one much about that person's identity, so did knowing whether a child was a good student color the evaluations which both teachers and fellow students formed about that individual. Competition also was important; the sexes were pitted against each other in the contest for grades and teacher favor.

Reasons for the Study

The initial investigations indicated that schools transmit skills, aspirations, norms, and behavior patterns both overtly and covertly. Overtly, they transmit cognitive skills such as reading, writing, and mathematics. Less obviously, they pursue non-cognitive objectives — norms, values and behavior patterns which are deemed important for socialization to adulthood. These objectives, and their articulation with the culture of minority children, were the focus of this study.

We felt that the noncognitive objectives of schooling were in many ways a reflection of the values, norms, and standards of behavior in a technological, competitive society. We felt that five of these norms (those pertaining to authority, time, achievement, work, and order) were heavily emphasized in schools for two reasons. First, the school is a task-oriented place where children, as well as teachers, work. Second, the tasks children engage in are performed and evaluated under normative constraints resembling those of adult life. Children have jobs to do and must carry out these jobs under strictures and criteria which may not be entirely comfortable. They work in crowded conditions, follow orders, and are evaluated much in the manner that they will be on the job in later life. The fact of school as a work place seemed to be one of the most salient aspects of schooling, one which markedly differentiated going to school from all other experiences children have. We chose, therefore, to concentrate on that aspect for this research. We subsumed these observations of classroom life into the five normative categories listed above.

We then needed to determine whether or not what we called "work norms" really did exist more generally, how they were effected in classrooms, and how much they were emphasized. We also wanted to generate some ideas as to the nature of their impact on children from ethnic minorities. For this a more systematic observation of teacher behavior was required; classrooms which differed in their ethnic composition were also necessary to establish variance both in teacher style and in teacher responses to student ethnicity.

The Sample

Four fourth grade classrooms in two schools in Albuquerque, New Mexico, were chosen for the study. The first school was in a semirural, lower income Mexican-American neighborhood; the second was located in a middle class neighborhood with a largely Anglo population. Three of the four teachers were Anglos; one was a Mexican-American. All were in their late twenties and early thirties; all had taught for five years, and none had previously taught fourth grade. Each teacher had about 30 children in a self-contained classroom; resource teachers, aides, and student teachers were not present. The children in one school were predominantly Mexican-American; in the other, they were predominantly Anglo-American. Schools with substantially different student clientele were chosen to determine whether the type of child taught affected how teachers acted with regard to student work behavior.

Although the teachers were not chosen specifically to represent different styles of teaching, their classrooms did range from rigidly structured and teacher-centered to highly individualized, open, and unconventional. In addition, their stated goals for students differed widely; the traditional teachers tended to emphasize basic skills and conformity to school rules while the less traditional teachers stressed creative writing, science, and student autonomy. The study, therefore, encompassed a wide spectrum of teacher behavior and philosophy, which facilitated an examination of the effect of teaching style and classroom environment upon the way teachers taught their students. Table 11.1 summarizes the teachers' styles and the composition of their classrooms.

TABLE 11.1   Classroom Composition and Teacher Characteristics

	Teacher A	Teacher B	Teacher C	Teacher D
School	Valley	Heights	Valley	Heights
Teacher's Ethnicity	Anglo	Anglo	Anglo	Mexican-American
No. of Students	25	30	29	30
% of Mexican-American Students	72%	20%	79%	10%
% of Female Students	36%	53%	58%	50%
Use of Materials	individualized instruction; unconventional curriculum; unconventional use of space and time	semi-individualized instruction; conventional curriculum, unconventional use of space and time	small group instruction; conventional curriculum; conventional use of space and time	large group instruction; conventional curriculum, conventional use of space and time
Teacher Style	student centered, open, therapeutic pupil-teacher relationship	teacher centered, open, therapeutic pupil-teacher relationship	teacher centered, authoritarian pupil-teacher relationship	teacher centered, authoritarian pupil-teacher relationship

Procedures

The sample was limited to four classrooms because of the intensive nature of the observations required in the study and the sheer numbers and range of the behavior to be enumerated. Chronicles of teacher verbal and quasi-verbal behavior were again recorded by the researcher. Coding of the chronicles or transcripts then took place in two stages.

First, the chronicles were used to develop categories of teacher behavior which reinforced the five management norms: Authority, Time, Achievement, Work, and Order. Indicators for several other areas were also developed, based upon what was observed in the classrooms and also upon behavior which teachers generally are exhorted to encourage in children. These were autonomy or self-initiative, punitiveness, and intrinsic and extrinsic motivations for achievement. Forty-one specific types of teacher behavior were delineated as reinforcers.

The second stage of coding consisted of assigning each behavior to the normative category, if any, to which it was related. Frequency counts of the behavior coded were calculated; these were converted into percentages of the total amount of teacher behavior coded. Classroom activities were also categorized so that both the amount of time spent in each type of activity and the categories which had the highest frequencies of behavior reinforcing the norms became apparent. In addition, the amount of time spent in each classroom activity was calculated by adding up the total time per activity. A random sample of transcripts were recoded by an independent rater. In general, interrater reliability was high for all coding categories, although some categories occurred so infrequently as to make statistical analysis of individual behaviors meaningless. The behavior categories were first grouped according to the five original variables — authority, work, achievement, time, and autonomy — in order to have numbers large enough for a statistical test. Frequencies for each group for each of the two raters were summed, and a Student's t statistic used to indicate differences. For grouped behavior, no significant differences appeared.

Each classroom was observed in turn over a period of nine months. At least 33 hours were spent in each of the four classrooms, and all times during the day were included to insure a representative sample of classroom activity.

Supplementary information on teachers was obtained by means of an interview with each teacher. The impact of their behavior on students was assessed by interviewing a representative sample of the children in each classroom, and by administering a pencil-and-paper questionnaire to each child on perceptions of his teacher's behavior.

Similarities Underlying Differences

Initial observation revealed four teachers whose styles differed radically. One ran an open classroom whose flexibility stretched school permissiveness to the limits. At the other extreme was a teacher whose classroom operated "by the book" and who never engaged in any activity not fully sanctioned by traditional practice.

Analysis of the behavior of these four teachers, however, indicated that *despite* the variation in the *Gestalt* of their classrooms, there were systematic similarities in their behavior which were centered around management and tasks.

Thus, our suspicion that work norms were heavily emphasized in all kinds of classrooms was confirmed. The frequency counts of specific work-norm reinforcing behavior indicated that all four teachers utilized it extensively. In particular, the analysis of classroom activities indicated that much emphasis was placed on independent or individual work by all four teachers. However, there also was a great deal of teacher behavior which was related not to work norms, but to other kinds of normative emphases.

Thus, we could place teacher behavior in two major categories. One, which we called the "management core," was related to the institutional and structural demands of school life. Another, the "discretionary area," was predicated upon individual teacher personality and needs and tended to create the variation in classroom style. Teacher behavior seemed to be a product of both discretionary and management behavior. The discretionary and management behavior displayed by the teachers in this study focused either upon initiative and autonomy, or upon achievement and attaining classroom order. Behavior which constituted the management core is displayed in Tables 11.2 and 11.3; the content and distribution of discretionary behavior is displayed in Tables 11.5, 11.6, and 11.7. It will be noted in the discussion which follows that the norm of achievement is discussed as discretionary behavior, not management. This is because it was heavily emphasized by only two of the four teachers, and because it was not related to structural demands for the order and task orientation which seemed to characterize the shared core of behavior.

The Management Core

All four teachers stressed work norms by means of constant verbal and nonverbal requests for certain kinds of student behavior. However, six of these requests occurred with particular frequency, constituting no less than 50 percent of the noninstructional talking teachers engaged in, and in the case of one, comprising over 60 percent. These six items of teacher behavior constituted what was termed in this study the "management core" of teacher behavior so named because the six behaviors in the management core expressed the work norms defined earlier and were central to all activities of all four teachers. Despite their otherwise very dissimilar classrooms, the four teachers in the study were alike in their use of the management core.

The management core seemed to arise from the structure and task orientation of the school, and it acted to constrain even the most unconventional teachers to conform. This was because it represented the minimal managerial demands which teachers could use to get children to perform their tasks in the crowded arena of the classroom. Table 11.2 shows behaviors which made up the management core, their distribution among the four teachers, and their percentage of the total behavior coded for each teacher.

TABLE 11.2   Indicators and Distribution of Management Core Behavior

Norm	Behavior Indicator	Teacher A		Teacher B		Teacher C		Teacher D	
		%*	n**	%	n	%	n	%	n
Acceptance of Authority	1) Statements spelling out teacher rules and expectations	16	124	10	68	18	167	17	120
	2) Reprimands	6	51	10	69	10	87	9	62
Orderliness	3) Statements limiting movement and talking	10	75	10	70	6	56	13	94
Task Orientation	4) Dispatching orders	5	41	7	49	6	50	7	49
	5) Get-moving statements	4	32	8	58	3	30	8	60
Time Orientation	6) Statements signaling beginnings and endings of activities	13	102	9	67	12	106	10	73
Total Management Core Behavior Coded		54	425	54	381	55	496	63	458
Total Behavior Coded			792		707		906		724

*Percent of Total Behavior Coded   **Total number of Statements

NOTE: Reprimands were seen as authority reinforcing, although they also can reinforce other norms.

Overall, almost 16 percent of the total number of statements coded for the four teachers were oriented toward establishing who was boss in the classroom. That the children did indeed accept the teacher as an authority was indicated in their interviews, where, regardless of their ethnicity, they said that they "had to do what the teacher said because she was the boss," and that children who did not do so were acting inappropriately. About 11 percent of the total number of messages coded had to do with a task orientation, keeping busy, getting to work, or being told what to do next. Ten percent reinforced a time orientation which emphasized and clarified the class schedule, while six percent were "get-moving" statements which told children to hurry up and not waste time. Children were also subjected to a very large number of messages (seven percent of the total coded) telling them to "sit down and shut up." That these norms were enforced was indicated by the number of reprimands — nine percent of the total. The management core did not seem to be optional; all teachers, regardless of their intentions, teaching styles, or ethnicity used the behavior it included in great quantity. In addition, they appeared to use it uniformly; there were no statistical differences among the teachers when the total frequencies of the six core management behaviors were examined using a test of differences among proportions. Some differences were revealed in the relative distribution of specific items within the management core; chi-square was significant at the .001 level for three of the six

TABLE 11.3   Percent of Management Core Behavior Related to Each of the Norms

Norm	Teacher A	Teacher B	Teacher C	Teacher D
Acceptance of Authority	41	36	51	40
Orderliness	18	18	11	21
Task Orientation	18	28	16	24
Time Orientation	24	18	21	16
Management Core as a Percent of Total Behavior Coded	54	53	55	63

TABLE 11.4   Percent of Total Student Time Spent in Given Activities

	Classroom A	Classroom B	Classroom C	Classroom D
Solitary Activities	42	53	30	48
Managerial Activities	25	19	20	21
Interactive Activities	21	18	38	20
Other	12	10	12	11

management core behaviors. These were: statements spelling out teacher rules and expectations; get-moving statements; and statements setting limits on talking and movement.

The differences in behavior emphasis may be because the same behavior may be used by a teacher to mean several things. That is, when a teacher tells a child she wants him to get back to work, she may also imply that she wants him to sit down and shut up. A teacher who spends a great deal of time explaining why children have to do certain things may have to spend less time telling children to get to work and be quiet, because the children understand the reasons why they are doing things. Thus, although behavior was coded as though it fell into only one category, many of them may have carried more than one meaning for children. It is the total impact which is important rather than the relatively small differences in allocation of the behaviors which constitute the management core. Table 11.3, which presents percentages of the behavior coded for each of the management norms, shows that when normative emphases are considered, the differences between teachers are actually very small.

A "hidden curriculum" existed, then, consisting in certain rules which children were expected to internalize in each classroom and which were embodied in management-type behavior. There rules were:

1. Do what the teacher says
2. Live up to teacher expectations for proper behavior
3. Stick to the schedule
4. Keep busy
5. Keep quiet and don't move too much

The message was reinforced by the fact that children in all four classrooms spent a great deal of time working alone at their desks in individual seatwork. Table 11.4 shows the allocation of time to various classroom activities, indicating that from 30 to 53 percent of the time spent in school was occupied with activities which did not allow children to move around or respond verbally to anyone but the teacher. Thus, keeping quiet and keeping busy were reinforced both by the structure of classroom activity and by what teachers actually said.

Within the limitations of the data obtained in this study, it was clear that the children had begun to internalize the work norms which were the focus of the study. When interviewed, children in all classrooms stated that classrooms were work places, not places for play, that classrooms had rules which had to be followed, and that there existed a timetable for things to be done. When children were asked what their teacher most wanted them to do, both Mexican-American and Anglos responded, "Be quiet, don't fool around, and get our work done on time."

The Discretionary Area

Once the management core had been outlined, however, it was still apparent that the four classrooms looked quite different from each other. For this reason, a

TABLE 11.5   Discretionary Behavior

Management

1. Establishing rituals which produce order
2. Interfering with a child's initiatives or preferences, not responding to a child or embarrassing him

Achievement

3. Encouraging a competitive atmosphere and anxious competition in question and answer sessions
4. Announcing or posting grades publicly

Autonomy

5. Stressing some kind of contract or reciprocal relationship between teacher and pupil
6. Explaining or clarifying policies, relationships, or problems encountered in school
7. Providing opportunities for the child to organize his own activities, schedule, or to do things himself
8. Stressing teacher pleasure as a sanction for obedience
9. Providing opportunities for the child to initiate topics for discussion

further examination of nonmanagerial teacher behavior was begun to determine what seemed to shape the atmosphere and climate of the classroom. We called this nonmanagerial behavior "discretionary" because it did not seem to be required of teachers for ordinary classroom management, and it was not shared by all of the teachers. Operationally, it was defined as any nonmanagement-core behavior which comprised at least two percent of the total verbal behavior recorded and coded for any given teacher. Discretionary behavior seemed to determine such things as the amount of initiative children were allowed to have, the emphasis on achievement, the degree of competition, the frequency and types of sanctions used, and how often the teacher explained rules and subject matter. Table 11.5 indicates the kind of behavior included in the discretionary area.

It should be noted that all teachers did not employ similar discretionary behavior. Tables 11.6 and 11.7 indicate how the discretionary behavior was distributed among the teachers observed. These differences in distribution appeared to affect greatly the atmosphere of individual classrooms.

Teacher A, for example, strongly emphasized student autonomy and decision-making, in that 69 percent of her discretionary behavior was devoted to this category; Teacher C and Teacher D both had highly competitive classrooms in which games and contests played an important pedagogic role. Nineteen percent of Teacher C's and 36 percent of Teacher D's discretionary behavior was devoted to stressing achievement and competition. These two teachers also employed a considerable amount of discretionary management behavior, which when combined with the relative lack of behavior stressing student initiative, gave a wholly different flavor to the climate and structure of their classroom.

Thus, teacher behavior could be divided into three groups, as illustrated in Figure 11.1. One group, *Area A*, represents management core behavior shared by

TABLE 11.6   Categories of Discretionary Behavior Used by Each Teacher

Management Behavior	Achievement and Competition	Autonomy and Decision-Making
	Teacher A	
1. Performance standards expressed in terms of teacher preference (3.0)*	(No discretionary achievement reinforcing behavior)	1. Opportunities for children to organize their own activities (5.0)
2. Lectures on differences between work and play (2.5)		2. Explaining and clarifying school rules and policies (4.3)
3. Citing activities as inappropriate for a given time (2.3)		3. Opportunities for children to initiate topics of discussion (4.0)
		4. Presentation of teacher's value convictions (4.0)
	Teacher B	
1. Statements reminding students of deadlines (5.0)	(No discretionary achievement reinforcing behavior)	1. Opportunities for children to organize their own activities (3.6)
2. Reprimands for not working (2.8)		2. Explaining and clarifying school rules and policies (2.6)
3. Schedules and agendas displayed on the blackboard (2.5)		

TABLE 11.6 (continued)

Management Behavior	Achievement and Competition	Autonomy and Decision-Making
	Teacher C	
1. Statements reminding students of deadlines (6.8)	1. Building competition in question and answer sessions (3.5)	(No discretionary autonomy reinforcing behavior)
2. Preparatory rituals signalling beginnings and endings of activities (4.0)		
3. Interfering with a child's initiatives; humiliating, embarrassing a child (2.4)		
4. Statements alluding to teacher's "hidden agenda" (2.0)		
	Teacher D	
1. Preparatory rituals signalling beginnings and endings of activities (3.9)	1. Building competition in question and answer sessions (3.5)	1. Opportunities for children to initiate topics for discussion (2.6)
2. Statements reminding students of deadlines (3.5)	2. Reprimands for bad work or for not knowing an answer (3.0)	
3. Interfering with a child's initiatives; humiliating or embarrassing a child (3.0)	3. Publicly praising a child for quality of work (2.3)	
4. Hurry-up comments, rushing (2.5)		

*Percentage of the total coded behavior for each teacher.

TABLE 11.7   Distribution of Discretionary Behavior

	Teacher A		Teacher B		Teacher C		Teacher D	
	%T*	%D**	%T	%D	%T	%D	%T	%D
Discretionary Management Behavior	7.8	(31)	10.3	(62)	15.2	(81)	12.9	(53)
Discretionary Achievement Behavior	0	(0)	0	(0)	3.5	(19)	8.8	(36)
Discretionary Autonomy and Decision-Making Behavior	17.3	69	6.2	38	0	0	2.6	11
Total Discretionary Behavior	25.1		16.5		18.7		24.3	

*Percentage of Total Behavior coded   **Percentage of Discretionary Behavior coded

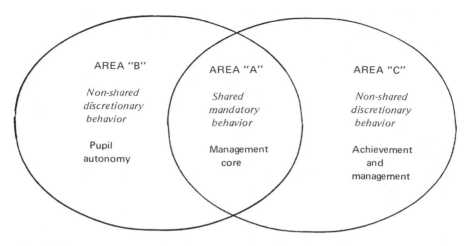

FIGURE 11.1   THREE AREAS OF TEACHER BEHAVIOR

the four teachers. The other two groups, *Area B* and *Area C*, represent discretionary behavior since it was not employed by all four teachers, and appeared to express idiosyncratic preferences and values held by individual teachers.

Area C behaviors were reflective of the management norms of authority, work, order, and time-keeping; teachers whose personal values led them to feel that these were of paramount importance devoted their discretionary realms to the emphasis of those norms and used the behaviors in Area C to do so. *Area B* behaviors stressed student autonomy, student decision-making, and specific personal conditions held by the teachers. A teacher whose behavior fell into Areas A and C would be oriented strongly toward conformity with institutional norms; because teachers who had this orientation also emphasized academic achievement and competition, these behaviors were also included in Area C. On the other hand a teacher whose behavior fell into Areas A and B would engage in the amount of management necessary to keep the school day moving, but would tend to stress other behavior emphasizing student autonomy.

Discussion

Most studies of teachers have stressed the variation which exists in teacher style and activity. However, this study has tried to point out that at least along one very important dimension, that of management, teachers tended to look rather alike. There were basic rules for school life which made it possible for teachers to survive in classrooms. Teachers employed management behavior because they had to; achieving cognitive objectives in classrooms meant activities had to be carried out in an orderly fashion. The exigencies of the crowded classroom and the task orientation of schooling dictated the management core; it represented the minimal demands of the school as an institution. This held true across all four of the classrooms studied, despite their variation in style. When differences in classroom management did exist, they seemed to be determined by the individual personality and philosophy of the teacher rather than by the institutional constraints of the management core, the ethnicity of the children or the sex distribution of the pupils in each classroom. The sample of teachers was too small to determine if their ethnicity affected styles of classroom organization.

It is our position that this division of teacher behavior between the management core and the discretionary area has great importance for the schooling experience of children. Specifically, we feel that the management core may represent values and norms which are facilitative and adaptive for the work world outside the classroom and are, therefore, crucial in the socialization process in Western societies. However, they may be at variance with training and predispositions which certain children, particularly those from ethnic minorities, bring from their home culture. The management core, therefore, may constitute a "hidden curriculum" which minority children disproportionately fail to master. By the same token, the discretionary area of behavior, while not a crucial component of the mainstream socialization process *per se*, may still provide enough flexibility in teacher behavior to lessen the immediate impact of the management core until children who have some difficulty with it are more able to cope with the demands of school.

The Learning Style of the School

In our study, the demands of management created a set of teacher expectations which formed a behavioral curriculum for children, no less important than reading, writing, and math. Children could, and did, get in more trouble faster for violating behavior rules than for failing subject matter. The latter merely created problems for an individual child; the former disrupted the entire classroom order. In addition, "real work" was that which children did by themselves; even when group work was encouraged, the only work which was seriously evaluated was individual tasks. Children had to succeed in the curriculum of rules and regulations as well as in purely cognitive material. Thus, schools required success, but also defined how that success was to be effected. Structural constraints and the evaluation of tasks created in classrooms the demand for a particular learning style to which children had to accommodate in order to achieve.

The problem in general appears to be that while some children accommodate well to this learning style, others do not. For these children to succeed, they must be stretched somehow to fit a common set of schooling expectations, just as the mythical Procrustes adjusted travellers to fit his guest bed. Further, having difficulty with the learning style of the school seems to correlate with cultural background; the children who do not fit seem to come disproportionately from minority cultures. Children whose cultures are not oriented to the formal authority, evaluative procedures and task orientation, competition, time schedules, and order of the classroom may not "make it." What seems to be immutable in the schooling and learning experience often faces something unalterable in the child. Thus, we support the position of those critics who say that schools have structural characteristics which create problems for minorities. We have outlined what some of these characteristics might be and why they exist. We feel also that the study indicated a way out for minority children, in that it outlined an area of flexibility contained in the discretionary area.

The Problem of Cognitive Style

Of particular interest to this study is the fact that differences in cognitive style are strongly correlated with differences in culture (Cole and Scribner, 1974; Gladwin, 1970). Mexican-American children tend to be field dependent while Anglos tend to be field independent (Ramirez, 1973). Mexican-Americans tend to be extra-sensitive to the social and ethnic climate of the school (Felice, 1973), prefer to work cooperatively and in a close affective relationship with the teacher, and are not as motivated by individualistic achievement incentives and competition as are Anglo children (Kagan and Madsen, 1971).

This cultural predisposition creates schooling problems for Mexican-American children because, according to Ramirez and Castañeda, public education in America reflects and rewards only a field-independent cognitive style, one with which Mexican-American children cannot cope as well as Anglo children (Ramirez and Castañeda, 1974). In a sense, Ramirez and Castañeda seem to be equating the term field independent, when applied to the classroom environment, with what might be called a traditional classroom — teacher centered, individualistic, achievement and task oriented — in other words, a classroom where the management core, as we have defined it, predominates. It is this type of environment which they and others feel is inimical to the scholastic success of "field sensitive" (their term for field dependent) children, a description which disproportionately describes Mexican-Americans. A "good" field independent teacher has the following characteristics:

1. Maintains formal relationships with students
2. Centers on instructional objectives rather than the social atmosphere
3. Encourages a task orientation and trial-and-error learning
4. Encourages independent student achievement and competition
5. Focuses on curriculum details, facts, principles and novel approaches to problem solving
6. Emphasizes inductive learning (Ramirez and Castañeda, 1974)

However, Ramirez and Castañeda also imply that there are good field independent and bad field independent teachers, just as there are good and bad traditional teachers. Many of their characteristics are quite similar to the norms and behavior emphasized in the management core; they are also the kinds of behavior which prepare a child for a professional work situation in adult life in American society. In the classroom, however, they may not articulate well with the social needs and learning style of Mexican-Americans (and others who are field "sensitive").

Ramirez and Castañeda suggest that an environment in which Mexican-American children could succeed academically would be one which begins with field sensitivity and moves a child gradually to field independence, such that he or she can operate successfully in both modes. This they call "bi-cultural democracy"; that is, while children in the end are required to succeed in terms of overall school requirements for formality, order, task orientation, obedience to authority, and achievement (the management core), they are induced to do so gradually until they can switch from field sensitive modes and affective skills to field independent and impersonal modes. They would not be expected to succeed immediately in tasks which were characterized as predominantly field independent.

Teacher A in the study we report here was indeed able to establish a highly ideographic classroom environment. Her students were mostly Mexican-American, and although she expected them to achieve, maintain order and operate within a formal setting, she did so by relying on strong personal rapport as a motivating device, employing no negative feedback and allowing children gradual experience in concept learning and organizing their work. She also gave them many mini-opportunities for decision-making. For example, she had wanted to establish an open classroom, yet she took all year to do so, gradually training the students to do without the structure and supports of the traditional classroom. We have already pointed out that Teacher A's classroom looked very different from the other three studied despite the fact that her emphasis on management core behavior was just as strong as that of the other teachers. What did distinguish her behavior was the wider range of discretionary behavior she employed. We do not know the effect of this teacher's work on the achievement of her students. Yet we feel that she exemplified the kind of teaching mix in behavior — combining institutional and management requisites with response to individual needs — which is advocated for children who cannot articulate well with conventional schooling demands.

We recognize that different minorities or subgroups might find different aspects of schooling difficult; while Mexican-Americans may tend to find the authority patterns, competition, and individualism of traditional classrooms to be a problem, other groups may have problems with other areas.

The Exacerbative Character of the Management Core

Because the management core is part of the management "system" of the school, it may act to enforce practices and behavior in schools which, while not necessarily offensive to minority cultures, may become so if emphasized. Behaviors which teachers see as deviant (or, what is worse, as an affront to their authority), will be defined as disruptive of classroom order and will result in reprimands, attempts to reinforce teacher dominance and get-to-work statements. While not all the behavior of minority children could possibly be classed as deviating from standard classroom practice, certain classes of behavior for certain ethnic groups are sometimes so designated. Social class and ethnic differences in language usage, for example, are among these behaviors.

Bernstein (1961) pointed out that there are social class differences in speech usage even within the same ethnic group, and that middle and upper-class language patterns, with their greater elaboration, use of inference and causality, as well as their formality, articulate better with school tasks and teacher talk. More recently, these differences have been observed in Chicago street gangs (Suttles, 1968), St. Louis ghetto classrooms (Smith and Geoffrey, 1968), and Navajo schools (Young, 1972). While there is some argument as to whether or not the differences Bernstein first isolated really do exist, the fact remains that for teachers, the "public language," or street talk, of students sounds strange. Children who cannot be understood by teachers (or who do not understand teachers) are often felt to be refusing willfully to learn, and may be punished or designated as stupid and recalcitrant. Here, language use is defined as a problem for the management system, and the management core exacerbates student problems.

Another problem area has been the social protocol surrounding speaking and interacting with elders among Native Americans.

> When the teacher called upon a pupil to recite, he would become the target of jibes and jokes whispered in Lakota and unperceived by the teacher, with the result that he (the student) would stand paralyzed and unable to respond; meanwhile, the teacher would be perplexed at her inability to secure responses . . . educators seemed unaware that individualistic achievement as they defined it is considered grossly immoral by Indian children. (Wax, Diamond, and Gearing, 1971, p. 7)

Similarly, Wolcott was never able to determine how much his Indian students knew because no matter what the assignment, no student could be induced to work solely for himself (Wax, Diamond, and Gearing, 1971). Here, what is essentially a cultural pattern was allowed to become a problem for the management system, with detrimental consequences for both pupils and teachers.

Conclusion

Barring radical changes in schools and in society such as those advocated by some school critics (Illich, 1972; Bowles and Gintis, 1976; Carnoy, 1974), children will have to continue to cope with the management core, the work ethic, achievement, and the timeliness discussed in this paper. We do not believe that culturally different children are forever barred by their culture from acquiring these norms and achieving in terms of them. We know, for example, that Mexican-American high school youth share the same view of the American Dream as other Americans (Gutierrez and Hirsch, 1973). Similarly, the children in this study clearly said that they shared the same work values as did Anglo classmates.

We feel that it is incumbent upon schools to teach children how to cope with the management core; not to do so would be to fail to stress the skills and attitudes necessary for many kinds of adult success. While it may not be fashionable to support such a position, in today's world children *do* have to pass tests, conform to authority and acquire certain job-related attitudes and behavior patterns. The child whose school allows him to believe that he does not have to do these things is the victim of a fraud no less cruel than the cruelty of racial bias. However, it may be that by utilizing the flexibility provided in outline in this research, teachers can adapt the learning style of the school to that of individual children so that children can be successful in a variety of modes, in school, on the job and in their own cultural milieu.

Note

1. Quasi-verbal behavior was that which substituted for teacher talk, such as when teachers wrote instructions on the blackboard, or pointed authoritatively to the seat in which the student was supposed to be sitting.

12

STRUCTURING CLASSROOM PARTICIPATION: THE USE OF METAPHRASING BY BLACK AND WHITE EIGHTH GRADE STUDENTS

Meredith Ludwig

This paper has two purposes: (1) to propose a model which describes the structuring of verbal interaction in classroom lessons and (2) to focus on one verbal strategy used by both black and white students to contribute to the structure of participation. The assumption in the development of this model is that verbal interaction in classroom participation is organized by a repeated sequence of four interactional times. These will be called: *Posing the Problem, Feeling Around, Redirection,* and *Finding the Problem.* This sequence is repeated many times in the course of each class period, functioning as a kind of turn-taking mechanism; within each time of interaction speaking and listening turns are enacted. Each complete sequence is focused on the resolution of a problem.

Either teacher or student may enact the time called *Posing the Problem* by identifying a question which establishes the focus for an exchange. *Feeling Around* is an optional time during which students may express confusion about or satisfaction with the structuring of participation; however, this interactional time does not always contribute to the production of an answer to the focus question. *Redirection* is a time in which either the teacher or a student explains or clarifies what is expected of the students in terms of task, interactional, and conceptual competence. *Finding the Problem* is a time in which students or the teacher demonstrate their knowledge of task requirements, conceptual requirements, and interaction standards by providing an acceptable answer to the focus question.

Metaphrasing is a strategy students use to comment on the negotiation of participation standards. This strategy helps students contribute to the structuring of participation by enacting a Feeling Around time. *Feeling Around*, an optional time, indicates a break in the complementary nature of student-teacher interaction and may indicate to the teacher that students are having difficulty accommodating to the teacher's expectations of competence. Three functions of metaphrasing will be discussed, using examples from videotape transcripts. These functions can be shown to relate to the knowledge participants share about appropriate behavior in the social situation of a classroom lesson.

The problem studied and the approach taken here have been defined in current research on the structuring of participation in classroom lessons (e.g., Mehan, 1974, 1978; Erickson and Shultz, 1977; Dorr-Bremme, 1976; Philips, 1972; Cazden, 1977). These researchers have focused on the conflicts which can occur when the "norms of interpretation" in the relevant "speech communities" (Hymes, 1972) differ between groups of students and between students and teacher in one educational setting. These researchers have talked about how such differences can lead to negative evaluation of student participation, differential treatment of students' similar answers and exclusion from participation.

This paper is based on ethnographic research in two eighth grade science classes in an urban, desegregated middle school in the eastern United States. My purpose in this research was to determine how similarities or differences in the participation structures of the two classes affected successful participation by students. Videotaping, interviews with participants who watched some of these tapes and observation records together provided a corpus of data from which a description of the structure of participation was established. In the methodology, a repeated sequence of taping and analysis, an attempt was made to follow the principles which Mehan (1978, p. 36) calls "retrievability of data, exhaustiveness of data treatment, convergence between the researchers' and participants' perspectives on events, and analysis at the interactional level." The basic data used in the analysis was the verbal interaction of the participants in both classes.

In this paper data from only one of the two classes in the original study is discussed. The paper is organized into three parts: (1) a brief description of the class and its members; (2) a presentation of the model of Posing the Problem, Feeling Around, Redirection, Finding the Problem; (3) a discussion of the strategy of metaphrasing and examples of its enactment. Some implications about the use of this strategy in situations where there is conflict created by sociocultural differences will also be discussed.

Description of the Class

Mr. Andrews' science class consisted of approximately 26 students: six white, two Asian, and eighteen black girls and boys. Mr. Andrews himself was a white male in his thirties who dressed casually and talked about himself as a "strong authority figure." Mr. Andrews was one of four teachers from different disciplines in the Alternative Program II. The Alternative Program II is one of two choices students in this middle school have when they enter the sixth grade. Alternative I is a traditionally structured class; Alternative II is distinguished from Alternative I by the type of choices teachers make of activities to meet the science objectives set for the entire school system. For example, one of the activities for the students in Mr. Andrews' class was the writing of research papers which included designing their own hypotheses and meeting the same stringent research guidelines that would be applied in high school and college. Admission to the Alternative Program II was through an application process, and the choice had to be endorsed by each student's parents. According to a representative of the administration of this school, a student's grades were not the chief criterion for admittance.

Over the course of the nine-week plus observation period, Mr. Andrews and his students were involved in several different work contexts. They reviewed the metric system and units of measurement; they studied lab equipment and its functions; they studied different forms of energy, simple and compound machines and the principles involved in their use. The students and the teacher worked with a physical science textbook, and much of their participation consisted of completing written word problems in their textbooks and then displaying the answers and the procedure used to complete the problems on a blackboard at the front of the room. The teacher was usually involved in directing the organization of activities. Mr. Andrews said that his chief objectives were teaching problem-solving skills which could be transferred to all types of problems and integrating communication skills from all disciplines. To accomplish these objectives he treated each task as a problem to be solved, and his verbal exchanges with students involved much deduction.

Mr. Andrews characterized the students in his class as being "all leaders, some more open-minded than others." He emphasized that the tasks selected and the opportunities provided for verbal interaction gave a quality of flexibility to the structure of participation in his class. Some students agreed with Mr. Andrews about this quality of flexibility. However, there were more students who expressed frustration with the teacher's contribution to the structure of participation.

The students whose names appear in the transcript excerpts in this paper are among those who were frequently taking part in verbal exchanges with Mr. Andrews. These students had different relationships with their teacher. Brit and Denise were two white female students who often worked together, consistently participating with success yet seldom volunteering to display their work on the board. Alice was a black female student who often acted as the teacher, assisting and evaluating student work from the teacher's vantage point — a desk at the front of the room. Sharon and Betty were two black female students who were successful in accomplishing their work and whose classroom participation was frequently marked by comments about the teacher's style of instruction. Tara was a black female student who often volunteered to participate and earnestly applied herself to accomplishing work. Sometimes she was impulsive in her responses and made errors which seemed to surprise the teacher and her classmates. Sonny was a black female student who was less successful in accomplishing homework and who seldom contributed to the class by displaying completed problems at the blackboard.

The students who are participants in the verbal exchanges presented here were all females. I did not intend to exclude males, but the fact was that female students were more numerous and more verbally active in this class. The verbal data from the males is extremely limited.

A Model for Structuring Verbal Participation

Participants in classroom lessons contribute to structuring classroom participation through the use of complementary interaction strategies (Mehan, 1978; Ludwig, 1978). As previously mentioned, the mechanism which structures the use of these strategies is called Posing the Problem, Feeling Around, Redirection, Finding the Problem. In my original study I found that student and teacher verbal behavior seems to follow this pattern — a sequence of four social contexts (Erickson and Shultz, 1977) — in exchanging information and in changing participation roles in the communication of curriculum content.

This pattern functions as a turn-taking mechanism in that each shift to a different time of interaction is marked by a change in speakers and anticipates the use of specific sets of verbal strategies from the participants. The whole sequence may be repeated each time there is a new focus question and the end of the sequence corresponds to the production of an answer to the focus question, whether by a student or by the teacher. The interpretation of social behavior in each time of interaction is negotiated as the situation warrants. Because enough participants in the study came to share information about how to act in each time of interaction the same kinds of verbal behaviors occurred repeatedly. I was thus able to abstract a framework which described the participants' tacit knowledge of how to exchange information about expectation and the matching interpretation of action.

Since Posing the Problem and Finding the Problem involves an exchange of information about interpretation and expectation, I found that analyzing instances of whole sequences would yield information about participation standards for task, interaction, and conceptual competence, as well as information about the complementary nature of student and teacher strategies. When exchanges ran smoothly, the sequence was resolved in its fundamental form. When there was a break in the exchange, the sequence became stuck in Redirection or Feeling Around. When an answer to the focus question was not forthcoming, the sequence would sometimes be abandoned for a new beginning and a reformulation, or a new question.

While analyzing sequences which were not smoothly resolved, I found that students used Feeling Around time to comment about or to translate the process of negotiating standards of participation. Metaphrasing was discovered to be an "improvisational" verbal strategy (Mehan, 1978) aimed at repairing the break in the complementary nature of teacher-student verbal action. This point will be discussed more fully in the next section. First, however, I will describe the identifying features of these four times of interaction and present two transcript excerpts which show how this model works to structure verbal participation.

Posing the Problem. Posing the Problem is a time in which a question or a statement about the focus of an exchange is presented by either student or teacher. The speaking turn may be in a one-to-one exchange between the teacher and a student, between two students, or between the teacher and the whole class. Mr. Andrews frequently said to his students: "I have a question" or "Does anyone see anything wrong with that?" These were cues that it was Posing the Problem time.

In initiating a time of Posing the Problem, students frequently asked for teacher assistance in clarifying a standard of social behavior or a task requirement. Posing the Problem required some kind of response from persons involved in the exchange. If no response was forthcoming, if the response was incorrect or only partially correct, or if the response was correct and was to be incorporated into the focus of another exchange, Posing the Problem led to a time of Redirection. Sometimes after the teacher enacted the time of Posing the Problem, a student responded to the question or the task requirement with a comment about its difficulty and an indication of his inability to accomplish the task. Then Posing the Problem led to a time of Feeling Around.

Feeling Around. When students expressed lack of knowledge, lack of direction, disagreement with the teacher's strategy, or frustration with the teacher's expectations, they enacted a time of Feeling Around. This interaction time has a noticeable decentering effect, pulling the attention of students (and sometimes the teacher) from the focus question and providing no contribution to the production of an answer to the question. Sometimes Feeling Around occurred when two students were working together and sometimes when a student was engaged in an exchange with the teacher. A student speaking in Feeling Around did not always elicit a verbal response from the teacher. Mr. Andrews occasionally argued with the student about the student's comment; frequently he ignored the comment; sometimes he gave a negative evaluation of the student who made the comment. The teacher's response seemed to be negotiated situationally and was apparently related to his regard for the student who had initiated the time of interaction. When metaphrasing occurred in Feeling Around, it served different functions and frequently signalled a break in the exchange of teacher-student verbal interaction.

Redirection. Redirection is a time of verbal interaction in which the teacher or a student attempts to organize the efforts of particular participants to answer the focus question. Redirection may come in the form of evaluations only, or of evaluation combined with any of these statements of information: additional information about task requirements, additional information about conceptual requirements, and clarification of the teacher's or the student's expectations for performance. When students are unable to meet the teacher's expectations for performance (when their answers are unacceptable or when they ask for clarifying and modifying information), the teacher may initiate this Redirection time. When students work together and their verbal interaction is organized in this same general sequence, Redirection involves an exchange of information which will help them accomplish the task. When Redirection is completed, the time of Finding the Problem may be enacted.

Finding the Problem. Finding the Problem is a time of interaction in which there is a resolution both of the focus of the exchange and the sequence which organizes it. Either students or the teacher may take speaking turns in Finding the Problem. Activities in which Finding the Problem was seen were taking tests, writing problems on the blackboard, reading answers from a textbook, volunteering answers to the teacher's questions, and students' giving each other the answer. As has been said, students may get help in Finding the Problem from the teacher's or another student's speaking turn in the time of Redirection. When students work together, success in finding the problem may depend on the actions of fellow classmates. When students are engaged in an exchange with the teacher, they must meet the teacher's expectations of task, interaction, and conceptual competence in order to find the problem.

The following examples illustrate the structuring of verbal interaction in this model.

Example 1: This exchange is from a lesson about the definition of the word "observation." Mr. Andrews indicated that he wanted the students to arrive at a workable, operational definition of the scientific terms they would be using in their classwork, and "observation" was one of those terms. Mr. Andrews threw a silver-colored cube to a student across the room from his desk and introduced Posing the Problem with a question which served to focus the exchange for the whole class: "What observations can you make?"

All the lines of verbal behavior in this exchange are identified as to the times that they represent in the sequence structuring participation.

Mr. Andrews: What observations can you make?	*Posing the Problem* 1
Student: It was in the air.	*Finding the Problem* 2
Mr. Andrews: How did you know if you didn't see the air?	*Posing the Problem* 3
(Students discuss this among themselves.)	
Tara: I observed it was traveling at a certain speed.	*Finding the Problem* 4
Lin: You put your arm in a certain position.	*Finding the Problem* 5
Mr. Andrews: Let's get back to speed.	*Redirection* 6
Speed in reference to what?	*Posing the Problem* 7
Tara: Line.	*Finding the Problem* 8
Mr. Andrews: Speed in reference to line?	*Posing the Problem* 9
No. In reference to a starting point or another body.	*Redirection* 10

Mr. Andrews' initial question was directed to the whole class, rather than to a particular student. This indicated that the teacher expected a response from the students in general. By using the word "observations" in the plural, Mr. Andrews indicated that there might be several responses which would be appropriate, and that Finding the Problem in this case involved giving several "observations." The teacher's question gave students information about his expectations for their participation.

Mr. Andrews responded differently to students' Finding the Problem responses, and this affected student participation. For example, when a student answered in line 2, "It was in the air," the teacher used a time of Posing the Problem to determine the basis of the student's observation. In presenting alternative responses to this new focus question the students explained that the only way they knew there was air was because they were able to breathe. This side discussion ceased when Tara returned to the time of Finding the Problem, answering the original question, line 4. Both Tara and Lin (line 5) provided observations that seemed to meet the teacher's expectations.

Mr. Andrews contributed to the structure of participation by initiating Redirection in line 6, returning student attention to Tara's answer about the speed of the object. This Redirection indicated to the students Posing the Problem was near. In fact, Mr. Andrews established another focus question in line 7: "Speed in reference to what?" When Tara's answer (Finding the Problem) indicated that she did not understand how speed is determined, Mr. Andrews repeated her answer. Then he evaluated Tara's answer combining this with information which clarified his standards for the correct answer.

This exchange between Mr. Andrews and his students showed that the interaction runs smoothly when participants remain within the sequence of times of interaction and when there is a match between the teacher's expectation of participation and student interpretation of that expectation. When there is an error or an answer which is unclear to the teacher, the time of Redirection is enacted to smooth the interaction and the production of the correct answer. In the next excerpt, there is a break in the exchange of interaction strategies which influenced the structure of participation so that the verbal exchange does not proceed as smoothly.

Example 2: This exchange comes from a lesson reviewing homework problems which required students to convert answers from millimeters and centimeters to meters. Mr. Andrews used an example from among those presented by the students as a basis for testing their knowledge of the principles involved in making these conversions.

Mr. Andrews: I've got a question.		1
How come 5500 mm is the same thing as 550 cm?	Posing the Problem	2
Here the problem is 550 cm and here the problem is 5500 mm.		3
You mean to tell me that 550 cm is the same thing as 5500 mm?	Posing the Problem	4
Students: Yes.	Finding the Problem	5
Mr. Andrews: Why?	Posing the Problem	6
Betty: Why do you want us to tell you? You know!	Feeling Around	7
(The teacher does not respond and there is a pause.)		
Tara: A centimeter is larger than a millimeter.	Finding the Problem	8
Mr. Andrews: Why are cm larger than mm?	Posing the Problem	9
I don't know how much larger until you tell me.	Redirection	10
Be precise.	Redirection	11
Say what you mean.		12

Mr. Andrews initiated this exchange by giving a cue to the coming enactment of the time of Posing the Problem. This cue — "I've got a question" — is part of the teacher's repertoire of strategies for focusing attention on a problem. Posing the Problem actually began when the teacher presented the focus question: "How come 5500 mm is the same thing as 550 cm?" Mr. Andrews frequently clarified his question as part of his contribution to Posing the Problem. This he did in line 3, before he rephrased his question to indicate the proper form for the students' responses. His question — "You mean to tell me that 550 cm is the same as 5500 mm" — showed that he was expecting students to tell him about the relationship between millimeters and centimeters.

Many students chimed in to answer his question by saying, "Yes" (Finding the Problem). Mr. Andrews indicated his interest in hearing the reason for this relationship, and his question, "Why?" presented a new focus question which narrowed the range of the answer he expected from students. This exchange was characterized by a flexibility in turn allocation. That is, there did not seem to be any restriction on the number of students who could speak at once. In the confusion which followed, Betty took the opportunity to speak out about her frustration with the teacher's strategy for structuring participation. Instead of using the time of Find the Problem (indicated by the teacher's question) Betty enacted Feeling Around time, and this disrupted the exchange between the teacher and other students. Betty used metaphrasing in Feeling Around to criticize the teacher's questions when she said, "Why do you want us to tell you? You know!"

Betty's question did not elicit a response from the teacher, but did lead some students away from the Focus Exchange between the teacher and other students. The number of student contributions dropped off. Others continued to respond as Tara did, contributing to Finding the Problem (line 8). Her answer, "A centimeter is larger than a millimeter," reestablished a complementary relationship with Mr. Andrews' questions. The teacher was then able to evaluate Tara's answer, which he did by incorporating it into a new focus question which clarified his expectations of student responses (line 9). This was followed by initiating Redirection (Lines 10-12), in which the teacher explained his evaluation of Tara's answer and provided further guidelines for successful participation: "Be precise. Say what you mean."

This excerpt shows the confusion and disorientatation created by difficulties in accommodating to the teacher's expectations for participation and shows how students can use metaphrasing to try to make sense of new or ambiguous contextual information. In the next section, metaphrasing will be described in detail and other transcript portions will be presented to illustrate its functioning within the model.

Metaphrasing: An Improvisational Strategy

A verbal strategy called metaphrasing was used by both black and white students to comment on the teacher's expectations for interactional competence and academic performance. Metaphrasing, a term taken from the *Webster's New World*

Dictionary, means: "To translate, especially literally, to change the wording of" (1964, p. 925). When observing verbal interaction in classroom lessons, one can recognize metaphrasing as a verbal comment by the student about the configuration of verbal and nonverbal behaviors in the negotiation of expectations of task, interaction, and conceptual competence.

I call this strategy an improvisational one because it seems to be a variation on a theme developed by Mehan (1978). He found that teachers use original methods of restoring the order of turn-taking in classroom lessons when there is a breakdown in the synchrony of the structuring of participation. He called such original methods Improvisational Strategies. The term *improvisational* indicates that someone is taking whatever is available to him or her and creating something new from it. In Mr. Andrews' class it was observed that when students were confused or frustrated by new or ambiguous information about how to behave they used the contextual features available to them to make sense of deviations from the normal order. Some contextual features which functioned as indicators of appropriate behavior were: previous experience with the task; previous experience with the teacher's strategy for structuring participation; knowledge of the teacher's expectations; knowledge of their classmates' abilities. The activity of interpreting these features comes to the surface, in metaphrasing, as a verbal comment which makes the individual's view of the social context explicit.

Metaphrasing seems to be initiated by students during Feeling Around time, which seems an appropriate context for the expression of an observation about the relationship between students and teacher. Both students and teacher seem to accept the use of this strategy during this time.

When metaphrasing occurs in Feeling Around, this time of interaction seems to serve as a "juncture" in the pattern of Posing the Problem — Finding the Problem. A reorientation of the participants occurs (Erickson and Shultz, 1977; Mehan, 1978) in which there is at least a partial shift of attention away from the focus exchange which involves the teacher and other students, toward the student who is metaphrasing. Since metaphrasing does not always elicit a teacher response, it sometimes divides the participants so that at least some students appear to draw together in mutual support. There is a shift in attitude and attention, with slight movements toward the student who is metaphrasing. Students remain in their seats but tend to look at, turn toward, or discuss the comment with that classmate, particularly those close by the speaker.

During a lesson the verbal exchanges can move from Posing the Problem to Finding the Problem via Redirection, with no Feeling Around time. Then it seems that the participants are successfully complementing each other, exchanging information about interpretation and expectation through strategies which make the communication of curriculum content proceed smoothly. When Feeling Around is enacted, it is a sign of a break in this exchange. This break informs teachers and other students of the difficulties in meeting standards for successful participation.

To understand how the metaphrasing strategy can function in the organization of classroom participation, it is necessary to consider a particular metaphrase in the light of the relationship between the participants in the exchange, the participants to whom it refers, and the information it contains about behavior in certain situations. During the research observations, most interactional work in Mr. Andrews' class took place when he involved the entire class in a task. Thus it was possible to locate focus exchanges involving the teacher and some students in most class periods. I was able to identify three functions of metaphrasing, each conveying information about the relationship between students and the teacher with regards to his expectations for participation.

Function 1: Identifying the perspectives of participants in the focus exchange

> *Topic:* What students and the teacher know about a task and about appropriate behavior in certain work contexts.

> *Relationship to the Focus Exchange:* Metaphrasing occurs outside the focus exchange, but simultaneous to it, during Feeling Around, without eliciting a reponse from the teacher.

Function 2: Identifying difficulties in accommodating to the teacher's expectations for participation

> *Topic:* Reasons why the teacher uses certain participation strategies rather than others and the probable effect of his expectations on successful participation.

> *Relationship to the Focus Exchange:* Metaphrasing may interrupt the sequence of Posing the Problem, Finding the Problem in a Focus Exchange, indicating that the teacher should clarify his expectations in a time of Redirection or that he should reformulate the focus question in a time of Posing the Problem.

Function 3: Rehearsing behavior standards — anticipating the teacher's role or expectations — to guide future interaction, making decisions about what to do in a particular social situation

> *Topic:* The teacher's previous responses to similar situations.

> *Relationship to the Focus Exchange:* Metaphrasing may occur outside the focus exchange, simultaneous to it, or without the existence of a focus exchange. It entails a totally different question from that which is the current focus of the teacher-student exchange and therefore, does not involve the teacher at all. It is a student-student exchange and assumes knowledge of the topic.

The following examples from transcripts show the different functions of metaphrasing and the relationship of metaphrasing to the model for structuring participation.

Example 1, Function 1: After Tara displayed her problem on the board, Mr. Andrews asked her (focus exchange) about her reasons for completing the problem in a certain way. Sonny and Alice used metaphrasing to identify the perspectives taken by Tara and Mr. Andrews.

Sonny: He knew what she meant.	*Metaphrasing*	*Feeling Around* 1
Mr. Andrews: Why are you changing it?		*Posing the Problem* 2
Tara: It's dealing with grams.		*Finding the Problem* 3

Sonny: He's mixing people up.	*Metaphrasing*	*Feeling Around*	4
Mr. Andrews: How's that?		*Posing the Problem*	5
Tara: Add up your ratio and divide by 20.		*Finding the Problem*	6
Mr. Andrews: Why are you dividing?		*Posing the Problem*	7
Tara: To get your ratio, to get your unit.		*Finding the Problem*	8
Mr. Andrews: You got to know what one unit is equal to.		*Redirection*	9
Alice: He's trying to act like a student and pretend he doesn't know nothing.	*Metaphrasing*	*Feeling Around*	10

Both students used metaphrasing during Feeling Around without eliciting a response from the teacher. Mr. Andrews was involved in the focus exchange. Metaphrasing was placed outside the focus exchange although it seemed to occur simultaneously. All three lines of metaphrasing seem to fit the function of identifying the perspectives of the participants in the focus exchange, although Sonny and Alice viewed the perspectives differently.

Sonny seemed to take the side of Tara by making statements about the effect of the teacher's instructional strategy on Tara and other students, as she saw it. Sonny's metaphrasing — "He knew what she meant" and "He's mixing people up" — indicated her conviction that the teacher was confusing students who already knew the answer. Sonny took the perspective of the student in the focus exchange, and her metaphrase is a statement of what she thinks Tara knows about the task and how to behave when working at the board.

Alice said of the teacher's structuring activities, "He's trying to act like a student and pretend he doesn't know nothing." This indicated that Mr. Andrews and Alice share quite a bit of knowledge about the structure of class participation. In fact Mr. Andrews did try to take the role of a student, while encouraging his students to act as if they were teachers.

The metaphrases of both students show the relationship of their comments to the focus exchange. Sonny and Alice spoke of the teacher and Tara in the third person, as if they were not present. They both addressed their comments to their classmates in an effort to establish a mutual understanding of the structure of participation and the purpose of the teacher's strategies.

Example 2, Function 2: This excerpt comes from a lesson on automotive systems. The students have previously had a lesson with another teacher (also a member of Alternative Program II) on this same material, when Mr. Andrews was absent. When he returned, he reviewed the content with them. During the lesson, it became apparent to the students that the two teachers had slightly different expectations with respect to the student's knowledge of the details of the same material. When the students found that a number of their answers were not meeting the expectations of Mr. Andrews, they defended them by saying that the other teacher had approved them. When this conflict had occurred a number of times, Sharon commented about the effect of the teacher's evaluation of answers and the difficulty in determining the teacher's expectations for the right answers.

Sharon: You are finding something wrong *Feeling Around* 1
with everything. He hasn't agreed with us
since we came in here. *Metaphrasing*   *Feeling Around* 2

Mr. Andrews: The point is not to agree
but to understand what's happening. *Redirection* 3

Sharon's use of the strategy of metaphrasing seems to fit the criteria which describe Function 2. The topic of the comment is the effect of the teacher's expectations on successful participation; the function is identifying the difficulties in accommodating to both teachers' expectations for participation. The metaphrasing interrupted the sequence of Posing the Problem, Finding the Problem, informing the teacher of a break in the complementary nature of the interaction and leading the teacher into Redirection to explain and clarify his attempts to structure participation.

Sharon's metaphrasing came after a comment addressed to the teacher about the conflict between his expectations and those of the previous teacher: "You are finding something wrong with everything." In her metaphrasing she referred to the teacher in the third person and seemed to be addressing her classmates, using "us" and "we": "He hasn't agreed with us since we came in here." Sharon's comment seemed to be intended to draw students together in restructuring the participation. In this instance metaphrasing did not lead to restructuring. However, the teacher did explain his intentions, and this seemed to satisfy some students.

Example 3, Function 3: In this verbal exchange, Brit and Denise discussed the assignments for the coming week with another student. They were trying to decide whether or not to ask the teacher for information about the work.

Brit: What do we do for Monday? *Posing the Problem* 1

Student: Tuesday we got a test, man. *Finding the Problem* 2
Monday you have to put it (homework) up for show.
Why don't you ask him? *Posing the Problem* 3
(referring to the teacher)

Brit: I won't ask him 'cause he'll tell us
and then I can say on Monday — *Finding the Problem* 4

Brit and Denise: I didn't know you
had to do that. *Metaphrasing*   *Feeling Around* 5

Denise: He doesn't fall for that anymore. *Metaphrasing*   *Feeling Around* 6

Brit and Denise used metaphrasing for rehearsal, anticipating their own and the teacher's roles in a focus exchange about being prepared for a test. The topic of the metaphrase is previous experience with similar situations and the teacher's previous responses. The metaphrasing occurred completely apart from any focus exchange which might have been taking place in the room at the time and assumed that the students shared knowledge about exchanging information in this social context.

The anticipation of Mr. Andrews' role by Denise — "He doesn't fall for that anymore" — expresses an awareness of the teacher's expectations of student responsibility. This exchange may help Brit and Denise decide what to do to avoid errors and subsequent negative evaluation by the teacher. Brit and Denise decided that the teacher would not accept ignorance as an excuse and they proceeded to check with him for details about their assignment.

In the nine-week observation period, I found 20 instances of metaphrasing. The number of instances of metaphrasing according to function and involvement of Black and White students is illustrated in Table 12.1.

TABLE 12.1   Number of Black and White Students Involved in Instances of Metaphrasing According to Each of Three Functions

Function	Number of Instances of Metaphrasing			Number of Different Students Involved in Metaphrasing	
	With Black Students	With White Students	Total	Different Black Students	Different White Students
Identifying Perspectives	8	1	9	5	1
Identifying Difficulties	6	1	7	5	1
Rehearsing Behavior Standards	1	3	4	1	2
Total	15	5	20	11	4

As Table 12.1 shows, of the nine instances illustrating Function 1, eight involved black students and one involved a white student. In a total of seven examples of Function 2, six involved black students and one involved a white student. Of the four instances of Function 3, one involved a black student, three involved white students. The table shows that both black and white students used metaphrasing for all three functions. Overall, black students used metaphrasing more than white students. (There are 15 instances of metaphrasing by black students and five instances by white students.) The frequency of black student use of metaphrasing for Function 1 and 2 contributed to this overall difference.

Eleven black students were involved in instances of metaphrasing. The same group of three students (Sharon, Alice, and Christina) used metaphrasing for Functions 1 and 2, sometimes more than once. Four other black students contributed to the totals for Functions 1, 2, and 3. Four white students used metaphrasing for all three functions. (Brit was a white student who was involved in more than one instance of metaphrasing for Function 3.)

Considering the small total number of instances of metaphrasing that were found (20), it is important to be cautious in drawing conclusions about the differences in the use of this strategy by black and white students. In Mr. Andrews' class there were three times as many black (18) as white students (six), which may account for some of the differences in the number of times black and white students were involved in metaphrasing. The use of metaphrasing for all three functions by both black and white students indicates that they seemed to share the knowledge that the structure of participation in this class permitted this use of language.

At the same time, questions should be raised about apparent cultural differences in the more frequent choice of metaphrasing for Functions 1 and 2 by black students and for Function 3 by white students. Function 3 differs from Functions 1 and 2 in its concern with rehearsing standards to act appropriately. Functions 1 and 2, which are concerned with identifying perspectives and difficulties, do not necessarily entail the student's ability to act upon this knowledge. While there is no evidence to suggest that the black students using metaphrasing for Functions 1 and 2 were unable to rehearse standards, it is clear they do so less frequently. Why does this happen? Were black students unwilling to discuss standards among themselves in class? Did they see more need to focus the attention of their classmates and the teacher on difficulties in accommodating expectations and on conflicts in perspectives? Were these students unwilling to cooperate within the structure of participation and, therefore, using metaphrasing to disrupt the synchrony of interaction and to avoid the task?

It is unlikely that metaphrasing was a strategy used by a particular group of students to deter the class from completing tasks or to avoid these tasks. Both successful and less successful black and white students used this strategy for all three functions. Those black students who did not use metaphrasing for Function 3 were no less effective in avoiding errors over the nine weeks than those students who did. Since black students — interviewed with white students while watching videotapes of their class — knew and described similar class behavior standards, it is likely that these students would have been able to rehearse the same standards if necessary during classroom lessons. Yet there was a difference in who spoke about these standards during class.

Some indication of the reason for this difference may be found in the interviews with black and white students. Both groups of students agreed on the way to be successful in meeting their teacher's expectations for participation. However, there was disagreement among students about whether it was worthwhile to point out difficulties and raise questions in class. Alice said that getting into discussions with the teacher was one way students learned about tasks and whether they knew the answers. On the other hand Cary, a white student, said that she was unwilling to raise the issue of difficulties in meeting Mr. Andrews' expectations. Cary claimed that when she did ask questions Mr. Andrews often told her that the class had been through that and she must not have been listening. Sharon agreed that the teacher was not always approachable for questions, even though he told the class that he liked a student who asked good questions. Sharon said that she would rather risk embarrassment by the teacher in order to ask questions, "cause you have to learn it somehow and after he's done his little act, he'll explain it."

Cary's suggestion that some students may have been keeping quiet in class to avoid embarrassment by the teacher indicates one reason why white students used metaphrasing less frequently than Blacks for Functions 1 and 2. Even though black and white students knew that the teacher approved of asking questions and getting into discussions about task requirements and behavior standards, it was apparent that certain black students were less reluctant to bring up issues of difficulties during classroom lessons. When they found it necessary, some black students did so frequently, thus fulfilling Functions 1 and 2.

Summary and Implications

This paper has presented an interactional model which describes the structuring of verbal participation in the lessons in an eighth grade science class. It was found that both black and white students in this class used a strategy called metaphrasing in commenting about the negotiation of standards for participation. This verbal strategy occurred in an interactional time called Feeling Around, part of the sequence of Posing the Problem, Feeling Around, Redirection, Finding the Problem. The use of the strategy signified a break in the complementarity of teacher-student perspectives on participation.

Three functions of metaphrasing were identified: (1) identifying the perspectives of participants in the focus exchange; (2) identifying difficulties in accommodating to the teacher's expectations for participation; and (3) rehearsing behavior standards to guide future interaction with the teacher. Metaphrasing was found to be taking place (1) outside the focus exchange but simultaneous to it; (2) within the focus exchange, where it operated as a sign that the sequence of times was breaking down; and (3) outside of, and unrelated to, any focus exchange.

The evidence that both black and white students used metaphrasing in Mr. Andrews' class indicates that students were knowledgeable about the opportunities for using language to comment on the ongoing interaction in classroom lessons. Mr. Andrews informed students that a certain amount of flexibility in their use of language and in their contributions to the structure of participation was permitted, through the use of participation strategies reflecting his objectives for the class and his expectations of student abilities. Although many students had worked with Mr. Andrews before, work and social contexts which Kochman (1972) might identify as "low contexts" still did occur during classroom lessons. Confused about expectations for their behavior when these contexts emerged, both black and white students found it desirable — although not always effective — to use language to structure their own participation. Therefore features of the participation structure of this class contributed to the possibility of using metaphrasing.

These same features may have contributed to cultural differences in the frequency of use of metaphrasing for all three functions. Black students more frequently used this strategy to point out difficulties in meeting expectations and to identify perspectives of participants in the focus exchange. White students more frequently used metaphrasing to rehearse behavior standards. There is no evidence to suggest that either black or white students were unable to use metaphrasing for other functions. However, many students were concerned with the teacher's response to their raising questions and making the kinds of comments indicative of Functions 1 and 2, even when they thought these comments were necessary to participate successfully. Certain black students were less concerned about this response and were less reluctant to risk using metaphrasing for Functions 1 and 2. This may explain the more frequent use of metaphrasing for Functions 1 and 2 by black students.

Considering the complexity of classroom participation and the difficulties in monitoring one's own behavior in moment-by-moment interactions, how is it possible to use metaphrasing to help improve teacher-student communication of participation standards? It seems that if teachers create opportunities for metaphrasing to occur, then students should learn to use it to express their difficulties in accommodating to ambiguous or new standards for behavior. If teachers listen to the messages in metaphrases, they might be able to identify students who are unsuccessful participants because they have not learned the standards for appropriate behavior in the classroom.

There has been much concern that a student's use of language in the classroom and in other school contexts may adversely affect his or her relationships with persons who make key decisions about "life chances" (Mehan, 1978). Encouraging the use of such improvisational strategies as metaphrasing in the classroom particularly when there are sociocultural differences among students or between students and the teacher, may be one means of allowing students to take more responsibility in structuring classroom participation and of helping them to develop skills transferable to other events and group situations.

13

SOCIAL CONTEXTS FOR ETHNIC BORDERS
AND SCHOOL FAILURE*

R. P. McDermott
Kenneth Gospodinoff

I. Introduction

This paper considers the recently popular claim that many minority children fail in school because there is a mismatch between their procedures or codes for making sense with each other and the codes used by their teachers who generally come from a socially more powerful group. In most claims, the emphasis is on the fact that the minority and majority group members have different languages, dialects, gestural systems, or interactional rhythms, etc., that they accordingly produce much miscommunication with each other, and that in the classroom such miscommunication leads to alienation and failure. This paper is different in that, while we do not deny that communicative code differences exist, we emphasize that they are secondary to the political relations between members of the different groups both in the classroom and in the larger community. We claim that constant miscommunication between teachers and their pupils is no accident, that it, in fact, represents an interactional accomplishment on the parts of all those involved given the conditions under which they are asked to come together either to teach or to learn how to read and write.

Primarily, we offer an analysis of only a few moments of some minority children miscommunicating with their teacher and failing in school. But we offer these moments as a systematic part of the contexts in which the teacher and the children are immersed. The most immediate context is that of the children and

*The same paper was originally published in Aaron Wolfgang (ed.), *Nonverbal Behavior: Application and Cultural Implications,* New York: Academic Press, 1979.

the teacher trying to understand each other while face-to-face during their reading lessons. At this level, everyone appears to make sense in that they simultaneously act upon and respond to each other's behavior in systematic ways. In terms of the organization of a given piece of face-to-face behavior, what appears to be a miscommunication may be a carefully arranged and sensible way for all the participants to proceed, given the interactional and pedagogical problems confronted by members of the classroom. We present an analysis of such a case in Section III.

By itself, the detailed analysis of the good sense of a miscommunication will leave the reader confused. What is needed is an account of how the classroom came to be organized in such a way that the development of codes for miscommunicating came to be a sensible adaptation. The usual account of miscommunication and school failure simply in terms of communicative code differences does not deal with this difficult task. Instead, it usually is assumed that people from different groups are naturally different and that their differences can be in the long run irremedial; with such an assumption in hand, it is not necessary to show how people develop vested interests in being different from one another. Our point is that without such vested interests being created from one moment to the next, people usually develop metacommunicative procedures for altering their communicative codes in order to make sense of each other. When communicative differences become irremedial, it is because there are sound political or economic reasons for their being so. No matter how hard the dominant group is trying to equalize access to resources, no matter how downtrodden the minority group, every group is somehow getting a maximum payoff, given their starting place within a political economy.

In order to give this point some substance, in Section II, we concentrate on the political circumstances in which people alternatively deemphasize, emphasize, and even create communicative code differences. And in Section IV, we attempt to sketch out the higher order contexts in terms of which the sensible, but ultimately damaging, miscommunication analyzed in Section III came to be, in the short run at least, adaptive for all. By way of conclusion, we suggest that in the long run such arrangements are maladaptive in that they have consequences that in no way maximize the potentials for the population under analysis, and we raise questions about the worth and morality of school systems that are geared to sorting young children into successful and unsuccessful categories instead of being geared to socializing everyone for a maximally rich experience of the world.

The setting for our analysis is a first-grade classroom in a comparatively successful school in a suburb not far beyond the New York City limits. School failure by minority group children was quite visible in this classroom. Shortly after the start of the school year, most children were ranked into one of three groups on the basis of the teacher's analysis of their reading abilities. The top group consisted of white children, primarily Italian and Jewish. The bottom, or least literate, group consisted of three Puerto Rican, one black and finally two white children, one of whom was considered the group's best reader and destined to move into a higher group, the other of whom was considered brain damaged. There was one other Puerto Rican boy who was originally assigned to the bottom group, but who had been put out for being too disruptive. Thereafter, the boy had no reading group, and he wandered around the classroom causing trouble. The one other minority child in the class belonged to the middle reading group.

So five of six minority children are in the bottom group or in no group at all, despite the efforts of a teacher who was considered excellent by her peers, and incidentally, by us. The teacher of this class gets the most difficult first graders into her room each year and is often successful in teaching them the basics of classroom behavior and reading. However, in the year under analysis, not all the children emerged with such survival skills, and by the end of the second year in school, two Puerto Rican children and one white boy, all from the bottom group, had been reassigned to special schools for various functional handicaps, namely, for being "slow," "emotionally disturbed," and "brain damaged." Essentially, the children were sent to special schools because their teacher found them impossible to work with in the classroom. The other children in the group were not doing too much better in that they were not learning to read up to grade level, a *sine qua non* of institutional success, but at least they had escaped placement (for the moment) in a slowed down program.

The process just described is in no way unusual to schools. Selection for failure is common in many kinds of social institutions (Auerswald, 1971; Moore, 1975). There are some who have mistakenly used ethnicity to explain this phenomenon in schools. The claim is that there is something about a child's membership in a certain group that is predictive and causally related to the child's success or failure in school. Two basic versions of this argument stand out. One is that there is something wrong with the children; because they are biologically incapable, cognitively or linguistically deficient, or motivationally misdirected, the children are unable to keep up in school. The other is that the children are merely different and misunderstood. Space does not allow for a discussion of the first set of theories, but there is good reason to reject each of them on the grounds that they are neither logically coherent nor descriptively adequate (Cole, Gay, Glick and Sharp, 1971; D'Andrade, 1973). Fortunately, the work showing the inadequacies of these theories is persuasive enough to allow us to direct our attention to the argument that minority children fail in school because they communicate differently and are accordingly unappreciated and misunderstood.

II. Ethnic Differences Do Not Cause Irremediable Miscommunication

According to the second set of arguments, which we call the communicative code account, members of minority groups do less well than others in school because the schools generally are staffed by majority group members who do not understand minority group children (more sophisticated versions of this argument point out that even when the schools are staffed by minority group members they are likely to behave in accordance with the majority group communicative code, resulting in the same sort of miscommunication taking place). This argument is most appealing when we consider large differences such as those that exist between a teacher who speaks only one language and students who speak only another. The case for the smaller systems of differences, i.e., systems of touching, spacing, gesturing, speaking rights, etc., can be argued along the same lines. People with different communicative codes may want the same things and work equally hard at achieving their goals, but, to the extent that they do not share codes for making sense with members of the dominant groups, they will misinterpret each other's behavior and eventually create unpleasant environments for each other. It is in such unpleasant environments that minority children begin to "act up" and become alienated from the teacher and the learning enterprise.

This stand is attractive. For one thing, it holds out great hope for the children; it assumes they can all do well in school if we could only build more sensitivity for communicative code differences into our teachers. It also has the advantage of not off-handedly condemning the teachers as incompetents or racists. Like all of us, they have had limited experiences with people in different cultures, and once they become sensitive to the codes of the children, they can be the helpful and loving teachers they no doubt would like to be.

As attractive as this stand is, we have been forced to conclude that it is much too simple. Certainly, when the communicative resources of two groups are different, the people will generate much miscommunication. But the question is why this keeps generating problems. Why do the people not repair the miscommunication? This line of thought leads to an even more difficult question, namely, why are there communicative codes at all? Increasingly, there is reason to take the position that different communicative codes represent political adaptations; in the course of talking or moving in one way rather than another, children and teachers are doing politics. If this is so, we all not only suffer from communicative conflicts, we help to make them. Our communicative codes, as persuasive and entrapping as they are, do not turn us into communicative robots incapable of coming to grips with other people simply because they communicate differently. The social world is subject to negotiation. If codes exist, it is because we all help create them in the very process of communicating. If codes are keeping us apart, it is because it is adaptive for us to do so, given the constraints imposed on our behavior in the social order constituted by the codes. Ways of speaking and moving harbor political systems that we all help to recreate with our every movement and utterance (Beck, 1975; Hymes, 1961, 1973; Labov, 1972a, b; Scheflen, 1973, 1974).

There are a number of reasons for understanding the communication problems between members of different groups as the accomplishments of people trying to get the most out of the political and economic contexts for their being brought together. We will briefly mention some examples from the growing literature on interethnic communication and then present a detailed analysis of a case of a child supposedly miscommunicating with his teacher. From the literature, three kinds of examples stand out: (1) there are cases in which members of different groups make an effort to move beyond a major communicative code difference, for example, a difference between two mutually unintelligible languages; (2) there are cases in which one would think it would be easy for members of different groups to put aside their communicative differences, the difference between dialects, for example, but they maintain them anyway in the face of differential institutional payoffs; and (3) there are cases in which members of different communities work hard at establishing communicative code differences in order to mark themselves off as coherent and often antagonist groups.

Before proceeding with the examples, we want to take care to point out that our position rests on some assumptions about the nature of ethnic groups and that these assumptions have proved helpful in explaining interethnic relations around the world. The case we are making for classrooms is manifested in many diverse situations in which groups of people find themselves at odds. In most cases, it has become clear that the differences between people are only incidentally a problem; the differences between people are as much a resource for mutual exploration and celebration as they are a resource for conflict (J. McDermott, 1976; R. McDermott, 1975). Our problem is not ethnicity, but ethnic borders. Our problem is not that people are different, but that the differences are made to make more of a difference than they must, that the differences are politicized into borders that define different kinds of people as antagonists in various realms of everyday life (Frake, ms.).

Barth (1969a,b) has articulated this view and shown how we must understand the ethnic identities of many people in terms of how these identities are related to the maximization of physical and economic security and/or identity enhancement in contrast to other available alternatives. Moerman (1965, 1968) has made the same point for groups in Northern Thailand. His point of departure was to try to answer the question, "Who are the Lue?" with a description of the behavior and attitudes of the Lue people. His job proved so difficult that he had to rephrase his question to when, where, why, and how are the Lue. The complexities of having a Lue identity could not be understood without a specification of the circumstances under which it made sense for the Lue to emphasize their Lue identity over the various alternative identities available to them. As we shall see, this phenomenon of identity switching in certain situations is not any less prevalent even in societies in which ethnic groups are divided by a clear physical marker such as skin color; for example, many Whites and Blacks in urban American cities have developed competencies for communicating and identifying with each other in certain situations in which racial differences are temporarily brushed aside.

1. The position that communicative codes do not form a simple exact calculus determinative of behavior is perhaps most available to us in the records of millions of immigrants who move to other lands and pick up new and diverse languages and customs in only a few years. Here the political circumstances for learning the ways of the people who control the resources of the new land is obvious. Sometimes, it is even necessary for immigrants to learn two languages, one of the poorer working-class people who surround them upon their entrance to the country, the other the language of the politically more dominant group. For example, the Italians who immigrated to the bilingual city of Montreal work with, live near, and intermarry with the French. But the majority of Italian parents send

their children to schools to learn English, which the parents feel is the language of the successful, a feeling they apparently share with both French and English speakers of Montreal (Boissevain, 1970; Frender and Lambert, 1973; Lambert, 1967). In New York City, Puerto Ricans are exposed mostly to Black neighbors and co-workers, and the children first become competent in Black language (Wolfram, 1973). Although Black English is useful in the most immediate politics of everyday life, in the long run the children are forced to learn a more standardized English in order to get by in the larger urban scene. The result in both these cases are populations with three different codes for their participation in the three different communities. People who do not become trilingual can suffer exclusion from certain institutions.

Along with their adoption of languages, immigrants and their children also make drastic shifts in their kinesic behavior. In a stunning effort, Efron (1941) long ago showed that the Jews and Italians of New York City altered their gestural patterns in accordance with the demands of the immediate situation. The same Jewish student who would barely gesticulate when he talked with his professors at Columbia University would be far more active the next day back in the Jewish community where he could wave his forearms and button-hole his friends without being considered conversationally aggressive.

Even without the extreme example of immigration, the social science literature is filled with accounts of people overcoming structurally complex communicative code differences in order to make sense of each other on certain occasions. The fascinating records of whole groups together generating pidgin and creole languages come from all parts of the world. Usually the processes are more complex than the "Me Tarzan, you Jane" model of pidginization, but this example serves the purpose of showing that when the circumstances are such that people must understand each other, they will find a way. Most often, such pidgins develop among different groups of people who have much interaction with each other in the market place of a third and more powerful group and, under such conditions, it is good to have a way of communicating with each other without becoming part of the dominating market society (DeCamp, 1971). Similar processes have been demonstrated on the kinesic level by Erickson (1975, 1976 and this volume), who has shown that members of different ethnic groups alter their communicative styles to fit "panethnic" groupings made up of various ethnic groups aligned according to the dictates of local politics; for example, Blacks and Puerto Ricans in Chicago would fall together against Irish, Poles, and Italians on one hand, and WASPs on the other.

2. The case of people's refusing to repair minor communicative code boundaries also makes the point that the divergence of communicative patterns into mutually exclusive codes must be understood in terms of their function in interaction and not simply in terms of structural differences. The differences between the vernacular English of many American Blacks or the creole English of many West Indians are minute compared to the differences between mutually unintelligible languages. Yet these smaller barriers to mutual intelligibility appear to be much more difficult to overcome in schools and other institutional settings (Caz-

den, et al., 1972; Craig, 1971). What makes a difference is the politicization of language and dialect differences in the schools in which the children are asked to learn.

In fact, some research efforts are beginning to show that dialect use by Black children in American schools actually increases as children proceed through school (Hall and Freedle, 1975; Labov, 1972a; Piestrup, 1973). Given the correlation between dialect use and success in school in numerous minority-dominant group settings, this is an important finding that can give us a rough sense for the social processes underlining the emergence of communicative code boundaries together with failing school records. Labov and Robins (1969) have shown, for example, that the use of dialect increases as peer-group participation increases and school performances decline. This result is further illustrated by Piestrup (1973) who found that in the first grades she analyzed, the Black children's use of dialect either stayed the same or soared in direct proportion to how much the children were hassled for their use of dialect. The more their speech was corrected, the more they used dialect, and in such classrooms, reading scores were low. In classrooms in which the children were allowed to express themselves and read orally in dialect, the use of dialect did not increase and their reading scores were higher, with many children above the norms.

The presence or absence of dialect in the children's speech is not the crucial determinant of successful communication in school. Rather, dialect appears to function as a focus for the relational work of the children and the teacher. If the teacher and the children are alienated from each other, their dialects will take center stage and the teacher and the children will battle each other about the proper way to speak. In this sense, the emergence of a dialect in each new generation of different minorities represents more than a passing on of a set of speaking skills. It also represents an active adaptation to conditions in classrooms across the country. And the conscious claiming of a dialect, or any other aspect of a communicative code, from a clenched fist to a particular kind of walk, represents a political activity, a statement of one's identity as a member of a particular community.

3. The point that communicative codes are not determinants of people's relations with each other, that they are in fact adaptations to the various relations between the people who use the codes, is most clearly made by cases in which a group invents a communicative code in order to build cohesion into the home community and to block out the surrounding communities (Halliday, 1976; Gmelch, 1976). The Pennsylvania Dutch (Amish) are a good example of people who work at keeping themselves different, and they specify these differences not only at the level of general values against modern life, but at the level of the minutiae of everyday communication, at the level of language and dress, right down to the kinds of hooks used to fasten their clothing together. Such communicative strategies can have an effect on classrooms. The code differences do not in and of themselves enhance or detract from the children's learning. But the work that the Amish do to make themselves different apparently does interfere with the children's performance in public schools, where they do not do well academically. But this same work apparently creates a communal learning environment in their own schools in which Amish children do well, even by the standards of state tests

(Hostetler and Huntington, 1971). These differential school results can only be understood in terms of the mutually distrustful relations between the Amish and the surrounding communities, on the one hand, and the positive relational environments generated by Amish teachers and children, on the other (McDermott, 1977).

The same may be true for Black Muslim schools, which have apparently been more successful than public schools in the education of Black children in America (Shalaby and Chilcott, 1972). Certainly the Black Muslims work hard at defining their school as a special place carved out of an ugly racist and criminal environment, and this work can be seen in their efforts to create a unique communicative system for members of their community to use in their dealings with each other and outsiders. The use of Islamic symbolism and food taboos does much to accomplish this goal and the Black Muslims until recently have given the impression of being dominated by the secrets of the esoteric wisdom of the East, by what new adolescent initiates in the mid-1960s called "heavy knowledge" (Labov, Cohen, Robins and Lewis, 1968). Members also developed a special code for addressing each other in Arabic and fictive kinship terms, and they dress in ways that mark them off from the Black and white communities in which they are immersed. Upon entering school every day, each child is searched for candy and other prohibited items, a fascinating communicative device that informs every child that the door to the school or mosque is no ordinary door and that behind it lies a whole new world of meaning. This is further reinforced by the children, particularly the boys, being taught to adopt a special military, square-cornered walk for their time in school. By building such elaborate communicative code differences with the surrounding communities, the children are made to feel like part of a coherent community that is cut off from the evils of the outside world.

The three kinds of examples we have just cited should demonstrate that an account of minority group problems in school in terms of communicative code differences is too simple. Certainly communicative differences exist across groups. And certainly, we notice these differences more among the children who are failing in school. But to suggest that these differences cause misbehavior and failure in school is to make a cause out of what is more likely only an effective medium for expressing the political and economic relations between the different groups. In order to disentangle this hypothesis, we will have to locate some situations in which some minority children are failing and specify the role of communicative code differences in their behavior with the teacher. Our notion is that when ethnically specific patterns are used and appear to cause trouble, the cause of that trouble will not be with the communicative code disparity but with the function of the disparity in the relations between the students and the teacher in the classroom. The relations between the teacher and the children will be the key to the member's interpretations and evaluations of the importance of ethnic borders and school learning in their lives with each other (McDermott, 1977). With this in mind, we will present an account of a teacher and a child having trouble with each other in ways that could be understood in terms of a communicative code conflict, but which upon analysis appears to be a function of much mutual understanding of their circumstances by the child and the teacher.

III. A Context Analysis of the Function
of a Miscommunication

In the classroom we introduced above, there was a Puerto Rican boy who was assigned to the bottom group for most of the year. There Juan (as we shall call him), made life miserable for all, and much of his time was spent being put out of the group or chastised while in the group. Although we never tracked this boy's activities alone, there were times when he would show up in our notes more than ten times an hour as the focus of a disruptive incident in classroom routines. Later in the year, the teacher became concerned enough to have the school officials discuss his case as a candidate for a special school for disturbed children. And this is where he is today. By the time the films were taken, this child was no longer a part of the bottom reading group. He was in no group at all, and he either busied himself with little projects the teacher gave him or he wandered around the classroom interacting with the other children, interactions that often led to disagreements. When the bottom group was at the reading table, he appeared to monitor their actions carefully, and any disturbance usually was followed by his showing up at the table anxious to participate.

We should mention how we came by our observations; one of us was in the classroom throughout the year observing behavior and recording it in a notebook, on Super-8 film mounted in one corner of the room and on videotape often centered on the reading groups. We did not attempt to code the data that we abstracted out of the records for purposes of statistical manipulation as it was our conviction that the patterned nature of the behavior in the classroom must emerge on the participants' own terms from an intensive analysis rather than by being imposed *a priori*. With that in mind we carefully analyzed tapes of the top and bottom reading groups at work and identified how the participants struggled to understand and organize their own behavior. The result was a complex structural analysis, only a diluted example of which will be presented in this section. By virtue of the extended observation in the classroom and a more detailed interactional analysis, as in McDermott (1976), we feel our statements about Juan and ethnic borders are warranted.

On one occasion, Juan came to the teacher complaining that another child was bothering him and that her intervention was necessary. It came at a time that the teacher was working with the bottom group in a reading lesson. She was standing in front of the group writing a word on the board. All were quite involved. At this point, the young boy started across the classroom shouting the teacher's name, "Hey, S____ , you better tell him to stop!" The teacher ignored the boy until he reached her and made contact by touching her on the buttocks. Thus, the boy violated two apparent rules of mainstream culture. He skipped the teacher's title and used only her last name in trying to get her attention.

He got her attention by contacting a prohibited area. The teacher immediately responded to the boy's touch and gave witness to the violation status of his attention-getting techniques. She turned quickly and left the bottom group without instruction as to what they should do next. She took the boy by the arm to a corner near her desk where she had a brief conversation with him before they broke contact.

The discovery of this behavior was easy. The boy violated not only the teacher's rules for contact, but our rules also, and we attended to his violation almost immediately. With a little more looking at the videotape it became proba- ble that the teacher was not pleased with the boy, for throughout the year, when the teacher was annoyed, the same arm raising procedure was used. The procedure consisted of the teacher raising the child's arm to a height that made the child dependent on guidance for a means of transport.

So we have some behavior that can be used as an anecdote relating ethnicity to miscommunication. The child wanted the teacher's attention, went about it in the wrong way, and got nothing but trouble for his efforts. The teacher in turn has the trouble of being hassled and having to hassle the child. No one is getting what the institution has defined as desirable. At first, we thought that the problem was simple. People from different cultures have different systems for doing touch. The teacher is a rather classic Northern and Eastern (non-Jewish) European in this regard, and she has little tactile involvement with other people in public. This should be difficult on the Mediterranean and Caribbean children who come from more tactile cultures and who could suffer relational mishaps with the teacher be- cause of their different ways of making sense (Efron, 1971; Hall, 1966; Scheflen, 1974). This little anecdote supports this notion. Numerous other examples can be found in the literature on cross-cultural communication in educational settings (Byers and Byers, 1972; Collier, 1973; Dumont, 1972; Erickson, 1975, 1976; Mehan, 1973; Philips, 1972).

With this supporting literature, it is easy to jump from the anecdote to con- clusions. One is that the boy is working with a different communicative code than the teacher and unwittingly causes some trouble for himself by not learning her code. The second response is that the teacher should be aware that the child has a different way of proceeding and should be more adaptable in order to give the boy the most satisfying relational environment in which to learn and adapt to mainstream culture. In this way, it might be possible to minimize miscommunica- tion and restrict the possibility that the boy might eventually work at achieving school failure, rather than school success.

But two other questions have forced themselves on us. One, given the adap- tability children display in many of their activities, why is it that this boy is not using the mainstream code to get the teacher's attention? Why is it that after nine months in school, he still has not figured out the teacher's rules for addressing and touching? Is it possible that there are other contexts for this behavior than is ob- vious in the anecdote? Two, might there be more reasons for the teacher being annoyed than is obvious in the anecdote? The teacher generally displays tremen- dous patience with the children. Is there something else going on than simply a touch deemed inappropriate in the teacher's native culture? Is it possible the boy is breaking more rules than those of the culture at large? Is it possible the boy is breaking rules that govern the relational work between the children of the class- room and the teacher? And is it possible the teacher's annoyance is only a part of more inclusive contexts for the sequencing of their behavior? The anecdotal description we offered cannot be used to address these questions. Instead, we need a description of the people's contexts for their behavior as they are defining those contexts and using them in the organization of concerted behavior. Fortunately, both the theory and the method of context analysis has been well worked out (Bateson, 1955; Birdwhistell, 1970; McQuown, Bateson, Birdwhistell, Brosin, and Hockett, 1971; Scheflen, 1966, 1973).

Perhaps the most immediate context or environment for people's behavior is the answer they might collectively give to the question "What is it that is going on here?" or "What's happening?" (Frake, 1964, 1976; Goffman, 1974). Many have shown that it is possible to locate people's answers to this question, because people must constantly inform each other of what is going on in order to continue producing concerted behavior with each other. So much of the behavior of members when face to face is related to this task that it would seem to be the *sine qua non* of any interaction (Birdwhistell, 1970). Verbally, they keep each other informed by formulating or keying what it is that they are doing for everyone to hear most clearly by naming, although usually members are less explicit (Hymes, 1974a; Sacks, 1974; Wieder, 1974). Kinesically, they do this by moving and positioning their bodies in relation to each other in particular ways at particular times. Thus, what it is that people are doing together can be seen in the positions or postural configurations they work out for each other (Kendon, 1973; McDermott, et al., 1978).

In the bottom group, the children and the teacher move in and out of three different major activity types, only three of which will be considered in this paper. These are the most immediate contexts for their answers to the question that they constantly put to each other and to themselves, namely, "What's going on?" As these were located primarily by an analysis of postural shifts performed by the members, we will call them positionings (Figures 13.1–13.3).

For our present purpose, it is only important to know that each of these positionings is marked by a different kind of work at the outer boundaries of the group. That is, depending upon which of the three positionings the children and the teacher assume, outsiders to the group appear to have different degrees of license to enter the group. This is not an unusual phenomenon, and an outsider's rights to enter a group have been clearly documented as subject to the postural work of the people already in the group (Kendon and Ferber, 1973; Scheflen, 1971, 1976; Schultz, 1976). For example, in the bottom group, when the teacher is out of the group and the children are waiting for her return (positioning III), outsiders are invited in to visit. When the children are struggling to get a turn to read from the teacher (positioning II), the children carefully monitor the teacher's activities; accordingly, no one is invited in, but if outsiders have business with the teacher, they will usually make an entrance. However, when the children are actively engaged in reading with the teacher no outsider enters the group. Interestingly, the top reading group assumes this organization throughout its reading lesson and is never disturbed by outsiders.

FIGURE 13.1   POSITIONING I: LOOKING AT THE BOOK

FIGURE 13.2   POSITIONING II: GETTING-A-TURN TO READ

FIGURE 13.3   POSITIONING III: WAITING FOR THE TEACHER

Now we must reconsider the boy's attention-getting behaviors in terms of the immediate contexts in which they occur. The behaviors occur at a special time and must be understood as they function at that time. With such a reconsideration, for example, the teacher does not have to be such a cultural imperialist to respond in the way she does. No one except this boy enters the reading table while the group is reading (positioning I). The top group is never disturbed, and when a member of the bottom group even went near the top group while the members were reading (positioning I), the teacher, three top group members and one member of the bottom group at the other end of the room conspired to prevent a possible disturbance by chasing the boy back to his part of the room. On the other hand, children from the top group often disturb the children of the bottom group while they are at the reading table, but never enter the table while the bottom group is reading (positioning I). This avoidance is no accident, for there are examples of a top group child entering the periphery of reading activity (positioning I), waiting until it is complete, and finally moving in to address the teacher at the start of the children calling for a turn (positioning II). The only case of a child violating a reading positioning comes when Juan enters and contacts the teacher's buttocks. Suddenly, this episode does not look like a simple case of culture conflict. The conflict at hand is not between the patterning of behavior of Caribbean Spanish versus that of Northern and Eastern European. It is far more localized than that. Given the particular ways of doing the order of the classroom, as that order is negotiated, formulated and done by the teacher and the students for their moment-to-moment life in school, the important question here asks how it is that this particular boy becomes involved in conflicts of scheduling as well as conflicts of naming and touching. Whatever the reasons, the teacher's reactions appear to be quite sensible.

More context must be considered for the boy's behavior. Recall that the boy was formerly a member of the bottom group and has since been put out. However, the boy still monitors the group's activities quite carefully. For example, every time there is a disturbance while the teacher is away from the reading table and the children struggle, squirm and fight, this boy shows up on the scene. During one such episode, a child takes a pencil belonging to another child and throws it to the floor at the other end of the reading table. The pencil has barely hit the ground as the boy in question runs across the room and picks the pencil up. Later, when two children square off in an argument, the prodigal child again appears on camera examining the scene. The boy monitors the group carefully and gives evidence of knowing the difference between the three positionings. More examples are possible, and each of them would contrast the boy's entering behavior in the buttocks scene to the boy's usual behavior during a reading positioning, in which he moves past the table the same as everyone else, without any disturbance whatsoever. So there is some reason to think that the boy moves to the table misaddressing and mistouching the teacher at a time that he understands as inappropriate.

Can we still talk about the teacher and the child miscommunicating? The child appears to have mastered the basic rules of the classroom and simply uses them for a different purpose. What could be the function of his behavior? Remember that the teacher takes the child to a corner and chastises him (unfortunately out of the range of the microphone). What happens next is interesting. The teacher then goes off camera to the back of the room where she is picked up by another camera. There she chastises the boy that Juan was complaining about. On her way, she is followed by Juan, in no way crushed, clapping his hands and delighting in the fact that his adversary is also getting into trouble. The plot thickens. In short, he received from the interaction what he might have wanted all along, namely, to get the other child in trouble, no mean feat in a classroom in which the teacher discourages snitching, particularly while she is busy working with a group. So the small anecdote locating a miscommunication, if properly contextualized, shows the miscommunication not only to be sensible, but quite functional as well.

It is not as easy to locate the teacher's behavior as functional. By placing her behavior in its larger context, we have located that her annoyance was based on more than a misunderstanding of cross-cultural norms for touching. Rather, her behavior appears to be based as well on a "knowledge" of the interactional norms governing her particular classroom. The boy breaks the rules and the teacher chastises him for it. Up to this point, her behavior makes sense, but then she crowns his efforts by attending to the matter he brought before her in the way he might have hoped. She breaks the first rule of classroom management by rewarding a person for breaking the rules and norms she otherwise enforces. Meanwhile, the bottom reading group is wasting its time on the other side of the room; a fight has started and reading has stopped. A good portion of the class is also disrupted by this episode. There is little reason for him not to proceed in the same way at another time. How then can we say that the teacher's behavior makes sense? The answer to this question is in no way complete, but consider the following pattern.

Often, as the bottom group gets into a positioning II in which they are struggling for a turn to read or a positioning I in which they are engaged in reading or some other lesson activity with the teacher, they are disrupted by the teacher yelling at the rest of the class or actually leaving the group to attend to outsiders. The teacher's attending to the boy's behavior in both a negative and positive way at a particular time may have to be understood in terms of this larger pattern of the teacher exiting from the bottom group at key points, when the group is highly focused around a particular task. By way of inference, it can be claimed that the teacher is uncomfortable with the bottom group once it is settled and ready for instruction. In terms of the readiness of some of the children to engage in reading activities, the teacher's response to the bottom group is quite understandable. It is easier to teach children how to read when they already know how to read. The top group does not present the problems the bottom group does. If this is the case, then the teacher's positive response to the boy's request appears to be a self-serving activity in that it is a way of getting out of the group for a little while. In the long run, everyone pays heavily for this escape, but in the short run it is to everyone's advantage; the boy gets someone in trouble and the teacher and the children in the bottom group get a brief rest from their intense organizational negotiations.

By placing the behaviors described in the anecdote within the contexts in terms of which the people engaged could possibly understand and act upon them, a quite different interpretation of this anecdote is possible. A miscommunication cannot be understood without asking about the constraints on each person in terms of which their miscommunication may be adaptive. After this question is answered in terms of the contexts negotiated by the participants, a miscommunication may look quite sensible. The little boy and the teacher appear to understand each other quite well, and they prey on each other's circumstances in order to enhance their respective standings within those circumstances. How then can we talk of communicative code differences causing misbehavior and failure in school? Juan demonstrates an understanding of the world in which he operates. It is hard to imagine how Puerto Rican culture inhibits his participation in the classroom. He and the teacher get a maximum amount of use of each other given the pressures of the classroom on each of them at that moment. The consequences of the adjustments they make to their circumstances are the mutually regressive understandings we see at evidence in this account. Juan and the teacher seem to have agreed unknowingly on how to miscommunicate with each other. Their choices are adaptive given their circumstances. We will now have to give some attention to what these circumstances might be and, in terms of these circumstances, we will have to consider the longterm consequences of their behavior.

IV. The Circumstances and Consequences of Miscommunication in School

Just what are the circumstances that make this miscommunication functional? In other words, how is it that things are set up so that many children, particularly minority children have the kinds of problems just detailed? Our argument is that schooling situations offer less of a payoff for many minority and poor children. Most often, it is not the case that the schools are staffed with teachers consciously trying to keep minority children from succeeding in school. Nor is it generally the case that there is something wrong with the children as they enter school. Although these two explanations are the most popular accounts of minority school failure, we suspect that cases to which they actually apply are rare, and we will not deal with them as such. Our problem is neither racist teachers nor dumb kids. Our problem is that our school systems are set up to have conscientious teachers function as racists and bright little children function as dopes even when they are all trying to do otherwise.

More specifically, our claim is that poor and minority children start school knowing less about how to read and write than do the children of the enfranchised groups that survive in the modern nations via literacy skills. This is in no way a deprivation argument. We are not suggesting that the children of the minorities do not have the skills for immediately learning how to read; we have only suggested that many have not learned how to read before they come to school.

From everything we know about the proper age for starting to learn how to read around the world, being more or less prepared at age six should have no effect on the eventual acquisition of literacy by the children (Wanat, 1976). Yet, given the nature of the classrooms in which the children are asked to catch up, learning to read at school becomes an organizational impossibility.

In the early grades, schools are best set up for reinforcing and practicing what children have already learned at home. When minority children show up in school not knowing how to read, they are placed in special groups like the one described in this paper. The teacher's job is not only to teach them how to read, but to make sure that they achieve a certain competence and demonstrate it on a standardized test by a certain date. In other words, the teacher is trained, paid, and held accountable for producing certain kinds of reading children by a certain date. Children in the bottom group create difficult organizational and pedagogical problems for the teacher. Many of the communication problems that exist between teachers and minority children can be understood as mutual adaptations to these organizational problems. For example, in the classroom we analyzed, the teacher handled the top and bottom groups quite differently. With the top group, the teacher likes to have the children take turns reading, one after the other, from left to right, around the table. This is not possible with the bottom group, because there are children who cannot be expected to read any page that comes along. So the teacher spares them some embarrassment and picks a special reader for each page. This means that she cannot divert her attention from this group for more than a minute without their needing her direction in picking a new reader. Concentrated attention with the bottom reading group is hardly possible while the teacher has two other groups and some stragglers busy (and not so busy) in other parts of the room. Accordingly, the members of the bottom group are often left without direction about how to proceed in their reading lesson, and they spend more than half their time waiting for the teacher or trying to get the teacher's attention to their pleas for a turn to read.

Recall the three positions that the members of the bottom group achieve with each other; two of them, getting-a-turn and waiting for the teacher (positionings II and III respectively) pit the children and the teacher in a struggle for each other's attention. The top group shares only the first positioning with the bottom group, the one in which all the members focus on reading. Now recall that these three positionings are different in that they allow different visiting rights for outsiders. The fact that the top group stays in the reading positioning (even when they are not actually reading) means that no outsiders enter the group during its lesson. However, by adapting to the teacher's procedures for calling on special children for special pages, the children in the bottom group arrange themselves into positionings II and III, and suffer constant interruptions from the children in the top group entering to ask the teacher questions during the bottom group's time at the reading table. Each of these interruptions further necessitates the elaborate procedures the children in the bottom group develop to get the teacher's attention in order to get a turn to read. Juan became so good at getting the teacher's attention in unorthodox, but situationally adaptive ways that he was put out of the bottom group. As we have seen, he still exercises his communicative skills by entering the group in the way that he does. Other children in the bottom group are developing similar skills.

The case we have made for circumstances that nurture miscommunication in the classroom is as follows: Various children, most of them poor or minority children who are not submerged in literacy skills at home, come into school behind their peers in reading and present difficult organizational and pedagogical problems for their teachers who are pressured to produce children with certain kinds of reading skills by a certain date; the teacher and the children make adjustments to each other's organizational quandaries; and the consequences of these adjustments are institutionally regressive, but sensible and functional forms of communication that appear to us as cases of miscommunication and misbehavior.

There are two important consequences of such apparent agreements to miscommunicate in the classroom. By way of their participation in such classrooms, the children from the bottom group fail in school and achieve the same places their parents hold in the social structure of the community. And in the case of the minority children in the bottom group, they acquire an ethnic identity that is not defined simply in terms of the values and behavioral styles of the group, but in terms of their group's antagonistic relations with the more dominant groups. Both these statements deserve some warrant.

We have suggested that the children in the bottom group come into the first grade not knowing how to read. They start off behind. Then they are put into the bottom group where they suffer the organizational problems we have described. The significant fact is that although they spend the same amount of time at the reading table as the children in the other groups, due to all the interruptions, two-thirds of them initiated by the other groups, they get only one-third the amount of time as the children in the top group get in a reading positioning. The rest of their time is spent in attentional struggles with the teacher. The net effect of this is that the children in the bottom group fall further behind the children in the top group for every day they spend in the classroom. The alternative to this is that they learn how to read at home. If they do not do this before school, they apparently do not do it after they enter school, and they get caught in the communicational systems that accentuate this discrepancy. Placement in the bottom group of this classroom (and classrooms without such tracking into ability groups appear to get much the same job done in different ways) works like a self-fulfilling prophecy in that the children in this group consistently get less concentrated, quality instruction than the children in the other groups. And this is the case for an excellent teacher who cares deeply about the children. We all know that teaching a first grade is a difficult job, and this particular teacher is excellent under the circumstances. We are only suggesting that learning to read in a first grade classroom may be even more difficult for the organizational reasons we have highlighted.

Without learning how to read, there are few other paths for upward mobility for minority children in modern nations. Thus the children achieve the same adaptational skills of their parents, and a new generation of the so-called disadvantaged takes its place in the world. If we wanted a mechanism for sorting each new generation of citizens into the advantaged and the disadvantaged, into the achieving and the underachieving, we could have done no better than to have invented the school system we have. Not only is it efficient in assigning many generations of the same people to the top and bottom slots, but, and this is one of the ironies of contemporary life, it does so in ways that make sense to the hard working, caring, and talented people who are trying to help break the cycle of the disadvantaged becoming more disadvantaged and the advantaged becoming more advantaged.

Lastly, we want to note that the ethnic border conflicts that mark all the nation states and plague most modern cities are reinforced in the classroom. People need a way to explain the persistent failure of minority children in schools. Rather than taking a look at how this is done, as we have tried to do here in only a limited way, most of us have ethnic labels available for talking about and explaining the failure of the different kinds of children. Ethnic group membership does not cause school failure or success, but after different kinds of children differentially succeed and fail, ethnicity becomes salient in negative ways. In the classroom we have just analyzed, at the beginning of the year, the white, Black, and Puerto Rican children divided their time with each other without regard to ethnicity. By the end of the year, the two Black children, the four Puerto Rican children and the eighteen white children began to form isolates. By late May, the terms "nigger" and "spic" began to show up, and border fights between members of the different groups became a daily occurrence. How this happened is worth another paper. We are pointing to this phenomenon now because we believe that it flows rather directly from the experiences we have described for the children in this classroom. For it is the minority children who engage in the bulk of the miscommunication with the teacher. Under these conditions, ethnic solidarity becomes a refuge from the negative relationships offered to the children in the classrooms. In this way, the experience of belonging to a group was transformed into an experience of having enemies. The problem in this classroom was not ethnicity, but a set of contexts in terms of which ethnic differences were turned into ethnic borders.

Hopefully, ethnic differences will survive the many homogenizing influences of the modern world. We will need these differences to keep us alive to the variety of ways we potentially have available for celebrating and humanizing each other. However, when ethnic differences become a source for ethnic borders, we must attempt to overcome the conflicts; we must attempt to locate for ourselves how we are helping to create the conditions for transforming differences into borders. Unfortunately, even if we achieve some semblance of intellectual clarity on the subject, there is considerable question as to whether we will be able to stop our own participation in the creation of borders without considerable change in the institutional demands with which we must deal in our everyday life. Many of our institutions certainly get in the way of maximizing the social and psychological potential of our children, and most of us do not have the foggiest notion of how to proceed in rectifying the situation. Efforts at achieving institutional reform consistent with our growing knowledge of the constraints and possibilities of human behavior, efforts such as those formulated in a stimulating paper by Church (1976), will have to form a far greater focus for our activities.

Acknowledgments. Most of the research reported in this paper was supported by predoctoral research grants to McDermott by the National Institute of General Medical Studies, the National Institute of Mental Health, and the National Science Foundation. McDermott's writing time was supported by Carnegie Corporation Funds to Michael Cole and the Laboratory of Comparative Human Cognition at the Rockefeller University. We both are indebted to Albert Scheflen who gave us some difficult problems to work on and the inspiration (and a place) to work on them. Bernard Strassberg did an expert job on our drawings. In addition Gospodinoff wishes to acknowledge numerous discussions over the past six years on many of the issues of this paper with Dr. E. H. Auerswald of the University of Hawaii Department of Psychiatry and the Maui Community Mental Health Center, who also provided financial support and critical comments. About one-third of this material has been adapted from the doctoral dissertation submitted by McDermott to the Department of Anthropology, Stanford University, 1976.

A Parting Note

14

PROSPECTS FOR INCREASING THE IMPACT OF ANTHROPOLOGICAL FINDINGS ON THE EDUCATIONAL ENTERPRISE

Solon Kimball

Recently, when I began to cast up, in a rough sort of way, the influence of anthropology on educational practices over the past twenty years I found that I experienced both pleasure and despair.

All of us know of specific instances in which some anthropological concept has influenced educational practice or been included in an educational program. One significant contribution has been the inculcation of an awareness that the various peoples of the world differ from each other in outlook and behavior but should, nevertheless, be respected for their differences. This cultural relativism, however, has won a place in the educational catechism as a label rather than becoming a dynamic principle affecting policy and program. Cultural variability, reduced to a static truism, justifies the adjustment of programs to fit Blacks, Chicanos, or Indians but ignores the dynamics of culture transmission characteristic of each group.

The response to other anthropological concepts seems equally inadequate in that these concepts may be readily incorporated as novelties but also as quickly forgotten or discarded where there is no intellectual soil in which they can take root. Such a deficiency can undoubtedly be traced to a teacher training process in which slogans become substitutes for systematic thought. Nevertheless, general recognition of an anthropological position continues to grow. For instance, anthropological references were included in desegregation literature issued by the United States Civil Rights Commission and by the 1972 San Francisco court decision of *Lau versus Nichols* involving the teaching of Chinese.

The most impressive growth, however, has been within the discipline of anthropology itself. This probably was a necessary development before an informed and continuous connection with educators could be established. These developments include the formation of the Council on Anthropology and Education with its successful quarterly journal and a large and lively membership. Evidence of an enormous expansion in research is found in the numerous books and monographs published in the anthropology and education series of Holt, Rinehart and Winston or Teachers College Press, as well as readers and monographs published elsewhere. In addition, many departments now offer one or more courses in the subject and a few institutions have developed a major program. Such an inventory testifies to a vigorous and expanding development in the field of anthropology and education within the discipline of anthropology.

When I assessed the influence of these activities within the educational establishment, however, I regret that my conclusions left me greatly saddened. My despair came from the realization that the efforts of so many of us over these years seemed to have had so little impact among professional educators. I venture to suggest that any systematic polling of educational personnel would reveal that most of those who had heard of anthropology continue to associate it with fossil man or vanished tribes. Only a fraction would accept that anthropology might make a contribution to the educational enterprise. What a startling contrast with any similar assessment of psychology. If such a conclusion is even approximately correct, it deserves serious investigation.

Perhaps some of us misjudged the significance of our message or have been overly optimistic of the receptivity of educators to findings relevant to the educational process. Possibly we have been inept in our approach, or perhaps the timing has been inappropriate. Conceivably, the basic barrier is an ideological one in the contrast of the natural history-experimental approach of anthropology versus a judgmental-programmatic one in education. Resentment and jealousies by educators of anthropological criticisms and proposals seem unlikely since the attempt of anthropologists to convince educators of the usefulness of the anthropological approach resembles the power of a gnat rather than a bulldozer.

There are some educational problems, however, where the anthropological contribution should be obvious. For example, there is no school program for which anthropological resources are more abundant nor more directly applicable than that of multicultural education. These resources include the substantive knowledge contained in the numerous cultural studies of ethnic groups, classroom ethnographies, learning and socialization, schooling and intelligence, sociolinguistics, and counseling. Any failure to utilize such a plethora of riches may be attributed to a combination of existing school organization and practices and the absence of educator-anthropologists who can translate knowledge into programs.

Also related to multicultural education are other areas in anthropology that have a broader applicability. These are:

1. *Learning Theory:* Anthropological studies of the biological basis of behavior, physical maturation in cultural settings, enculturation, socialization, and schooling offer significant cross-cultural insights into the consequences of humans achieving maturity in social groups. The recent attention to the significance of play as an instrument of development provides a specific example. Practically no educators and probably few anthropologists are aware of the developments in this

area. Anthropological conclusions are sometimes complementary, sometimes anti-thetical to those of psychology, but the utilization of these findings is essential for programs involving minorities and educational development in Third World countries.

2. *Curriculum:* There have been three projects engaged in the preparation and introduction of anthropological materials for classroom instruction. The Anthropological Curriculum Study Project and "Man, A Course of Study," have been funded by the National Science Foundation. The Center of Cognitive Studies at Cambridge, Massachusetts, produced "Man, A Course of Study," which has evoked protests from some fundamentalists. A joint project of the College of Education and the Department of Anthropology at the University of Georgia has produced other materials. Each of these projects had somewhat different objec-tives, and no attempt to measure their impact has been made. The introduction of anthropology as subject matter is of lesser importance, in my judgment, than the task of deciding the cultural heritage which is to be transmitted from generation to generation. A democratic society does not assign official responsibility for such a function. The training of professional educators, however, does not produce competence in this area. Anthropology's humanistic tradition, combined with the wisdom derived from cross-cultural knowledge, uniquely prepares anthropologists for participating in such efforts.

3. *Organization:* Broadly stated, this area is concerned with the settings in which learning occurs. Specifically, it addresses problems of school administra-tion, classroom management, and formal and informal student systems. Our knowledge of beneficial changes that could be made in the latter two areas far exceeds any evidence that school officials either understand or are interested in our findings. And certainly we have established our capability to conduct studies on the functioning of school bureaucracies.

4. *School and Community:* The fiscal and legal focus which is imposed on school administrators and policymakers tends to overshadow the kinds of knowl-edge which they ought to be concerned with in school operation. As an example, of great significance would be an understanding of the subcommunity perspective which the child brings into the classroom and which conditions his behavior and affects his response to the teaching process. In a few places, such as Hawaii, some limited and temporary success has been achieved in bringing an awareness of cul-tural diversity in pupils and consequent adjustment of school programs.

5. *Sociolinguistics:* This is one of the areas which has attracted interest from educators who are faced with teaching minority students, particularly Blacks. When teachers do not understand what their students are saying and are unsuc-cessful in either communicating or getting them to modify their speech patterns, then it is fairly obvious that those who possess linguistic skills are needed. Utiliza-tion of language skills, however, extends beyond culturally deviant groups.

Prospects

Some portion of the failure to influence the educational enterprise may be attri-buted to the absence of an adequate assessment of the problem. In particular, certain organizational aspects have been ignored. There have been no studies, for example, of teacher training institutions and their related laboratory schools, of state departments of education, of the Office of Education in Washington, of the operation of international organizations, or agencies operating on an international level. These bureaucracies are powerful sources of control and regulation. Those who have had dealings with them have probably encountered intellectual myopia, bureaucratic obtuseness, and self-serving perpetuation. Such a characterization, however, may evidence more judgmental bias among anthropologists than useful assessment of the agencies' functioning.

Anthropologists should not be discouraged by the limited extent to which their findings have influenced the educational establishment. The neglect is much more a consequence of the inability to inform educators of the desirable results to be obtained by utilizing an anthropological approach than by any conscious rejection. Ongoing systems acquire a resistance which protects them against innovation. Insiders feed the system. Outsiders are naive if they believe that their ostensibly superior ways will be readily accepted.

Mutuality of interest leads to such unusual consequences as the proverbial strange bedfellows of politics and the joining of practitioners in the professions with the scholar of the disciplines. Such a commonality encompasses multicultural bilingual education and anthropology. The multicultural bilingual classroom is a situation which offers an unusual opportunity to observe the utilization of anthropological resources in an educational problem.

The capabilities include an initial assessment of the problem, preparation of a plan, and putting a program into operation. First, we use ethnographic field methods to assemble the information about behavior and groupings in the context of the setting of school and community. This operation also provides us with a definition of the problem. Next, through sociolinguistic observations the situational variations between culture and speech are catalogued. From such data it is then possible to fashion contextual objectives in contrast to those arising from such nonrelevant abstractions — that is, goals become a function of the situation and not of some idealized standards. Finally, from applied anthropology come the principles which shape procedures and organization.

No one can guarantee that such a combination of research, planning, and program based upon the anthropological approach can solve all the problems of multicultural and bilingual education. There are other ingredients which affect the outcome, of course. However, such a joining of anthropology and education offers some fascinating possibilities which may have broader implications for cooperation in other areas.

BIBLIOGRAPHY

Alu Like, Inc. "Analysis of Needs Assessment Survey and Related Data." Honolulu: Alu Like, Inc., 1976.

American Institute for Research (AIR). "Evaluation of the Impact of ESEA Title VII Spanish/ English Bilingual Programs." Vol. 1, *Study Design and Interim Findings,* AIR Report No. 48300-2/77-FIRU.

Amidon, Edmund J. and N. Flanders. *The Role of the Teacher in the Classroom.* Minneapolis: Paul S. Amidon Associates, 1963.

Aspira vs. Board of Education of the City of New York. No. 72 Cir. 40002 (filed August 29, 1974) (J. Franel).

Atiles, Emilio Gonzales, P. Pedraza, A. C. Zentella. "Toward a Language Policy for Puerto Ricans in the United States." In press.

Au, Kathryn H. *KEEP Reading Research: 1972–75.* Honolulu: The Kamehameha Early Education Program.

——— and C. E. Speidel. *Hawaiian Creole Speakers' Listening Comprehension Abilities in Standard English and Hawaiian Creole.* Honolulu: The Kamehameha Early Education Program, 1976.

Auerswald, E. H. "The Noncare of the Underprivileged: Some Ecological Observations." *International Psychiatry Clinics,* 8 (1971):43–60.

Bagely, William C. and John A. H. Keith. *An Introduction to Teaching.* New York: Macmillan, 1924.

Baratz, J. "Teaching Reading in an Urban Negro School." In F. Williams (ed.), *Language and Poverty.* Chicago: Markham, 1970.

——— and S. Baratz. "Early Childhood Intervention: The Social Science Base of Institutional Racism." *Harvard Educational Review,* 40 (1970):29–50.

Barker, R. G. *The Stream of Behavior: Explorations of Its Structure and Content.* New York: Appleton-Century-Crofts, 1963.

———. "Explorations in Ecological Psychology." *American Psychologist,* 20 (1965):1–14.

———. *Ecological Psychology.* Stanford: Stanford University Press, 1968.

Barnett, P. A. *Common Sense in Education and Teaching: An Introduction to Practice.* London: Longmans Green, 1905.

Barth, F. "Introduction." In F. Barth (ed.), *Ethnic Groups and Boundaries.* Boston: Little, Brown, and Company, 1969.

———. "Pathan Identity and Its Maintenance." In F. Barth (ed.), *Ethnic Groups and Boundaries.* Boston: Little, Brown, and Company, 1969.

Bateson, G. "The Message 'This is Play.'" In B. Schaffner (ed.), *Group Processes.* New York: Josiah Macy, Jr. Foundation, 1955.

Battiste, M. and G. Mohatt. *Evaluation of Lakeview Immersion Project.* West Bay, Ontario, 1977.

Bauman, Richard. "An Ethnographic Framework of the Investigation of Communicative Behavior." In R. D. Abraham and R. C. Troike, *Language and Cultural Diversity in American Education.* Englewood Cliffs, N. J.: Prentice-Hall, 1972.

——— and J. Sherzer. "The Ethnography of Speaking." *Annual Review of Anthropology,* 4 (1975):95–119.

Beck, H. "Ethological Considerations on the Problem of Political Order." *Political Anthropology,* 1 (1975):110–132.

Bereiter, Carl, et al. "An Academically Oriented Preschool for Culturally Deprived Children." In F. M. Hechinger (ed.), *Preschool Education Today.* New York: Doubleday, 1966.

Berliner, D. C. and L. S. Cahen. "Trait-Treatment Interaction and Learning." In F. N. Kerlinger (ed.), *Review of Research in Education I.* Itasca, IL: F E. Peacock Publishers (for AERA), 1973.

Bernstein, Basil. "A Critique of the Concept of Compensatory Education." In C. B. Cazden, V. P. John, and D. Hymes (eds.), *Functions of Language in the Classroom.* New York: Teachers College Press, 1972.

———. "Social Class and Linguistic Development: A Theory of Social Learning." In A. H. Halsey, J. Floyd, and C. A. Anderson (eds.), *Education, Economy, and Society.* New York: Free Press, 1961.

Birdwhistell, R. *Kinesics and Context.* Philadelphia: University of Pennsylvania Press, 1970.

Bissell, Joan, S. White, and G. Zivin. "Sensory Modalities in Children's Learning." In Gerald S. Lesser (ed.), *Psychology and Educational Practice,* pp. 130–155. Glenview, IL: Scott, Foresman and Co., 1971.

Blom, J. and J. Gumperz. "Social Meaning in Linguistic Structure: Code-Switching in Norway." In J. Gumperz and D. Hymes (eds.), *Directions in Sociolinguistics.* New York: Holt, Rinehart and Winston, 1972.

Boggs, Stephen T. "The Meaning of Questions and Narratives to Hawaiian Children." In C. B. Cazden, et al. (eds.), *Functions of Language in the Classroom.* New York: Teachers College Press, 1972.

Boissevain, J. *The Italians of Montreal.* Ottawa: Crown Copyrights, 1970.

Bowles, Samuel and H. Gintis. *Schooling in Capitalist America.* New York: Basic Books, 1976.

Bremme, Donald. "Accomplishing a Classroom Event: A Micro-ethnography of 'First Circle.'" Working Paper No. 3, Newton Classroom Interaction Project, Harvard Graduate School of Education, 1977.

——— and F. Erickson. "Relationships Among Verbal and Non-verbal Classroom Behaviors." *Theory into Practice,* 16 (1977) 5:153–162.

Bruck, M. and J. Shultz. "An Ethnographic Analysis of the Language Use Patterns of Bilingually Schooled Children." *Working Papers on Bilingualism,* Issue No. 13, Toronto: Ontario Institute for Studies in Education, 1977.

Bryde, J. "Indian Students and Guidance." *Guidance Monograph.* New York: Houghton-Mifflin, 1977.

Byers, P. and H. Byers. "Non-verbal Communication and the Education of Children." In C. B. Cazden, et al. (eds.), *Functions of Language in the Classroom.* New York: Teachers College Press, 1972.

Cardenas, B. "It's a Circle for Everybody to be Involved In." *Colloquy* (1972):18–23.

Cardenas, J. A. "An Educational Plan for the Denver Public Schools." San Antonio: National Educational Task Force de la Raza, 1974. Excerpts reprinted in *Bilingual-Bicultural Education, A Handbook for Attorneys and Community Workers.* Cambridge: Center for Law and Education, 1975, pp. 8–19.

Carnoy, M. *Education as Cultural Imperialism.* New York: David McKay Company, Inc., 1974.

Carrasco, R., A. Vera, and C. B. Cazden. "Aspects of Bilingual Student's Communicative Competence in the Classroom: A Case Study." In R. Duran (ed.), *Latino Language and Communicative Behavior.* Norwood, NJ: Ablex Publishing Co., in press.

Cazden, C. B. "The Neglected Situation in Child Language Research." In F. Williams (ed.), *Language and Poverty.* Chicago: Rand McNally, 1970.

———. "Approaches to Dialects in Early Childhood Education." In R. Shuy (compiler), *Social Dialects and Interdisciplinary Perspectives.* Arlington, VA: Center for Applied Linguistics, 1971.

———. "Teaching as a Linguistic Process in a Cultural Setting." In N. L. Gage (ed.), *NIE Conference on Studies in Teaching.* Washington, DC: National Institute of Education, 1974.

———. "How Knowledge About Language Helps the Classroom Teacher—Or Does It; A Personal Account." *The Urban Review,* 9 (Summer, 1976):74–90.

———. "The Student as Teacher." Paper presented at the American Educational Research Association Annual Meeting, New York, April 5, 1977.

———, et al. "You all Gonna Hafta Listen: Peer Teaching in a Primary Classroom." In W. A. Collins (ed.), *Children's Language and Communication,* 12th Annual Minnesota Symposium on Child Psychology, Hillsboro, NJ: Lawrence Erlbaum, in press.

———, et al. (eds.), *Functions of Language in the Classroom.* New York: Teachers College Press, 1972.

——— and V. P. John. "Learning in American Indian Children." In M. L. Wax, S. Diamond, and F. O. Gearing (eds.), *Anthropological Perspectives on Education.* New York: Basic Books, 1971.

Center for Applied Linguistics. *Recommendations for the Implementation of the Guidelines for the Preparation and Certification of Teachers of BBE Through Inservice Training.* Arlington, VA: Center for Applied Linguistics, 1974.

———. *Handbook for Staff Development Workshops in Indian Education.* Arlington, VA: Center for Applied Linguistics, 1976.

———. *Bilingual Education: Current Perspectives Vols. 1–5.* Arlington, VA: Center for Applied Linguistics, 1977.

———. *Response to the AIR Study.* Arlington, VA: Center for Applied Linguistics, 1977.

——— and Citizens' Task Force on Bilingual Education. *A Master Plan for Bilingual-Bicultural Education in the San Francisco Unified School District, Part 4.* Arlington, VA: Center for Applied Linguistics, 1975.

Center for Law and Education. *Bilingual-Bicultural Education: A Handbook for Attorneys and Community Workers.* Cambridge: Center for Law and Education, 1975.

Chomsky, N. *Aspects of the Theory of Syntax.* Cambridge: M.I.T. Press, 1965.

Church, J. *Psychology and the Social Order.* The New York Academy of Science, 270 (1976): pp. 141–151.

Cicourel, A. "Basic and Normative Rules in the Negotiation of Status and Role." In D. Sudnow (ed.), *Studies in Social Interaction.* New York: Free Press, 1972.

———. *Cognitive Sociology: Language and Meaning in Social Interaction.* London: Penguin, 1973.

———. *Cognitive Sociology.* New York: The Free Press, 1974b.

———, et al. *Language and Use and School Performance.* New York: Academic Press, 1974a.

Coburn, J. *Proposal for 1976 Northwest Indian Reading and Language Development Program.* Portland, OR: Northwest Regional Educational Laboratory, 1975.

Cole, M., J. Gay, J. Glick and D. Sharp. *The Cultural Context of Learning and Thinking.* New York: Basic Books, 1971.

——— and S. Scribner. *Culture and Thought: A Psychological Introduction.* New York: John Wiley and Sons, Inc., 1974.

Collier, J. *Alaskan Eskimo Education.* New York: Holt, Rinehart and Winston, 1973.

Corbiere, E. *Rules for Play and the Group Teaching Method in Odawa Homes.* Unpublished paper, 1976.

Craig, D. "Education and Creole English in the West Indies." In D. Hymes (ed.), *Pidginization and Creolization of Languages.* London: Cambridge University Press, 1971.

Cronbach, L. J. and R. E. Snow. *Aptitudes and Instructional Methods: A Handbook for Research in Interactions.* New York: Irvington, 1977.

Crowell, D. *Description of the KEEP Reading Program for Grades 1, 2, and 3: 1976–1977.* Honolulu: The Kamehameha Early Education Program, 1977.

D'Andrade, R. "Cultural Constructions of Reality." In L. Nadar and T. Martezki (eds.), *Cultural Illness and Health.* Washington, DC: American Anthropological Association, 1973.

DeAvila, E. A. and S. E. Duncan. "Research on Cognitive Styles with Language Minority Children: Summary of Pilot Study Design and Data Analysis." Report presented at the National Association for Bilingual Education Conference, San Juan, Puerto Rico, April 16, 1978.

DeCamp, D. "Introduction." In D. Hymes (ed.), *Pidginization and Creolization of Languages.* London: Cambridge University Press, 1971.

Denzin, N. *The Research Act: Introduction to Sociological Methods.* Chicago: Aldine, 1970.

Deutsch, Martin, et al. *The Disadvantaged Child.* New York: Basic Books, 1967.

Dorr-Bremme, D. *See* Bremme, 1977.

Dreeben, R. *On What is Learned in School.* Reading, MA: Addison-Wesley, 1968.

Dumont, R. V., Jr. "Learning English and How to be Silent: Studies in Sioux and Cherokee Classroom." In C. B. Cazden, V. P. John, and D. Hymes (eds.), *Function of Language in the Classroom.* New York: Teachers College Press, 1972.

Duncan, S. "Some Signals and Rules for Taking Speaking Turns in Conversations." *Journal of Personality and Social Psychology,* 23 (1972):283–292.

Dunkin, M. J. and B. Biddle. *The Study of Teaching.* New York: Holt, Rinehart and Winston, 1974.

Durkheim, E. *The Rules of Sociological Method.* Glencoe, IL: Free Press, 1958. (Original, 1895).

Eddy, E. M. *Becoming a Teacher.* New York: Teachers College Press, 1969.

Efron, D. *Gesture and Environment.* New York: King's Crown Press, 1941.

Elías-Olivares, L. "Ways of Speaking in a Chicano Community: A Sociolinguistic Approach." Ph.D. dissertation, University of Texas at Austin, 1975.

Erickson, F. "Afterthoughts." In A. Kendon, R. Harris, and M. R. Key (eds.), *Organization of Behavior in Face-to-Face Interaction.* The Hague: Mouton, 1975.

———. "Gatekeeping and the Melting Pot: Interaction in Counseling Encounters." *Harvard Educational Review,* 45 (1975): 1:44–70.

———. "One Function of Proxemic Shifts in Face-to-Face Interaction." In A. Kendon, M. R. Key and R. Harris (eds.), *The Organization of Behavior in Face-to-Face Interaction.* The Hague: Mouton, 1975.

———. "Gatekeeping Encounters: A Social Selection Process." In P. R. Sanday (ed.), *Anthropology and the Public Interest: Fieldwork and Theory.* New York: Academic Press, 1976a.

———. "Talking Down and Giving Reasons: Hyperexplanation and Listening Behavior in Interracial Interviews." Paper delivered at the International Conference on Non-verbal Behaviour, Toronto, Canada, May 11, 1976.

———. "What Makes School Ethnography 'Ethnographic'?" *Council of Anthropology and Education Quarterly,* 4 (May, 1976) 1:10–19.

———. Discussant's comments in C. Jordan, et al. (eds.), *A Multidisciplinary Approach to Research in Education Program.* Honolulu: The Kamehameha Early Education Program, 1978.

———. "On Standards of Descriptive Validity in Studies of Classroom Activity." Paper delivered at the Annual Meeting of the American Educational Research Association, Toronto, Canada, March 29, 1978.

Erickson, F., et al. "Inter-Ethnic Relations in Urban Institutional Settings." Final Technical Report for Project MH18230 and MH21460 submitted to Center for Studies of Metropolitan Problems, National Institutes of Mental Health, MD by the Harvard Graduate School of Education, December, 1973.

———, S. Florio and D. Bremme. "Children's Sociolinguistic Performance and Teacher's Judgements of Children's Competence." Paper delivered at the Annual Meeting of the American Educational Research Association, Washington, DC, April 2, 1975.

——— and J. Shultz. "When is a Context: Some Issues and Methods in the Analysis of Social Competence." *Quarterly Newsletter of the Institute for Comparative Human Development,* 1 (February 1977):5–10.

Ervin-Tripp, S. *Language Acquisition and Communicative Choice.* Stanford, CA: Stanford University Press, 1977.

——— and C. Mitchell-Kernan (eds.). *Child Discourse.* New York: Academic Press, 1977.

Feinberg, S. E. "The Collection and Analysis of Ethnographic Data in Educational Research." *Anthropology and Education Quarterly,* 8 (May 1977) 2:50–57.

Felice, L. "Mexican American Self-Concept and Educational Achievement: The Effects of Ethnic Isolation and Socio Economic Deprivation." *Social Science Quarterly,* 53 (1973) 4:716–727.

Firth, R. "Social Organization and Social Change." *Journal of the Royal Anthropological Institute of Great Britain and Ireland,* 84 (1954).

Fishman, J. A. "The Social Science Perspective." *Bilingual Education: Current Perspectives, Vol. 1.* Arlington, VA: Center for Applied Linguistics, 1977.

Flanders, N. A. *Analyzing Teacher Behavior.* Reading, MA: Addison-Wesley, 1970.

Florio, S. "Issues in the Analysis of the Structure of Classroom Interaction." Qualifying paper, Harvard Graduate School of Education, 1976.

———. *Learning How to Go to School: An Ethnography of Interaction in a Kindergarten/First Grade Classroom.* Ph.D. dissertation, Harvard University, Graduate School of Education, 1978.

Fox, Mary Lou. *Pauses in Odawa Speech.* Unpublished paper, 1976.

Frake, C. "A Structural Description of Subanun 'Religious' Behavior." In W. Goodenough (ed.), *Explorations in Cultural Anthropology.* New York: McGraw-Hill, 1964.

———. "Interpretations of Illness." Paper presented to the New York Academy of Sciences, March 8, 1976.

———. "The Emics and Etics of Ethnicity: Cultural Boundaries in the Sulu Sea." Unpublished manuscript, n.d.

Frender, R. and W. Lambert. "Speech Style and Scholastic Success." In R. Shuy (ed.), *Sociolinguists.* Washington, DC: Georgetown University Press, 1973.

Fuchs, Estelle. *Pickets at the Gates.* New York: The Free Press, 1966.

——— and R. Hainghurst. "To Live on this Earth." *American Indian Education.* New York: Anchor Books, 1973.

Gallimore, R. "The Role of Dialect and General Verbal/Cognitive Abilities in School Performance of Hawaiian Creole Speakers." In C. Jordan, et al. (ed.), *A Multidisciplinary Approach to Research in Education.* Honolulu, HI: The Kamehameha Early Education Program, 1978.

———, J. Boggs, and C. Jordan. *Culture, Behavior, and Education: A Study of Hawaiian-Americans.* Beverly Hills, CA: Sage Publications, 1974.

——— and R. G. Tharp. *Studies of Standard English and Hawaiian Islands Creole English: KEEP Linguistic Research, 1971–1975.* Honolulu: The Kamehameha Early Education Program, 1976.

———, R. G. Tharp, and K. C. W. Sloat. *Analysis of WPPSI and WISC-R Scores for the Kamehameha Early Education Program, 1972–1978.* Honolulu: The Kamehameha Early Education Program, 1979.

———, et al. "The Relationship of Sibling Caretaking and Attentiveness to a Peer Tutor." *American Educational Research Journal,* 15 (1978) 2:267–273.

Garcia, E. "Chicano Cultural Diversity: Implications for Competence-Based Teacher Education." In W. A. Hunter (ed.), *Multi-cultural Education through Competency-Based Teacher Education.* Washington, DC: American Association of Colleges for Teacher Education, 1974.

——— and R. L. Carrasco. "An Analysis of Bilingual Mother-Child Discourse." In R. Duran (ed.), *Latino Language and Communicative Behavior.* Norwood, NJ: Ablex Publishing Corp. In press.

Garfinkel, H. *Studies in Ethnomethodology.* Englewood Cliffs, NJ: Prentice-Hall, 1967.

Gearing, F. and L. Sangree. *Toward a General Theory of Education.* The Hague/Chicago: Mouton/Aldine, in press.

Geer, B. "First Days in the Field: A Chronicle of Research in Progress." In G. J. McCall and J. L. Simmons (eds.), *Issues in Participant Observation.* Reading, MA: Addison-Wesley, 1969.

Genishi, C. S. "Rules for Code-Switching in Young Spanish-English Speakers: An Exploratory Study of Language Socialization." Ph.D. dissertation, University of California at Berkeley, 1976.

Gibson, M. A. "Approaches to Multicultural Education in the U.S.: Some Concepts and Assumptions." *Anthropology and Education Quarterly,* 7 (1976) 4:7–18.

Gilmore, Perry (ed.). *Ethnography and Education: Children in and out of Schools.* Philadelphia: University of Pennsylvania, in press.

Gladwin, T. *East is a Big Bird.* Boston: Belknap Press, 1970.

Gmelch, S., P. Langan, and G. Gmelch. *Tinkers and Travellers.* Montreal: McGill-Queen's University Press, 1976.

Goffman, E. "The Nature of Deference and Demeanor." *American Anthropologist,* 58 (1956): 473–502.

———. *Encounters—Two Studies in the Sociology of Interaction.* New York: Bobbs-Merrill Co., 1961.

———. "The Neglected Situation." In J. J. Gumperz and D. Hymes (eds.), "The Ethnography of Communication." *American Anthropologist,* 66 (1964) 2:133–136.

———. *Frame Analysis.* New York: Harper Colophon Books, 1974.

———. *Interaction Ritual: Essays on Face-to-Face Behavior.* Garden City, NJ: Doubleday, 1976.

Good, T. L. and J. E. Brophy. *Looking in Classrooms.* New York: Harper and Row, 1973.

Goodenough, W. "Cultural Anthropology and Linguistics." In D. Hymes (ed.), *Language in Culture and Society.* New York: Harper and Row, 1964.

———. "Rethinking 'Status' and 'Role': Toward a General Model of the Cultural Organization of Social Relationships." In M. Banton (ed.), *The Relevance of Models for Social Anthropology.* London: Tavistock, 1965.

———. *Culture, Langauge and Society.* Reading, MA: Addison-Wesley, 1971.

———. "Multiculturalism as the Normal Human Experience." Paper presented at the Annual Meeting of the American Anthropological Association, San Francisco, 1975. Also appears in *CAE Quarterly,* 7 (1976) 4:4–7.

Grambs, J. "The Roles of the Teacher." In J. Clulcott, N. Greenberg and H. Wilson (eds.), *Readings in the Socio-cultural Foundations of Education.* Belmont, CA: Wadsworth, 1969.

Grant, B. M. and D. G. Hennings. *The Teacher Moves: An Analysis of Non-Verbal Activity.* New York: Teachers College Press, 1971.

Griffin, P. "Three Social Factors Involved in Language and Bilingual Education Programs." *Language Development in a Bilingual Setting.* Los Angeles: National Dissemination and Assessment Center, 1978.

——— and F. Humphry. "Task and Tack." In R. Shuy and P. Griffin (eds.), *Children's Functional Language,* 1978.

——— and R. Shuy (eds.). *Children's Functional Language.* Final Report to the Carnegie Corporation of New York. Arlington, VA: Center for Applied Linguistics, 1978.

Gump, P. V. "Intra-Setting Analysis: The Third Grade Classroom as a Special but Instructive Case." In E. P. Willens and H. L. Raush (eds.), *Naturalistic Viewpoints in Psychological Research.* New York: Holt, Rinehart and Winston, 1969.

———. "What's Happening in the Elementary Classroom." In I. Wesvurg and A. Bellack, *Research into Classroom Processes.* New York: Teachers College Press, 1971.

——— and L. R. Good. "Environments Operating in Open Space and Traditionally Designed Schools." *Journal of Architectural Research,* 5 (1976) 1:20–27.

——— and R. Ross. "Problems and Possibilities in Measurement of School Environments." Paper presented at Conference of the International Society for the Study of Behavioural Development, University of Surrey, Guildford, England, July 1975.

Gumperz, John. "Linguistic and Social Interaction in Two Communities." In J. Gumperz and D. Hymes (eds.), *"The Ethnography of Communication," American Anthropologist,* 66 (1964): 137–153.

———. *Language in Social Groups.* Stanford, CA: Stanford University Press, 1971.

———. "Langauge, Communication and Public Negotiation." In Peggy R. Sandy (ed.), *Anthropology and the Public Interest.* New York: Academic Press, 1976.

——— and E. Herasimchuk. "The Conversational Analysis of Social Meaning: A Study of Classroom Interaction." In R. Shuy (ed.), *Sociolinguistics: Current Trends and Prospects,* (23rd) Annual Round Table, Monograph Series on Languages and Linguistics. Washington, DC: Georgetown University Press, 1970. Also in M. Sanchez and B. Blount, *Sociocultural Dimensions of Langauge Use.* New York: Academic Press, 1975.

Gutierrez, A. and H. Hirsch. "The Militant Challenge to the American Ethos: Chicanos and Mexican Americans." *Social Science Quarterly,* 53 (1973) 4:830–846.

Hall, E. T. *The Silent Language.* New York: Doubleday, 1959.

———. *The Hidden Dimension.* New York: Doubleday, 1966.

———. *Beyond Culture.* New York: Doubleday, 1976.

Hall, W. S. and R. O. Freedle. *Culture and Language: The Black American Experience.* New York: Halstead Press, Division of John Wiley and Sons, 1975.

Halliday, M. "Antilanguages." *American Anthropologist,* 78 (1976):570–578.

Hallowell, A. I. *Culture and Experience.* Philadelphia: University of Pennsylvania Press, 1955.

Hawaii State Department of Education. *Supplemental Information for Local Education Agency Grants under the Emergency School Aid Act,* 05/62 523-2. Hawaii: Hawaii State Department of Education, 1978.

Herskovits, M. J. *Cultural Anthropology.* New York: Knopf, 1955.

House, E. R. *School Evaluation: The Politics and Process.* Berkeley: McCutchan, 1973.

Hostetler, J. and G. Huntington. *Children in Amish Society.* New York: Holt, Rinehart and Winston, 1971.

Hymes, D. "Functions of Speech." In F. Gruber (ed.), *Anthropology and Education.* Philadelphia: University of Pennsylvania Press, 1961.

———. "Introduction." In C. Cazden, V. John, and D. Hymes (eds.), *Functions of Language in the Classroom.* New York: Teachers College Press, 1972.

———. "Speech and Language: On the Origins and Foundations of Inequality in Speaking." *Daedalus,* 102 (1973):59–86.

———. *Foundations in Sociolinguistics.* Philadelphia: University Press, 1974a.

———. *Reinventing Anthropology.* New York: Random House (Vintage Books), 1974b.

————. "On Ways of Speaking." In P. Bauman and J. Sherzer (eds.), *Explorations in the Ethnography of Speaking*. New York: Cambridge, 1974c.

————. "Qualitative/Quantitative Research Methodologies in Education: A Linguistic Perspective." *Anthropology and Education Quarterly,* 8 (1977) 3:165–176.

————. Untitled Manuscript, University of Pennsylvania, School of Commerce, April 15, 1977a.

Illich, I. *Deschooling Society.* New York: Harper and Row (Harrow Books), 1972.

Intercultural Development Research Association." The AIR Evaluation of the Impact of ESEA Title VII Spanish/English Bilingual Education Programs: An IDRA Response." San Antonio, TX: IDRA, 1977.

Jacob, E. and P. R. Sanday. "Dropping Out: A Strategy for Coping with Cultural Pluralism." In P. R. Sanday (ed.), *Anthropology and the Public Interest: Fieldwork and the Theory.* New York: Academic Press, 1976.

Jackson, G. and C. Cosca. "The Inequality of Educational Opportunity in the Southwest: An Observational Study of Ethnically Mixed Classrooms." *American Educational Research Journal,* 10 (Summer, 1974):219–229.

Jackson, P. W. *Life in Classrooms.* New York: Holt, Rinehart and Winston, 1968.

Jensen, A. R. "How Much Can We Boost IQ and Scholastic Achievement?" *Harvard Educational Review,* 39 (1969) 1:1–123.

————. "Can We and Should We Study Race Difference?" In C. L. Broce, et al. (eds.), *Race and Intelligence,* Anthropological Studies, No. 8. Washington, DC: American Anthropological Association, 1971.

John-Steiner, V. and H. Osterreich. *Learning Styles Among Pueblo Children.* Final Report HEW: NEG-00-3-0074. Albuquerque: University of New Mexico, 1975.

Jordan, C. "Proposal for a Study of Teaching and Learning Modes Among Hawaiians." Working paper. Honolulu: The Kamehameha Early Education Program, 1974.

————. "Teaching Behaviors of Hawaiian Mothers and School Success of Their Children: A Consideration of Two Explanations." Working paper, Honolulu: The Kamehameha Early Education Program, 1975a.

————. "The Place of Cultural Knowledge in Adjusting Schools to Serve Minority Populations." Working paper, Honolulu: The Kamehameha Early Education Program, 1975b.

————. *Maternal Teaching Modes and School Adaptation.* Honolulu: The Kamehameha Early Education Program, 1976.

————. *Maternal Teaching, Peer Teaching, and School Adaptation in Urban Hawaiian Population.* Honolulu: The Kamehameha Early Education Program, 1977.

————. "Teaching/Learning Interactions and School Adaptation: The Hawaiian Case." In C. Jordan, et al., *A Multidisciplinary Approach to Research in Education: The Kamehameha Early Education Program.* Honolulu: The Kamehameha Early Education Program, 1978a.

————. "Hawaiian Peer Interaction in a Classroom Context." Paper presented at the Annual Meeting of the Society for Cross-cultural Research. New Haven, CT., 1978b.

————, et al. *A Multidisciplinary Approach to Research in Education: The Kamehameha Early Education Program.* Technical Report No. 81. Symposium delivered at the Meeting of the American Anthropological Association, Houston, Dec., 1977.

———— and R. Tharp. "Culture and Education." In A. Marsella, et al. (eds.), *Perspectives in Cross-cultural Psychology.* New York: Academic Press, 1979.

Kagan, S. and M. C. Madsen. "Cooperation and Competition of Mexican, Mexican-American and Anglo-American Children of Two Ages Under Four Instructional Sets." *Developmental Psychology,* 5 (1971):32–39.

Kelly, J. G. "Naturalistic Observations in Contrasting Social Environments." In E. P. Willems and H. L. Raush (eds.), *Naturalistic Viewpoints in Psychological Research.* New York: Holt, Rinehart and Winston, 1969.

Kendon, A. "Some Functions of Gaze Directions in Face to Face Interaction." *Acta Psychologica,* 26 (1967):22–63.

————. "The Role of Visible Behavior in the Organization of Social Interaction." In M. von Cranach and I. Vine (eds.), *Social Communication and Movement.* New York: Academic Press, 1973.

———— and A. A. Ferber. "A Description of Home Human Greetings." In R. Michael and L. Pearson (eds.), *Comparative Ecology and Behavior Primates.* New York: Academic Press, 1973.

————, et al. *Organization of Behavior in Face-to-Face Interaction.* Chicago: Mouton, 1975.

Kinietz, W. Vernon. *The Indian of the Western Great Lakes: 1615–1760.* Ann Arbor: University of Michigan Press (1st ed., 1940), 1972.

Kinsley, A. "Reading and Mathematics Achievement of Indian and Non-Indian Elementary School Children in the Same School." Master's Thesis, University of South Dakota, 1976.

Kleinfeld, J. S. "Intellectual Strengths in Culturally Different Groups: An Eskimo Illustration." *Review of Educational Research,* 43 (Summer, 1973):341–359.

Kluckhohn, Clyde. *Mirror for Man.* New York: McGraw-Hill, 1949.

——— and W. H. Kelly. "The Concept of Culture." In R. Linton (ed.), *Science of Man in the World Crisis.* New York: Columbia University Press, 1945.

Kochman, T. "Black American Speech Event and a Language Program for the Classroom." In Cazden, et al., *Functions of Language in the Classroom.* New York: Teachers College Press, 1972.

Kogan, N. "Educational Implications of Cognitive Styles." In G. S. Lesser (ed.), *Psychology and Educational Practice.* Glenview, IL: Scott, Foresman, 1971.

Kounin, J. S. *Discipline and Group Management in Classrooms.* New York: Holt, Rinehart and Winston, 1970.

Kroeber, A. L. *Anthropology: Race, Language, Culture, Psychology, Prehistory.* New York: Harcourt, 1948.

——— and C. Kluckhohn. "Culture: A Critical Review of Concepts and Definitions." Papers of the Peabody Museum of American Archaeology and Ethnology, Harvard University, Vol. 47 (1952):1.

LaBelle, J., L. Moll, and T. Weisner. "Context-Based Educational Evaluation: A Participant Research Strategy." *Educational Evaluation and Policy Analysis,* 1 (1979) 3:85–93.

Labov, W. "The Logic of Non-Standard English." In F. Williams (ed.), *Language and Poverty.* Chicago: Rand McNally, 1970.

———. *Language in the Inner City.* Philadelphia: University of Pennsylvania Press, 1972a.

———. *Sociolinguistic Patterns.* Philadelphia: University of Pennsylvania Press, 1972b.

———, P. Cohen, C. Robins, and J. Lewis. "A Study of the Nonstandard English of Negro and Puerto Rican Speakers in New York City." Cooperative Research Project No. 3288, Office of Education, 1968.

——— and D. Fanshel. *Therapeutic Discourse: Psychotherapy as Conversation.* New York: Academic Press, 1977.

——— and C. Robins. "A Note on the Relation of Reading Failure to Peer-Group Status in Urban Ghettos." *Florida FL Reporter,* 7 (1969):54–57, 167.

Lambert, W. "A Social Psychology of Bilingualism." *The Journal of Social Issues,* 73 (1967):91–109.

Lancey, D. F. *The Beliefs and Behaviors of Pupils in an Experimental School.* Pittsburgh: University of Pittsburgh, Learning Research and Development Center, 1976.

Landes, Ruth. *Culture in American Education: Anthropological Approaches to Minority and Dominant Groups in the Schools.* New York: Wiley, 1965.

Leach, E. R. "Culture and Social Cohesion: An Anthropologist's View." In G. Holton (ed.), *Science and Culture.* Boston: Beacon Press, 1967.

Leacock, E. B. "Race and the We-They Dichotomy in Culture." *CAE Quarterly,* 8 (1977) 2:152–159.

Lee, P. C. and N. B. Gropper. "Sex-role Culture and Educational Practice." *Harvard Educational Review,* 44 (1974) 3:369–410.

Leiter, K. "Ad Hocing in the Schools: A Study of Placement Practices in the Kindergarten of Two Schools." In A. Cicourel, et al., *Language Use and School Performance.* New York: Academic Press, 1975.

Lesser, G. S. "Matching Instruction to Student Characteristics." In G. S. Lesser (ed.), *Psychology and Educational Practice.* Glenview, IL: Scott, Foresman, 1971.

Lewis, D. K. "The Multi-cultural Education Model and Minorities: Some Reservations." *CAE Quarterly,* 7 (1976) 4:32–37.

Linton, R. *Acculturation in Seven American Indian Tribes.* New York: Appleton-Century, 1940.

Lofland, J. *Doing Social Life: The Qualitative Study of Human Interaction in Natural Settings.* New York: John Wiley and Sons, 1976.

Ludwig, M. "Posing the Problem... Finding the Problem." Paper presented at the American Anthropological Association 1978 Annual Meeting, Los Angeles, Nov. 16, 1978.

Malinowski, B. *Argonauts of the Western Pacific.* New York: Dutton (Original ed., 1922), 1961.

Mays, V., et al. *Selection of Children for KEEP Demonstration School: Criteria, Procedures and Results (1972–73 and 1973–74).* Honolulu, HI: The Kamehameha Early Education Program, 1975.

McCall, G. J. and J. L. Simmons. *Issues in Participant Observation.* Reading, MA: Addison-Wesley, 1969.

McDermott, R. P. "Achieving School Failure: An Anthropological Approach to Illiteracy and Social Stratification." In G. D. Spindler (ed.), *Education and Culture Process.* New York: Holt, Rinehart and Winston, 1974.

———. "Toward an Embodied Map of Urban Neighborhoods: How It May Be that New York City Taxicab Drivers Make Sense and Generate Social Structure." Paper presented to the Anthropological Society of Washington, May 14, 1975.

———. *The Culture of Experience.* New York: New York University Press, 1976.

———. *Kids Make Sense: An Ethnographic Account of the Interactional Management of Success and Failure in One First-Grade Classroom.* Ph.D. dissertation, Stanford University, 1976.

———. "School Relations as Contexts for Learning in School." *Harvard Educational Review,* 47 (1977):298–313.

———. "Relating and Learning: An Analysis of Two Classroom Reading Groups." In R. Shuy (ed.), *Linguistics and Reading.* Rowley, MA: Newbury House, in press.

———, et al. "Criteria for an Ethnographically Adequate Description of Concerted Activities and Their Contexts." *Semiotica,* 24 (1978) 3/4:245–275.

——— and K. Gospodinoff. "Social Contexts for Ethnic Borders and School Failure: A Communicative Analysis." In A. Wolfgang (ed.), *Nonverbal Behavior.* London: Academic Press, 1979.

McKinley, F., S. Bayne, and G. Nimnicht. "Who Should Control Indian Education?" Berkeley: Far West Laboratory for Educational Research and Development, Feb., 1970.

McQuown, N., et al. *The Natural History of an Interview.* University of Chicago Library Microfilm Collection of Manuscripts in Cultural Anthropology, Series 15, Nos. 95–98, 1971.

Mehan, Hugh. "Assessing Children's School Performance." *Recent Sociology,* 5 (1973):240–264.

———. "Accomplishing Classroom Lessons." In A. Circourel, et al. (eds.), *Language Use and School Performance.* New York: Academic Press, 1974.

Mehan, H. "Students' Interactional Competence in the Classroom." *Institute for Comparative Human Development Quarterly Newsletter,* 1 (Sept., 1976) 1:7–10.

———. "Structuring School Structure." *Harvard Educational Review,* 45 (1978) 1:311–338.

———. *Learning Lessons.* Cambridge: Harvard University Press, 1979.

———, et al. *The Social Organization of Classroom Lessons.* La Jolla, CA: Center for Information Processing, University of California, San Diego, 1976.

Merian, L. (ed.). *The Problem of Indian Administration.* Baltimore: Johns Hopkins Press, 1928.

Moerman, M. "Ethnic Identification in a Complex Civilization: Who Are the Lue?" *American Anthropologist,* 67 (1965):1215–1226.

———. "Uses and Abuses of Ethnic Identification." In J. Helm (ed.), *Essays on the Problem of Tribe.* Seattle: University of Washington Press, 1968.

Moore, S. "Selection for Failure in a Small Social Field." In S. Moore and B. Meyerhoff (eds.), *Symbols and Politics and Communal Ideology: Cases and Questions.* Ithaca: Cornell University Press, 1975.

Nadel, S. *The Theory of Social Structure.* London: Cohen and West Ltd., 1957.

National Institute of Education. *Multicultural/Bilingual Division Fiscal Year 1976 Program Plan.* Washington, DC: National Institute of Education, 1976.

National Puerto Rican Development and Training Institute, Inc. *A Proposed Approach to Implement Bilingual Education Programs: Research and Synthesis of Philosophical, Theoretical and Practical Implications.* New York: National Puerto Rican Development and Training Institute, Inc., n.d.

Office of Civil Rights. "Task Force Findings Specifying Remedies Available for Eliminating Past Educational Practices Ruled Unlawful Under Lau vs. Nichols." Washington, DC: Department of Health, Education and Welfare, 1975. Also reprinted in *The Linguistic Reporter,* 18 (1975) 2:1.

Ogbu, J. U. *The Next Generation: An Ethnography of Education in an Urban Neighborhood.* New York: Academic Press, 1974.

———. "Social Stratification and the Socialization of Competence." *Anthropology and Educational Quarterly,* 10 (1979) 1:3–20.

Ornstein, J. *The Sociolinguistic Studies on Southwest Bilingualism: A Status Report.* San Diego: Institute for Cultural Pluralism, 1974.

Peltier, S. *How Commands Become Requests.* Unpublished paper, 1976.

Pelto, P. *Anthropological Research: The Structure of Inquiry.* New York: Harcourt, Brace, 1970.

Philips, S. "Participant Structures and Communicative Competence: Warm Springs Children in Community and Classroom." In C. Cazden, D. Hymes, and V. J. John (eds.), *Functions of Language in the Classroom*. New York: Teachers College Press, 1972.

———. "The Invisible Culture: Communication in Classroom and Community in the Warm Springs Reservation." Ph.D. dissertation, University of Pennsylvania, 1974.

Piestrup, A. *Black Dialect Interference and Accommodation of Reading Instruction in First Grade*. Berkeley: Monographs of the Language-Behavior Research Laboratory, 1973.

Pike, K. *Language in Relation to a Unified Theory of the Structure of Human Behavior*. The Hague: Mouton, 1967.

Polanyi, M. *The Tacit Dimension*. New York: Harper and Row, 1962.

Powdermaker, H. *Stranger and Friend: The Way of an Anthropologist*. New York: W. W. Norton, 1966.

Provus, M. *Discrepancy Evaluation for Educational Program Improvement and Assessment*. Berkeley: McCutchan, 1971.

Ramirez, Manuel III. "Cognitive Style and Cultural Democracy in Education." *Social Science Quarterly*, 53 (1973) 4:895–905.

———. "Reading Strategies for Different Cultural and Linguistic Groups." National Institute of Education Conference on Studies in Reading, Report of Panel 9. Washington, DC: National Institute of Education, 1975.

——— and A. Castañeda. *Cultural Democracy, Bicognitive Development, and Education*. New York: Academic Press, 1974.

———, et al. "The Relationship of Acculturation to Cognitive Style Among Mexican Americans." *Journal of Cross-Cultural Psychology*, 5 (Dec., 1974):424–433.

——— and D. R. Price-Williams. "Cognitive Styles of Children of Three Ethnic Groups in the United States." *Journal of Cross-Cultural Psychology*, 5 (June, 1974):212–219.

Riesman, D. *The Lonely Crowd*. New York: Doubleday, 1955.

Rist, R. C. "Student Social Class and Teacher Self-fulfilling Prophecy In Ghetto Education." *Harvard Educational Review*, 40 (Aug., 1970) 3:411–450.

———. "On the Relations Among Educational Research Paradigms: From Disdain to Detente." *CAE Quarterly*, 8 (1977) 2:42–49.

Rodriquez, E. E. "More on Teacher Attitudes and Assessment of Student Capabilities: A Researcher's Quest for Epiphanal Experiences in the Field." Unpublished manuscript, Harvard University, Graduate School of Education, April 18, 1978.

Rosenthal, R. and L. Jacobson. *Pygmalion in the Classroom: Teacher Expectation and Pupils' Intellectual Development*. New York: Holt, Rinehart and Winston, 1968.

Ruiz, S. "Use of Space in the Classroom." Research Report N. 11, Center for Urban Affairs, Michigan State University, 1971.

Runcie, J. F. *Experiencing Social Research*. Homewood, IL: Dorsey, 1976.

Sacks, H. "An Analysis of the Course of a Joke's Telling." In R. Bauman and J. Sherzer (eds.), *Explorations in the Ethnography of Speaking*. London: Cambridge University Press, 1974.

Sànchez, R. "Nuestra Circunstancia Linguística." *El Grito*, 6:1 (1972):45–74.

Sanday, P. R. "Cultural and Structural Pluralism in the U.S." In P. R. Sanday (ed.), *Anthropology and the Public Interest: Fieldwork and Theory*. New York: Academic Press, 1976.

Sapir, E. "Sound Patterns in Language." *Language*, 1 (1925):37–51.

Sarason, S. *The Culture of the School and the Problem of Change*. Boston: Allyn and Bacon, 1971.

Schatzman, L. and A. Strauss. *Field Research: Strategies for a Natural Sociology*. Englewood Cliffs, NJ: Prentice-Hall, 1974.

Scheflen, A. E. "The Significance of Posture in Communication Systems." *Psychiatry*, 27 (1964):316–331.

———. "Natural History Method in Psychotherapy." In Gottschalk and A. Auerback (eds.), *Methods of Research in Psychotherapy*. New York: Appleton-Century-Crofts, 1966.

———. "Living Space in an Urban Ghetto." *Family Process*, 10 (1971):429–450.

———. *Communicational Structure Analysis of a Psychotherapy Transaction*. Bloomington, IN: Indiana University Press, 1973.

———. *How Behavior Means*. New York: Anchor Press, 1974.

———. *Human Territories*. Englewood Cliffs, NJ: Prentice-Hall, 1976.

Schensul, S. "Skills Needed in Action Anthropology: Lessons from El Centro de la Causa." *Human Organization*, 33 (Summer, 1974) 2:203–209.

Schutz, A. *Collected Papers I: The Problem of Social Reality.* The Hague: Martinus Nijhoff, 1962.

Scribner, S. and M. Cole. "Cognitive Consequences of Formal and Informal Education." *Science,* 182 (1973):553–559.

Seligman, C. R., et al. "The Effect of Speech Style and Other Attributes on Teachers' Attitudes Toward Pupils." *Language in Society,* 1 (1972):131–142.

Shalaby, I. and J. Chilcott. *The Education of a Black Muslim.* Tucson, AZ: Impresora Sahuero, 1972.

Shatz, M. and R. Gelman. "The Development of Communication Skills: Modifications in the Speech of Young Children as a Function of Listener." *Monographs of the Society for Research in Child Development,* Serial No. 152, 38 (5), 1973.

Sherzer, J. "Ethnography of Speaking." Paper presented for the Bilingual Symposium, Linguistic Society of America, San Francisco, Dec., 1975.

Shultz, J. *A Microethnographic Analysis of Game Playing in a Kindergarten/First Grade Classroom.* Unpublished paper, Harvard University, April, 1972.

———. "It's Not Whether You Win or Lose, It's How You Play the Game. A Microethnographic Analysis of Game Playing in a Kindergarten-First Grade Classroom." Working paper No. 2, Newton Classroom Interaction Project: Harvard Graduate School of Education, Feb., 1976. Also paper presented to the American Educational Research Association Annual Meeting, New York, April 5, 1977.

———. "Language Use in Bilingual Classrooms." Unpublished manuscript, Harvard Graduate School of Education, n.d.

——— and S. Harkness. "Code-switching in a Bilingual Classroom." Unpublished paper, Harvard University, April, 1972.

Shuy, R. and P. Griffin (eds.), *The Study of Children's Functional Language and Education in the Early Years.* Final Report to the Carnegie Corporation of New York. Arlington, VA: Center for Applied Linguistics, 1978.

Sinclair, J. McH. and R. M. Coulthard. *Towards an Analysis of Discourse: The English Used by Teachers and Pupils.* London: Oxford University Press, 1975.

Smith, L. M. "An Evolving Logic of Participant Observation, Educational Ethnography, and Other Case Studies." In L. Shuman (ed.), *Review of Research in Education.* Chicago: Peacock, 1979.

——— and P. C. Carpenter. *General Reinforcement Package Project: Qualitative Observation and Interpretation.* St. Ann, MO: CEMREL, Inc., 1972.

——— and W. Geoffrey. *The Complexities of an Urban Classroom: An Analysis Toward a General Theory of Teaching.* New York: Holt, Rinehart and Winston, 1968.

Speidel, G. E. and R. G. Tharp. *Developing Children's Oral Language: A Study of the Effectiveness of Minicourse Instruction with Hawaiian Creole-Speaking Children.* Honolulu: The Kamehameha Early Education Program, 1978.

Spradley, J. *Culture and Cognition: Rules, Maps and Plans.* San Francisco: Chandler, 1972.

——— and D. W. McCurdy. *The Cultural Experience: Ethnography in Complex Society.* Chicago: Science Research Associates, 1972.

Stodolsky, S. S. and G. S. Leser. "Learning Patterns in the Disadvantaged." *Harvard Educational Review,* 37 (Fall, 1967):546–593.

Suttles, G. *The Social Order of the Slum.* Chicago: University of Chicago Press, 1968.

Tharp, R. G. "Peer Orientation, Industriousness and Learning to Read: Experience with the Hawaiian Child." In C. Jordan, et al., *A Multidisciplinary Approach to Research in Education.* Honolulu: The Kamehameha Early Education Program, 1978.

———. *The Direct Instruction of Comprehension Within an Integrated Reading Curriculum: Description and Results of the Kamehameha Early Education Program (KEEP).* Honolulu: The Kamehameha Early Education Program, 1979.

——— and R. Gallimore. *The Mutual Problems of Hawaiian-American Students and the Public Schools.* Honolulu: The Kamehameha Early Education Program, 1975.

——— ——— ———. *The Uses and Limits of Social Reinforcement and Industriousness for Learning to Read.* Honolulu: The Kamehameha Early Education Program, 1976.

——— ——— ———. "The Ecology of Program Research and Development: A Model of Evaluation Succession." In L. B. Sechrest (ed.), *Evaluation Studies Review Annual,* Vol. 4. Beverly Hills, CA: Sage Publications, 1979.

Tikunoff, W., et al. *Special Study A: An Ethnographic Study of the Forty Classrooms of the BTES Known Sample.* San Francisco: Far West Laboratory for Educational Research and Development, 1975.

Tobias, S. "Achievement Treatment Interactions." *Review of Educational Research,* 46 (Winter, 1976):61–74.

Tylor, E. B. *Primitive Culture.* 1st edition. New York: Brentano, 1871.

United States Commission on Civil Rights. *Mexican American Educational Study, Report V.* Washington, DC: U.S. Government Printing Office, 1972.

———. Teacher and Students. *Differences in Teacher Interaction with Mexican American and Anglo Students.* Washington, DC: U.S. Government Printing Office, March, 1973.

United States Office of Education. *National Study of American Indian Children and Youth.* Project No. 8-0147. United States Office of Education, OEO-0-8-0147-2805.

United States Senate. Special Subcommittee on Indian Education of the Committee on Labor and Public Welfare. *A National Tragedy-Challenge,* United States Senate, Ninety-first Congress, Senate Report, No. 91-501. Washington, DC: U.S. Government Printing Office, 1969.

Valentine, C. A. *Culture and Poverty: Critique and Counter-Proposals.* Chicago: University of Chicago Press, 1968.

———. "The Culture of Poverty: Its Scientific Significance and its Implications for Action." In E. B. Leacock (ed.), *The Culture of Poverty: A Critique.* New York: Simon and Schuster, 1971.

Wallace, A. F. C. *Culture and Personality.* (2nd ed.). New York: Random House, 1970.

Waller, W. *The Sociology of Teaching.* New York: John Wiley and Sons, Inc., 1932.

Wanat, S. "Reading and Readiness." *Visible Language,* 10 (1976):101–127.

Watson-Gegeo, K. A. and D. T. Bogg. "From Verbal Play to Talk Story: The Role of Routine in Speech Events among Hawaiian Children." In S. Ervin-Tripp and C. Mitchell-Kernan (eds.), *Child Discourse.* New York: Academic Press, 1977.

Wax, M., S. Diamond, and F. Gearing. *Anthropological Perspectives on Education.* New York: Basic Books, 1971.

——— and R. Thomas. "American Indians and White People." *Phylon,* 22 (1966):305–317.

———, R. Wax, and R. Dumont, Jr. *Formal Education in an American Indian Community.* Kalamazoo, MI: The Society for the Study of Social Problems, 1964.

Webster's New World Dictionary of the American Language. New York: The World Publishing Company, 1964.

Weisner, T. "The Hawaiian American Cultural and Familial Context: What Can it Tell Us?" In C. Jordan, et al. (eds.), *A Multidisciplinary Approach to Research in Education: The Kamehameha Early Education Program.* Honolulu: The Kamehameha Early Education Program, 1978.

———, R. Gallimore, and S. Omori. *Social and Demographic Description of KEEP Families, 1974–75.* Honolulu: The Kamehameha Early Education Program, 1978.

Whyte, W. F. *Street Corner Society* (2nd ed.). Chicago: University of Chicago Press, 1955.

Wieder, D. *Language and Social Reality.* The Hague: Mouton, 1974.

Witkin, H., R. B. Dyk, H. F. Faterson, D. R. Goodenough, and S. A. Karp. *Psychological Differentiation: Studies of Development.* Potomac: Erlbaum, 1974 (originally published in 1962).

——— and D. R. Goodenough. *Field Dependence and Interpersonal Behavior.* Research Bulletin. Princeton: Educational Testing Service, 1976.

———, H. B. Lewis, M. Hertzman, K. Machover, P. B. Meissner, and S. Wapner. *Personality Through Perception: An Experimental and Clinical Study.* Westport, CT: Greenwood Press, 1972 (originally published in 1954).

———, et al. "Field-Dependent and Field-Independent Cognitive Styles and Their Educational Implications." *Review of Educational Research,* 47 (Winter, 1977):1–64.

Wittgenstein, L. *Philosophical Investigations.* New York: Macmillan, 1953.

Wolcott, H. F. *A Kwakiutl Village and School.* New York: Holt, Rinehart and Winston, 1967.

Wolfram, W. "Objective and Subjective Parameters of Language among Second Generation Puerto Ricans in East Harlem." In R. Shuy and R. Fasold (eds.), *Language Attitudes.* Washington, DC: Georgetown University Press, 1973.

Young, R. "Language in Culture." In R. Abrahams and R. Troike (eds.), *Language and Cultural Diversity in American Education.* Englewood Cliffs, NJ: Prentice-Hall, 1972.